'I could have played for either one of the Irish international teams as my mother hails from Bangor, County Down. Indeed, my son Alex made his debut for the Republic of Ireland in 2007. John's book reveals the history of the Irish and their love for Manchester United. I have played alongside many wonderful Irish footballers, including Norman Whiteside, Mal Donaghy, Kevin Moran, Paul McGrath, Denis Irwin and Roy Keane, and John's book tells the story of every Irish Red and United's proud Irish tradition.'

Steve Bruce, Manchester United 1987–96

'The Irish and Manchester United enjoy a unique marriage which has lasted since a bunch of railway workers formed the club in 1878, then known as Newton Heath Lancashire & Yorkshire Railway Football Club. Both of my parents were Irish, born and bred in Gweedore, County Donegal, and I love spending time there. I love the Irish people and, having met tens of thousands of them during my travels with United, both as a player and working for MUTV, I can tell you that they are all mad – mad Manchester United fans that is! What a magnificent following Manchester United has in the Emerald Isle.'

Paddy Crerand, Manchester United 1963–71

'I am honoured to be part of John's story covering the history of United and the Irish. It was always a dream for me to play for the club I supported as a boy and I can still recall going to Carryduff to have my photograph taken with the Premier League trophy, FA Cup and European Cup in February 2000 when John persuaded United to let the Carryduff MUSC borrow them for a weekend.'

Jonny Evans, Manchester United 2006–

'John's book is a fitting tribute to the many wonderful Irish players who have proudly worn the jersey of Manchester United Football Club and, indeed, the many Irish fans the club has. Whenever I visit Ireland it never ceases to amaze me just how many Irish fans we have, and of course thousands of loyal Irish Reds cross the Irish Sea every other weekend to watch the team play. For me, the Mancunians and the Irish share a unique bond and John's book tells the story of this very special relationship and, of course, what part his fellow Irishmen have played in the history of our magnificent club.'

Sir Alex Ferguson CBE, Manager of Manchester United 1986–

'Manchester United has a long and illustrious association with Ireland. In fact, the reason I started supporting United was watching George Best and becoming instantly hooked. The many thousands who cross the Irish Sea every week to support the team home and away are a key part of our loyal fan base. It is little wonder then that one of the first names suggested for a new club after the bankruptcy of Newton Heath was Manchester Celtic. John's book brings out the passion he and his fellow Irishmen have for the club.'

David Gill, Chief Executive of Manchester United 2003–

'John's book is the definitive story of the Irish's love affair with Manchester United. His book is crammed full of personal insights from former Irish United greats and contains so many wonderful stories from the fans themselves giving their own account of just why Manchester United is in their lifeblood.'

Harry Gregg MBE, Manchester United 1957–66

'Inside John's book you will find all of the information you ever wanted to know about the Irish players that have played for Manchester United and just why United are so special to the Irish people. John has managed to bring back so many wonderful memories that I have from my own career at Old Trafford.'

Sammy McIlroy, Manchester United 1971–82

'John's book is an intriguing insight into United's Irish connection, which pre-dates the club's formation and takes us on a magical historical tour right up to the present day. *Irish Devils* is a fascinating story charting the history of Ireland's love affair with the world's greatest club, Manchester United.'

Kevin Moran, Manchester United 1979–88

'With detailed biographies of the players, coupled with stories from many of the fans who recall the moment they fell in love with the greatest football team in the world, it tells the story of the unique bond that exists between Manchester United and the people of Ireland. A thoroughly enjoyable read.'

Jimmy Nicholl, Manchester United 1975–82

'This book does exactly what it says on the cover. It tells the story of Ireland's connections with Manchester United and my fellow countrymen's love affair with the club. It is a fascinating read which begins in 1830 with many Irishmen, women and children leaving their homes in Ireland behind them to start a new life in Manchester and takes us right up to the present day when Manchester is regularly invaded by Ireland's Red Army.'

John O'Shea, Manchester United 1999–2011

'It is great to see a fellow Belfast man writing a book about all of the Irish players who have played for Manchester United. I am proud to say that I am one of those players and I will never forget my time at the club. Looking back over my career, I played with many wonderful players at United and a lot of them were Northern Ireland and Republic of Ireland internationals. And, of course, United would not be United without the dedication and loyal support their army of fans from the Emerald Isle gives the team week in and week out.'

Norman Whiteside, Manchester United 1982–89

Foreword

United and the Irish, now there's a story or a thousand! I was absolutely delighted when John asked me to write the Foreword to this book, his sixth about Manchester United, a team we both follow with tremendous passion. Like John, I too grew up in Belfast, and although many of my schoolmates supported Glasgow Celtic or Leeds United there was only one team for me and that team was Manchester United.

From an early age, all I ever wanted to do was play for United alongside my boyhood hero George Best. Looking back now, it was all just a pipe dream; but hey, I enjoyed it up until George effectively ended his career on New Year's Day 1974, when I was just 14 years old.

I was born the year after the Munich Air Disaster when eight Busby Babes tragically lost their lives on that snowy runway in Germany on 6 February 1958. This disaster ripped the heart out of Manchester United, but history shows us that football fans united and collectively mourned their loss. Ireland's very own Liam 'Billy' Whelan perished in the disaster, and no Manchester United fan should ever forget the heroism of Northern Ireland's Harry Gregg, who helped his team-mates, including his fellow countryman Jackie Blanchflower, from the burning fuselage. Sadly, as a result of the injuries Jackie sustained in the crash, he never played football again, a huge loss not only to Manchester United but to Northern Ireland's international side also.

Thankfully Matt Busby, who almost lost his own life in

Munich, had the strength to rebuild the team and oversee the club rise from the ashes and be crowned champions of Europe ten years later. I will forever remember that wonderful night of 29 May 1968, when United defeated the mighty Benfica at the old Wembley Stadium in the European Cup final, and the role played that balmy evening by United's trio of gifted Irishmen: Shay Brennan, Tony Dunne and of course my idol, the Belfast boy himself, George Best.

Looking back now, perhaps Manchester United's huge Irish following rose with the team from the ashes post-Munich Air Disaster, but for me and many kids just like me, the Irish's love affair with Manchester United really took off when a skinny kid from the Cregagh Estate in East Belfast burst onto our TV screens and took the English game to new heights. George Best was Northern Ireland's first internationally recognised football superstar and made the game look easy as he glided past defenders before delivering a killer pass to a team-mate or firing the ball into the net.

One of my best ever memories as a Red simply has to be the first time I saw the team play, Manchester United versus Newcastle United at Old Trafford on 17 March 1973. I was only 13 years old and going to Old Trafford, the place of my dreams as a young boy, was quite a daunting and emotional experience for a kid from Belfast. My only regret was that Bestie had not played since November and was not in the United line-up that memorable day, nor was Denis Law.

There I was with my hat, scarf, rattle and of course my sprig of Shamrock – well, it was St Patrick's Day! I cheered as I watched my heroes take to the pitch: 1. Jimmy Rimmer, 2. Tony Young, 3. Steve James, 4. George Graham, 5. Jim Holton, 6. Martin Buchan, 7. Willie Morgan, 8. Brian Kidd, 9. Bobby Charlton (captain), 10. Lou Macari, 11. Mick Martin. We won 2–1 that magical day, with goals from Jim Holton and Dublin's Mick Martin.

Since then, I have lost count of the number of times I have had the pleasure of watching my team play. Every time I visit Manchester on a match day, it reminds me so much of home because of the many Irish fans I meet in and around Old Trafford. Honestly, it is like the Irish have taken over the Trafford area for the day, and if United win, I don't need to tell you how long into the night we Irishmen celebrate the team's success. And, of course, we love nothing better than sharing our night's *craic* with our English hosts in the numerous hotels we fill to bursting in the city.

And so to John's superb book. I love the stories that John has written about the many wonderful Irishmen who have proudly worn the red of Manchester United and the way he manages to reveal how Manchester United's Irish fanbase has developed since the club's formation as Newton Heath Lancashire & Yorkshire Railway Football Club in 1878 up to the present day. I have witnessed first-hand on countless occasions just how Manchester United has brought together opposing sides of Northern Ireland's religious divide through their shared love for a team they cross the Irish Sea in their thousands to watch every season.

That is why I accepted John's invitation to become the president of the George Best Carryduff Manchester United Supporters' Club (MUSC), which he formed in 1991. The first time I met the members of the branch in their local pub, the Royal Ascot in Carryduff, will always live with me. I walked into the pub and found myself in a room full of people who, under any other circumstances, would not normally associate with one another. But then that is exactly how Manchester United manages to break down a religious barrier that to this day still divides the two sides of the community in some areas of my city of birth.

My saddest moment as a Manchester United fan came on 25 November 2005 when I heard the news that my boyhood idol had died. I was so very proud to be invited by the Best family to open the eulogies at the funeral of the greatest footballer who ever lived. And it was moving to see so many fans around the country (regardless of the team they supported) pay tribute to the shy Belfast boy, who helped make Manchester United into a global phenomenon, with a minute's applause held in honour of our George prior to that weekend's league fixtures. That day George brought the football world together, because no one could deny that the boy from the Emerald Isle was the greatest footballer ever. Just ask the legendary Pelé.

So enjoy John's book, and thank you George and Manchester United for giving this Irishman so many magical memories to cherish following Ireland's most loved club.

Eamonn Holmes

Introduction

Who? What? Where? When? Why? Five great questions each of which can start a debate. Who was the first Irishman to play for Manchester United? What great Irish internationals have worn the famous red jersey of Manchester United? Where in Ireland does Manchester United's most fervent support exist? When did the Irish first decide that Manchester United was their team and thereafter decide to go to watch them on a regular basis? Why do the Irish love Manchester United so much? I hope that by the time you have read this book I will have answered all of these questions (and many more), as we look at the magical journey that is the history of Manchester United and its Irish connection.

I was born and bred in Harper Street the Short Strand area of East Belfast and kicked a football in the streets with my mates (Danny Young and the boys) not far from where George Best grew up. When I was a young boy, I dreamt that one day a scout would spot me, as Bob Bishop had done for Best, so that I could follow in my idol's footsteps and wear the world-famous red jersey of Manchester United Football Club. That dream has long since gone, but my love affair with the club is never ending.

I have always been intrigued as to why so many Irish football fans have flocked to Old Trafford over the past 50 years or so to watch Manchester United. Why, for example, do more football fans in Belfast not go to watch any one of the local teams that play in the IFA Premiership? Or why do football fans in Dublin not tend to watch any one of the big teams in that city that play in the

FAI Premier League of Ireland? In particular, during the Troubles in Northern Ireland, what tempted so many to venture away from the relative safety of their communities to go to watch a game of football in Manchester? This book will hear the stories from many who made the decision that their football heart should lie in Manchester rather than Ireland.

I know because I was one of them. When I set foot on the Belfast to Liverpool ferry for the ten-hour crossing to attend my first game at Old Trafford, I was extremely nervous, and even a little frightened, about the journey. I was 17 years of age and various thoughts raced through my mind: would my Irish accent, and the fact that I was a Roman Catholic, leave me open to abuse or even harm from English United fans, angry at the IRA bombing campaigns? And how would Protestant United fans feel about travelling to Manchester with Catholics, given the sectarian divide? As the vast majority of MUSCs in those days identified you as being a Catholic or a Protestant, it would be hard to hide my background, even though it was not my intention to do so.

As it turned out, I need not have worried. The date was 26 April 1980 and United were playing Coventry City in the old English First Division in their last home game of the season. I think the thing that struck me most about the day was the fact that I heard so many different Irish accents; whether it was a group of fans standing chatting before the game; a fan purchasing a bite to eat from one of the chip vans in and around the stadium; or indeed the many Irish voices I heard pouring out of the Trafford Bar (I did not dare to venture inside). Much to my utter joy, United won the game 2–1 as I sat at the back of the Stretford End watching my heroes play before my transfixed eyes.

At the time the Stretford End was split into two parts; a seated section at the back of the stand and a terraced area at the front where United's diehard fans traditionally congregated. The noise and roar that came up from those fans standing in front of me was deafening. For me, a teenager who had been out of Northern Ireland only twice before (once on a day trip to the Isle of Man and the other time when some of us from my primary school spent a week in London with an English family at the height of the Troubles during the early 1970s), Old Trafford was the most exciting place in the world. I immediately felt a sense of belonging, and more than 30 years later that bond grows stronger by the day.

For the record, the attendance that day was 52,154, with about 20,000 of us occupying the Stretford End, all of us cheering on our idols who lined up as follows: 1. Gary Bailey, 2. Jimmy Nicholl, 3. Arthur Albiston, 4. Sammy McIlroy, 5. Kevin Moran, 6. Martin Buchan, 7. Steve Coppell, 8. Jimmy Greenhoff, 9. Joe Jordan, 10. Lou Macari, 11. Mickey Thomas (Tom Sloan came on as a substitute for Jimmy Greenhoff).

Four Irishmen starred for United that day, including Sammy McIlroy, who, like me, is from East Belfast. Although we are from opposite sides of the religious divide, I saw immediately how United broke down the intense hatred that often existed between Catholics and Protestants. After all, we were all members of the Church of Manchester United. Sammy scored both United goals that magical day to help Dave Sexton's side to runners-up place behind Liverpool in the league. After the match I bought an 'I'm a Stretford Ender' patch for my Wrangler jacket and a lapel badge that read 'Stretford Enders Rule OK!' My purchases helped me convince myself that I was now officially part of the United family, because I had at long last been to see my team play at Old Trafford and I could prove it.

Naturally, things have changed since then. But I can't think of any single experience that surpasses the camaraderie, emotion, excitement, joy and occasional pain that a trip from Belfast to Manchester to see United play throws up time and time again. And so, from the moment I book my journey to Old Trafford, whether I am flying in and out of England on the same day or I am going on a weekend trip with the George Best Carryduff MUSC, of which I am the founder member and branch secretary, a tingle runs down my spine. I can't recall the last day when

United did not take up some part of my life, ranging from organ-
ising branch trips (booking travel for 50 people, sourcing
accommodation and securing match tickets) to, well, writing a
book about them.

Today, thousands of fans from the Emerald Isle, north and
south of the border, invade Manchester on a regular basis throughout the season. Men, women, boys and girls of all ages and from
all walks of life leave the green, white and orange, or the red, white
and blue, behind them for a day or two and don the red, white
and black of Manchester United as they embark on a pilgrimage
across the Irish Sea. In fact, the red, white and black tricolour is
often the only flag that Northern Ireland's Manchester United fans
will wrap around their necks or wave in the air.

Once we're in England, I love nothing better than walking
through the John Lennon International Airport in Liverpool
wearing my United shirt. In many ways it reminds me of *The
Warriors*, the film about a gang from Coney Island who have to
make their way back from the Bronx, New York, to the safety of
their home turf. Here we are strolling through the home city of
one of our biggest rivals on our way to Old Trafford. And you
know that, whether they are Liverpool or Everton fans, they are
hoping we will be disappointed at the end of our journey, seeing
us as some sort of invading army. Which, in some ways, is exactly
what we are: the Irish regiment of Fergie's world-conquering red
and white army. As we walk out of the airport, heads held high
and chests bursting with pride, you know that the taxi drivers are
fearing that they may be the ones selected to take a United fan to
the place of their worst nightmares: Old Trafford. What could be
better?

Because so many of us share this same experience, I wanted to
tell the story of how Manchester United became the most popular football club in Ireland, and to show how players from Ireland
have played such a crucial role in the club's history, especially since
the war. With contributions from fellow Reds across all of Ireland,
as well as insights from current and former players, this book will

reveal the very special relationship that exists between the people of Ireland and Manchester United, and explain how and why the two have become so closely linked. As Morrissey famously sang: 'Irish blood, English heart, this I'm made of.'

John D.T. White

Chapter 1

When the Irish First Came to Manchester

Manchester's Irish connection goes back much further than many realise. What brought them to the city initially was not, as now, the footballers in action at the Theatre of Dreams, but cotton and construction. In 1830, more than 100,000 people were employed in the rapidly growing cotton industry of Lancashire. This boom attracted the first wave of immigration from across the Irish Sea. By 1841, a tenth of Manchester's population was Irish, many of whom lived in the district known as Little Ireland, a slum area in the Ancoats area of the city, while an area off Rochdale Road was known as Irish Town because of its high proportion of Irish inhabitants. The majority had come from the West of Ireland, where most had lived in windowless single-roomed mud cabins with little furniture. Although conditions in their new city were poor, they were still better than what they had left behind.

The jobs they took in factories not only provided regular income, but were much more highly paid than anything they were likely to get at home. For this reason, employers liked Irish labourers, as they would work for less than the locals. This willingness to undercut the native workforce did cause problems for the Irish as they tried to integrate into the city.

In his book, *Condition of the Working Class in England 1844*, which set out to depict the horrors of the new factories and the conditions faced by the workforce, Friedrich Engels described Little Ireland as 'the most disgusting spot of all'. The 22-year-old Engels had been sent to Manchester in 1842 from his home in Prussia to work for the textile firm of Ermen and Engels in which his father was a shareholder. He was horrified by what he saw, and it inspired his political thinking.

When the Great Famine began in 1845, the numbers leaving Ireland escalated rapidly, with two million emigrating, many to the United States and Canada. But of course the north-west of England took in a large number of them. Because of this, Little Ireland became even more overcrowded, and by the time of the 1851 census about half the men living in Ancoats had been born in Ireland (a figure that would drop only slightly, to 40 per cent, by the end of the century), while the figure across the whole of Manchester was about 15 per cent.

Engels paints a bleak picture of life for the Irish emigrants living and working in Manchester at this time. He wrote: 'The New Town, known also as Irish Town, stretches up a hill of clay, beyond the Old Town, between the Irk and St. George's Road. Here all the features of a city are lost. Single rows of houses or groups of streets stand, here and there, like little villages on the naked, not even grass-grown clay soil; the houses, or rather cottages, are in bad order, never repaired, filthy, with damp, unclean, cellar dwellings; the lanes are neither paved nor supplied with sewers, but harbour numerous colonies of swine penned in small sties or yards, or wandering unrestrained through the neighbourhood.'

Engels gained a particular insight into the plight of the Irish in Manchester through Mary Burns, with whom he had a 20-year relationship. The local-born daughter of Michael Burns, who had emigrated from Ireland, she lived in the slum district around Deansgate and helped guide him around Manchester. Engels' portrait of the average Irishman living in Manchester was anything but rose-tinted: 'He builds a pigsty against the house wall as he did at home, and if he is prevented from doing this, he lets the pig sleep in the room with himself. The Irishman loves his pig as the Arab his horse, with the difference that he sells it when it is fat enough to kill. Otherwise he eats and sleeps with it, his children play with it, ride upon it, roll in the dirt with it.'

The Irish were crammed into houses in Buxton Street, Gibraltar Lane, Long Millgate Street, Mill Street and Wakefield Street, with little clean air and hardly any natural light. A tax on windows led to landlords blocking up as many openings as possible, making the houses dangerously dark and lacking ventilation. With toilet facilities often shared between many houses, and no proper sewage system, cholera was a common summer visitor to the city, though it was the airborne diseases, such as pulmonary tuberculosis, that were the biggest killer. In 1992, the City of Manchester placed a red plaque in Great Marlborough Street, Chorlton-on-Medlock, to commemorate Little Ireland. Plaque No. 773 reads: 'Site of Little Ireland. Large numbers of immigrant Irish workers lived here in appalling housing conditions. Built c.1827, vacated c.1847, demolished c.1877.'

When the Irish got to the factories, conditions were little better, and there were, of course, no health and safety precautions or safeguards in place. The other major industry for Manchester's Irish immigrants was construction. As well as the labourers and builders, there were the 'navvies' (navigators), who learnt their trade in building canals (of which Manchester had many), before adapting to work in railway and road construction. Many women became domestic servants; a surprisingly high number of Irishmen found jobs in the armed forces; and a few became prize-fighters, finding fame and small fortune in the process.

When the famine finally ended in Ireland, most of the Irish who had settled in Manchester chose to remain there, and continued to integrate themselves within the local community. In 1877, and again in 1879, heavy rainfalls wiped out most of that year's potato crop in Ireland. Famine was about to take another grip on the country, which resulted in a second wave of immigration to

Manchester, just at the time Newton Heath (the forerunners of Manchester United) was being founded. By this stage, some of the earlier immigrant Irish generations had begun to establish themselves in Manchester, becoming merchants and shopkeepers.

But poverty was still rife among the Irish population of Manchester. During the first season of Newton Heath's existence, 1878–79, the Manchester & Salford District Provident Society's Poverty Fund revealed that the vast majority of qualifying applicants were casual and seasonal workers – among them were warehousemen, builder's labourers, general labourers, storemen and transport men – and most of these were of Irish descent. In the days before any welfare provision, there was no sick pay – if you couldn't work, you didn't receive any money.

In 1887, Irish labourers and navvies were heavily involved in the construction of the Manchester Ship Canal, a 36-mile long river navigation system. It took six years to construct, at a cost of £15 million, and it would transform the economy of the city. Where previously cotton and other goods traded had to go via Liverpool docks, adding hugely to costs and time, now ships could sail all the way to Manchester, and the docks in the city would become one of the busiest in the country.

As working hours had been reduced by this time, many now had Saturday afternoons off as well as Sundays, which meant people had more time for leisure pursuits. No wonder, then, that some of the Irish workers would be seen at North Road watching Newton Heath play, especially because of the club's links with the railway industry that employed so many of them. Little did they know it at the time, but the Heathens' Irish fans were watching their team play in the very same colours that would one day represent the colours of the Irish national flag. Newton Heath's green and gold jerseys and white shorts bore a striking resemblance to the Irish tricolour. It was at this time that the seeds of future generations of Manchester United fans from the Emerald Isle were well and truly sown. Eugene Bryson from Derry points out how central the Irish must have been to the club in its early days: 'The name Manchester Celtic was toyed with prior to Manchester United being selected, further evidence of the Irish connection.'

For any who want to know more about the history of the links between Manchester and Ireland, the Irish World Heritage Centre on Queen's Road in Cheetham Hill is a great place to start. Opened in 1984, it reflects the central role Manchester played in the story of the Irish diaspora around the world. But the sad truth of the matter is that the first wave of Irish support for the club that became Manchester United was down in large part to the waves of immigration caused by the famines in Ireland in the 1840s and 1870s. Manchester United would probably not enjoy the unique marriage it has with the Irish today were it not for those great tragedies.

Chapter 2

The Early Years

In 1873, *Kelly's Manchester Directory* described Newton Heath as: 'A township and ecclesiastical parish, within the parish and parliamentary borough, but not within the municipal boundary of Manchester, situated a mile and a half to the east of that city, in the union of Prestwich, and county court district of Manchester, rural deanery of Cheetham, and archdeaconry and diocese of Manchester.' Within a few years it would become famous as the birthplace of Manchester United.

Around this time, most of the major team sports in the UK – football, cricket and rugby – had recently become fully codified, with standardised rules, and the popularity of sport as a spectator activity was beginning to grow, as factory hours were reduced, giving working-class people more free time on Saturday afternoons. But some were more interested in using their leisure hours not only to watch but instead to participate in sport.

In late 1877, a number of workers from the Carriage & Wagon Works of the Lancashire & Yorkshire Railway in Newton Heath spent their lunchtime kicking a leather football around. As more and more of the railway employees took an interest, the workers obtained permission from the local church to play evening games

IRISH DEVILS

The Official Story of Manchester United and the Irish

JOHN D.T. WHITE

**SIMON &
SCHUSTER**

London · New York · Sydney · Toronto · New Delhi

A CBS COMPANY

First published in Great Britain in 2011 by Simon & Schuster UK Ltd
A CBS COMPANY

Copyright © by Manchester United Football Club Limited 2011

The right of John D.T. White to be identified as the author
of this work has been asserted by him in accordance with sections 77
and 78 of the Copyright, Designs and Patents Act, 1988.

1 3 5 7 9 10 8 6 4 2

Simon & Schuster UK Ltd
1st Floor
222 Gray's Inn Road
London
WC1X 8HB

www.simonandschuster.co.uk

Simon & Schuster Australia
Sydney

Simon & Schuster India
New Delhi

A CIP catalogue for this book is available
from the British Library.

ISBN: 978-0-85720-644-2

Typeset by M Rules
Printed and bound by CPI Group (UK) Ltd, Croydon, CR0 4YY

Contents

About the author

John D.T. White is the author of numerous football books, but the Red Devils have always been his first love, and this is his seventh book about his beloved United. He is the founding member and branch secretary of the George Best Carryduff Manchester United Supporters' Club, the largest official supporters' club in Ireland. He has been a season ticket holder at Old Trafford for the past 20 years. He lives in Carryduff, County Down, with his wife Janice and two sons, Marc and Paul.

on a disused piece of grassless chalk land belonging to the church, situated at North Road (now known as Northampton Road), off Monsall Road, Newton Heath. And so the club had its first ground close by where its members worked. In 1878, they formed Newton Heath Lancashire & Yorkshire Railway Football Club; they were to be the forerunners of Manchester United Football Club. They played local friendlies and purchased a set of cashmerette jerseys of green and gold halves. By the following year, the team had become more widely known as Newton Heath (L&YR) FC.

Times were hard for the players on and off the field of play, with no changing facilities and a pitch described by the local press as 'hard as flint with ashes underneath that had become like iron, and in other places thick mud'. Prior to home games, the players all met at The Three Crowns Inn on Oldham Road, half a mile from North Road, got changed there and then walked to the ground to play their opponents. However, the players were a fiercely determined bunch and were dominant in their early inter-railway games, resulting in the club looking for more testing opposition from further afield.

As the club continued to grow and develop, in 1882, Frederick Attock, the Carriage & Wagon superintendent, accepted the invitation to become the club's first president, while the management of the team fell to the dining room committee of the Lancashire & Yorkshire Railway. In 1883–84, Newton Heath entered the Lancashire FA Senior Cup, their first senior competition, but lost to Blackburn Olympic's reserve team. The price of admission to the game at North Road was 3d. Even in those very early days, there were many Irish railway workers in the crowd, finding a common bond with the indigenous Mancunians in their shared passion for football.

As professionalism became permitted in football in 1885, Newton Heath decided to follow suit if they wanted to attract the best players to their team. But most of their early recruits from outside the area came from Wales, not Ireland. The club had plenty of success in the Manchester FA Senior Cup, and in 1886–87 Newton Heath entered the FA Cup for the first time, but lost their first tie.

In 1888 the Football League, the oldest such competitive football league in the world, was formed, featuring professional clubs from the Midlands and the north of England. But Newton Heath's application to join the Football League received only a single vote, forcing the club to join the Football Combination, comprised of teams that failed to be admitted to the Football League. They were crowned the unofficial winners of the inaugural competition. But the Football Combination lasted just a solitary season and most teams, including Newton Heath, became founder members of the Football Alliance in season 1889–90.

It was during that season that we have the first official record of any link between the club and Ireland. On Christmas Day 1889, when most workmen and footballers were sitting at home with their families enjoying Christmas, Newton Heath welcomed the players of Belfast Distillery to North Road for a friendly. Belfast Distillery were the reigning Irish Cup and County Antrim Shield holders, and an excellent crowd turned up at the ground to see the Heathens lose 2–1.

Distillery historian Dawson Simpson describes it thus: 'Both teams changed in the Newton Heath Hotel and went to the field about half a mile away, where there was about 7,000 people around the ropes . . . [After Distillery went 1–0 up in the first half, their keeper Billy] Galbraith had just cleared, he fell off-balance and [Edgar] Wilson sent in a high drooping shot for Newton Heath's equaliser. The home crowd went wild, with handkerchiefs, hats and caps being thrown into the air amid intense cheering. The rest of the half, surprisingly after their arduous overnight journey, saw the Whites the fresher of the two teams.'

Eventually, Olphie Stanfield scored Distillery's second and winning goal (Jack Reynolds had scored the first). At the end of the game: 'The final whistle went to signal a tremendous 2–1 victory for Distillery in a brilliant hard-fought match. Spectators swarmed on to the ground and Galbraith was hoisted on to their shoulders and carried in triumph by an enormous crowd back to the hotel. En route they showed their appreciation of a tremendous display by filling his pockets with cigars. The proprietor of the hotel was jubilant – he was an Irishman – and a great night was had by all. So much so that the team were very ragged the following day and were easily beaten 3–1 by Denton.'

After such a successful occasion, not only in terms of the attendance but also for the breweries, this game laid the foundation for a relationship that would flourish over the subsequent years. The two sides met again, in Belfast at Grosvenor Park, on 24 May 1890 at the end of the season. The Irish side won that game 5–1.

The men from Belfast decided to return to Manchester to play Newton Heath on Christmas Day 1890 in another friendly, although they lost this one 8–4. On 4 February 1893, Newton Heath travelled across the Irish Sea to play Linfield Athletic at Windsor Park, Belfast. Their star player was a skilful Irish international outside-left named John Peden. It was not the last the Manchester side would see of him.

With the Heathens' links with Ireland being so strong, and the club having a large Irish contingent among its fans, it was not surprising that the summer of 1890 witnessed the first recorded arrival at the club of a player from Ireland, Thomas O'Shaughnessy. He was primarily a reserve team player during his two years with the club, although his big moment to impress the selectors came on 25 October 1890 when he was chosen to play against Bootle Reserves away in an FA Cup second qualifying round game. However, they lost the tie 1–0. O'Shaughnessy never played a senior game again for the club, as he broke his leg in a collision with the keeper in a friendly against a Canadian touring side on 2 January 1891. The injury effectively brought the curtain down on his career before it could even get started.

The early 1890s witnessed a number of English clubs paying notice to the talents on show week in and week out in the Irish League, and so began the steady flow of Irish players across the

Irish Sea to begin a career as a professional footballer in England. Newton Heath, with its established connections, was not going to miss out.

After purchasing two grandstands in summer 1891, each one capable of accommodating 1,000 spectators, the Heathens had a great season and finished runners-up to Nottingham Forest in the Football Alliance, which was good enough to secure their place in the Football League the following season. At this time the club also dropped the letters 'LYR' from their name, effectively severing their original links with the Lancashire & Yorkshire Railway, and was now known as Newton Heath FC.

However, playing in the Football League was a big step up and the Heathens ended their first season in last place, five points adrift of Accrington. There were highlights, however, and their first victory in the Football League was a 10–1 hammering of Wolverhampton Wanderers on 15 October 1892 at North Road, which remains the club's biggest in league football to date. The club remained in the Football League thanks only to an end-of-season victory in two 'Test Matches' against Small Heath (later Birmingham City).

Matters off the field came to a head at the end of the 1892–93 season when the club's landlords issued Newton Heath with a notice to quit their North Road home. The club had no option but to pack up and move three miles across the city to a piece of muddy wasteland situated at Bank Street, Clayton. This venue was hardly better than what they had been used to, and the neighbouring chemical works spewed out noxious fumes that were capable of putting off visiting teams unused to the foul stench.

That summer, Newton Heath welcomed their first Irish professional footballer, John Peden, who was signed from Linfield Athletic in Belfast. The 28-year-old Peden (born at The Maze, Lisburn, on 11 March 1865) was a founder member of Linfield Athletic in March 1886, scoring against Distillery in their first game. Before he came to Newton Heath he scored 108 goals in just 130 games – no wonder he is seen by many to have been the George Best of his day.

He won his first cap in Ireland's 4–1 defeat to Scotland on 19 February 1887 and scored his first international goal in his next match, on 12 March, in a 4–1 win over Wales. The highlight of his international career was when he scored a hat-trick in a 4–3 victory over Wales on 5 April 1893. No wonder Newton Heath were keen to bring him to Manchester that summer. In all, he won 24 caps for Ireland, scoring seven goals.

In fact, Peden had been signed even before that hat-trick. On 25 February 1893, he had played for Ireland against England at Wellington Road, Perry Barr, Birmingham (home to Aston Villa prior to Villa Park) and club officials in the stands watched him ease past the English defence with the ball seemingly tied to his boots. Following the game, they immediately got him to sign amateur forms and a Football League registration form, before returning home. It seems he had no immediate intention of moving to England, possibly because once he signed professional forms he would have to give up his place in the international team (professionalism was banned in Ireland until the end of 1894). However, Peden started the 1893–94 season playing as a professional for Newton Heath.

Peden made an instant impact in his first match, against Burnley on 2 September 1893. He set up the first goal in 3–2 home win with the local weekly sports newspaper, *Athletic News*, reporting: 'Peden was a success, and was carried off after the match, he and Fitzsimmons making a grand wing.' His first goals for Newton Heath came seven games into the season when he scored twice against West Bromwich Albion in a 4–1 victory, again at Bank Street, making him the first Irish player to score for the club. Criticism of the team's 'rough, brutal and cowardly' tactics, littered with 'dirty tricks' was published in a Birmingham newspaper. The club sued for libel, but won just a farthing in damages and had to pay their own costs.

Peden also scored against Middlesbrough in their 4–1 FA Cup

first round win on 27 January 1894 to become the first Irish player
to score for the club in the competition. But those wins were rare
events, and at the end of the season the Heathens were relegated,
their away form having been particularly dire all campaign.
Because of falling attendances and the legal costs associated with
the libel action, the Heathens were in deep financial trouble.

This may have been one reason why they sold Peden to
Sheffield United after they had been relegated. Peden himself
would have been initially happy with the move, as the Yorkshire
club was not only a Division One side, but there was the added
incentive of playing with their centre-forward, Bob Hill, a team-
mate in his Linfield days. However, he failed to settle at Bramall
Lane and soon returned to Ireland, which now accepted professionalism, at the end of 1894. He signed for Distillery, who
offered him a substantial wage of £1 a week, said to be the highest in Irish football. He subsequently rejoined Linfield during the
1898–99 football season.

So what sort of player was Peden, the first true Irish Devil?
Comments on his play suggested that he was more of an individual than a team player, and that he was often guilty of 'playing to
the gallery'. However, his style was popular with the fans, who
referred to him as 'the People's John'. In March 1898, *Ireland's
Saturday Night* commented: '[He] exercises a lot of judgment in all
his play. Has never failed to come up to expectations in an important match.' His obituary in the same newspaper (16 September
1944) notes: 'He was an artist on the field. His sprinting abilities,
which won him many trophies at athletic meetings, made him one
of the fastest wingers of his day. His ball control was a treat to
watch, and he was adept at drawing the defence, cutting in and
shooting with terrific power.' John Peden's importance in the history of Irish soccer is not only that he was a great talent, but a
player who was immensely popular with the fans.

And so although the initial Irish connections with the
Manchester team didn't last long, a bridgehead had been established and soon there would be a constant stream of Irish

footballers, from north and south, making their way across the Irish Sea to join the club.

The Heathens were unbeaten at home in Division Two in 1894–95, but it wasn't enough to win promotion. Meanwhile, money remained very tight, and the club was in danger of going under. Thankfully, in Alf Albut, Newton Heath had a very shrewd secretary who employed various ruses to drum up support for the club, but he couldn't win promotion.

In 1897–98 an Irish League XI side played their second game on English soil. They came to Manchester to play an English League XI, but the game took place at Hyde Road, home of Manchester City. Despite that, the fact that Manchester was chosen as the venue shows yet again how close the ties were between the city and Ireland. The Irish League XI would return to Manchester in 1905, further sealing the Mancunian-Irish links.

For 1900–01, James West was appointed secretary-manager, but he had joined a club on the brink of bankruptcy. The financial plight of Newton Heath was so bad that the fans conducted whip-rounds to pay for the team's railway fares to away fixtures. Newton Heath organised a Grand Bazaar at St James's Hall, Oxford Street, Manchester late in the season in an effort to boost finances and raise £1,000 to prevent the club from becoming bankrupt. At the bazaar the club captain's dog, Harry Stafford's St Bernard named Major, walked around the stalls in the hall with a collection box fastened around his collar so children could drop some pennies in his box. According to one possibly apocryphal story, Major wandered off and turned up at the home of John H.Davies, a very wealthy local brewery owner, whose daughter instantly fell in love with the dog. Stafford is believed to have tracked down the dog after placing a notice in a local newspaper and fell into conversation with Davies, informing him of the Heathens' precarious financial position. As a direct result of their chance meeting, Davies saw a new business opportunity and, as a benefactor of other sports, decided that he would get involved to financially support the Heathens. It was one of the most decisive moments in the club's history.

But the turnround was not immediate. In January 1902, the club's crippling debts amounted to £2,670 and a number of creditors pressed for payment. The club simply did not have the money and so they were declared bankrupt. With the gates to Bank Street locked, Harry Stafford decided to call in Davies's promise to help. A meeting of the club's shareholders was held at Islington Town Hall, Ancoats, on 18 March 1902. At the meeting, Stafford said that he knew of four local businessmen, Davies and three others, who were each prepared to put up £500 to guarantee the existence of the club, in return for them taking control. Newton Heath's existing board of directors agreed to the takeover, but the FA said the re-formed club would need to have a new name.

On 23 April 1902, Newton Heath beat Chesterfield 2–0 at home in Division Two and finished 15th in the table, their last league game under that name. Five days later, it was agreed at a key meeting to form a new club. Those present were invited to suggest a new name. Manchester Celtic and Manchester Central were both suggested, the former perhaps reflecting links with the Irish community, before the name of Manchester United was agreed. The team's new colours would be red jerseys and white shorts, although the team had played in red and white as early as 1892.

Over the summer of 1902, the first board of directors of Manchester United Football Club was established. Not surprisingly, Davies was appointed the club's first chairman and president. He was supported by five directors, including J.J. Bentley, who was the president of the Football League. James West continued in post as secretary-manager, while Harry Stafford took charge of team affairs.

That same summer, Tommy Morrison was signed from Burnley, one of six players bought by the club as they sought to build a squad to win promotion. Morrison was born in Belfast on 16 December 1874, the youngest of five sons born to James and

Annie Morrison. Football ran in the family, with two of his brothers playing for local teams, Robert for Linfield and Alex for Glentoran. Morrison had made his debut for Glentoran aged 16, and attracted the attention of several English sides, eventually signing for Burnley in early March 1894, but early the next season his contract was cancelled and he returned to Glentoran. In early April 1895, he was invited to play in a trial game by Glasgow Celtic and made his first team debut for the Hoops in their 2–0 home win against Clyde on 27 April 1895 and stayed with the club for almost two years. He was a fiery character and Willie Maley, the secretary-manager, had to tell him to curb his tongue and put an end to what was referred to as his 'Sandy Row antics'.

Morrison returned to Turf Moor in Febuary 1897, re-joining Burnley for £300 and was eventually appointed player-coach. While still there, on 22 March 1902, he won his seventh and final cap for Ireland when they lost 1–0 to England at the Balmoral Showgrounds, Belfast.

After joining United in the summer of 1902, Morrison had to wait until Christmas Day to make his debut for the team in the Manchester derby against City at Bank Street, thereby becoming Manchester United's first Irish player. A bumper gate of 40,000, Clayton's largest-ever crowd, turned up to see the 1–1 draw. The very next day he scored his first goal for United in their Boxing Day 2–2 home draw versus Blackpool. With the exception of United's FA Cup ties and their last two league games, he was ever-present in the Manchester United side for the rest of the season, making a total of 20 appearances and scoring seven goals in the process.

In season 1903–04, he found it more difficult to command a regular place in the United line-up at either of his two favoured positions, inside-right or outside-right. During the season he made 16 starts for United, seven of which were in the FA Cup with four of these ties against Small Heath, as it took three replays to overcome the Birmingham side. Morrison also starred for United in an FA Cup first-round replay when they caused a huge upset by beating First Division Notts County 2–1 at home on 10 February 1904, scoring the opening goal of a memorable game. Unfortunately for Morrison and United, their FA Cup run came to a juddering halt at Hillsborough, when they were thrashed 6–0 by The Wednesday in the second round. He made just two more appearances for Manchester United after that FA Cup exit, with his last match coming on 19 March 1904 away to Preston North End in a 1–1 draw. Thus Morrison's career at United ended as it began, in a 1–1 draw. In total he played 36 times for United and scored eight goals. After leaving United in September 1904, he joined Colne, who played in the Lancashire Combination and stayed there until 1906 when he signed for Burnley for a third time, before returning to Glentoran in 1907 for the final season of his playing career.

Morrison died on 26 March 1940 aged 65. He was a player who had tremendous ball control, possessed a powerful shot and was a very tricky winger. During his playing career he was nick-named 'Ching', which is believed to derive from the 1896 play entitled *Ah Sin* written by Bret Harte and Mark Twain. The play is about a Chinese laundryman who outsmarts and exposes the villain card sharp and murderer, and so fans likened his style of play to Ah Sin's jugglery with a deck of playing cards.

Part of the reason Morrison didn't get as many games in 1903–04 was that the club continued to recruit new players in their bid for promotion. Alex Bell, Harry Moger and Thomas Arkesden were all brought in to drive the team on to greater things. But after a disappointing start to the season, James West resigned from his position as secretary-manager at the end of September.

The decision to appoint Ernest Mangnall as West's successor proved to be a masterstroke by the directors. Just like Sir Matt Busby and Sir Alex Ferguson after him, Mangnall possessed an unquenchable thirst for success, he was a highly motivated indi-vidual who strove for perfection in everything the team did and had a keen eye for spotting up-and-coming talent. Recruited from

Burnley, Mangnall's recipe for success was simple: supreme physical fitness and an unbreakable team spirit.

Backed by Davies's money, he continued to recruit new players, signing Dick Duckworth from Newton Heath Athletic, who he converted from inside-forward to half-back. In April 1904, Mangnall signed Charlie Roberts from Grimsby Town, which proved to be an inspired decision and a bargain at £600. He was a quick-thinking footballer, strong in the tackle, a good passer of the ball and had an abundance of natural pace. At the start of the 1904–05 season, Mangnall made Roberts captain and set about creating arguably as strong a half-back line as ever played for United with Duckworth, Roberts and Bell, but they still could not win promotion.

The next Irish recruit joined United in late October 1905. Bernard Donaghy was a 22-year-old inside-forward from Derry Celtic. He was born in Londonderry on 23 December 1882 and came to the attention of Mangnall when he played a second game for the Irish League XI, against the Football League at Hyde Road, Manchester, on 14 October 1905. Despite the visitors losing the game 4–0, Donaghy's performance stood out on the day. Within two weeks, he was a Manchester United player. On 4 November 1905, he made his debut for United in their 2–0 Division Two home win against Lincoln City. He played in United's next game a week later, a 1–0 defeat at Chesterfield, and played his third and last game for the club on 25 April 1906, helping United to a 3–2 win at Lincoln City.

After the 1905–06 season, Donaghy was one of three players released by the club. He returned to Ireland in August 1906 and re-joined Derry Celtic. In season 1907–08 he tried his luck once more in England, this time with Burnley, but made just five appearances for the Lancashire side. In the First World War, he served as a soldier with the Royal Inniskilling Fusiliers and was killed in action on the first day of fighting in the Battle of the Somme, 1 July 1916.

Donaghy may not have played much part in the campaign, but

Mangnall's United finally brought an end to a 12-year sabbatical away from the top flight. They were back in the big time after ending the 1905–06 season in the runners-up spot behind Bristol City, who finished four points clear of United.

Having achieved promotion, in October 1906 Mangnall made one of the most important signings in the history of Manchester United when he persuaded the Welsh international outside-right, Billy Meredith, to join the club. Meredith was a household name in Manchester long before he arrived at Bank Street, having played for local rivals Manchester City since 1894. City had been heavily fined for making illegal payments to players and 17 of them were suspended until 31 December 1906. In order to pay the numerous fines imposed, City were forced to sell their best players in an auction. Mangnall stepped in quickly to snap up Meredith, plus three of his City team-mates: Jimmy Bannister, Herbert Burgess and Sandy Turnbull. With these four players trading the blue of City for the red of United, the first golden era of United was about to begin.

Within two years of winning promotion, United were crowned champions of England in season 1907–08 for the first time in the club's history, thanks to their famous half-back line, Meredith's outstanding displays on the wing and Turnbull's goals. The team played some wonderful attacking football throughout the season, thrilling fans up and down the country, a style of play United fans would become accustomed to over the next century and beyond. Their winning margin of nine points over second-placed Aston Villa shows how much they dominated that campaign.

Around this time, the supply of footballers from the Belfast area dried up. When the White Star Line placed an order for three Olympic-class passenger liners with the Harland & Wolff shipyard in Belfast in 1908, this effectively halted the influx of Irish players to English clubs. Many of the footballers who turned out for the Belfast teams on a Saturday afternoon were now guaranteed work in the Belfast yard building the leviathans, RMS *Olympic*, RMS *Titanic* and RMS *Gigantic* (later changed its name to HMHS

Britannic). With 3,000 men needed to build each one of the sister ships, a job in the yard coupled with weekend football close to home far outweighed most Irish players' desire to try their luck across the water on the mainland. Wages at the Belfast yard were not bad either, with skilled workmen receiving £2 per week.

United's defence of their title in 1908–09 never got going, as they finished a disappointing 13th in Division One, but they gave the fans something much more to cheer about when they lifted the FA Cup for the first time in the club's history, defeating Bristol City 1–0 in the final at the Crystal Palace, thanks to a goal from Sandy Turnbull.

As more and more fans wanted to see Manchester United play, including their huge Irish following, John H. Davies decided it was time that the club had a home befitting their status as one of the best teams in the country. Davies loaned United £60,000 to build Old Trafford which, when completed, was planned to have a capacity of 100,000. Davies had an appropriate site, adjacent to the Bridgewater Canal just off the north end of the Warwick Road in Old Trafford. Archibald Leitch, the architect who had previously designed Ibrox Park, Anfield and Stamford Bridge, was given the task of designing United's new home. Many men from Ireland crossed the Irish Sea to find lodgings in Manchester in order to take up offers of work from contractors Humphreys of London to help build Old Trafford.

United played their last game at Bank Street on 22 January 1910, beating Tottenham Hotspur 5–0 in Division One, with Billy Meredith credited with scoring the last goal at the ground that had been home for almost 18 years. In early February 1910 the finishing touches were put to Old Trafford, which had the largest grandstand in the Football League, a gymnasium, massage room, plunge baths, bars, lifts and tearooms. However, the final capacity had been reduced to 80,000, as spiralling costs during the construction phase meant it would have cost an extra £30,000 to achieve the intended capacity.

The inaugural game at United's new home was a Division One

clash with Liverpool on Saturday 19 February 1910. A crowd of 45,000 watched the visitors spoil the party by winning 4–3, with United's Sandy Turnbull scoring the first goal at their new home. After the game a reporter for the *Sporting Chronicle* described Old Trafford as: 'The most handsomest, the most spacious, and the most remarkable arena I have ever seen. As a football ground it is unrivalled anywhere in the world.'

After all the efforts and costs in building their new stadium, fifth place in the league in 1909–10 was a decent enough performance. But there was more to shout about at their new home the following season when United were crowned champions again. Mangnall added to his title-winning squad by capturing Mickey Hamill from Belfast Celtic. But, with the club burdened by debts from building Old Trafford and the squad ageing, they performed poorly once again in defence of their title and were only good enough to finish 13th in the table.

Hamill was born in West Belfast on 19 January 1885, the second youngest of a family of six children. He grew up in the family home located in Leeson Street, just off the Falls Road area of the city. As a young boy, he played more Gaelic football than association football at school, but increasingly the latter sport dominated and he began to turn out for St Paul's Swifts and Belfast Rangers. He was tracked by the scouts of various clubs and was very close to signing for Distillery until Belfast Celtic stepped in to secure his services. The inside-right made his senior debut for the club on Good Friday 1909, against Bohemians from Dublin.

However, he didn't fully establish himself in the team until the 1910–11 season, when he shone in a Christmas exhibition game against Glasgow Celtic. One of Manchester United's scouts was at the game, and on 31 December 1910 signed him for the club. United paid a transfer fee of £175 for Hamill and also agreed to play a friendly against Belfast Celtic at Celtic Park the following Easter. Even 100 years ago, Manchester United were a big box office attraction in Ireland, and the Belfast side knew that gate receipts would add substantially to the fee they had received for Hamill.

Hamill made his United debut on 16 September 1911 in a 1–0 away defeat at The Hawthorns against West Bromwich Albion in Division One. According to reports, the young Irishman was homesick and found it difficult to settle in Manchester, but through the intervention of nuns in Belfast and Manchester he found lodgings with his great-grandparents in St Patrick's Parish, North Manchester. Hamill was a devout Roman Catholic and attended mass regularly in Manchester. He also became very friendly with a local family named Ball and ended up moving in with them.

On 10 February 1912, Hamill won his first Ireland cap, scoring against England, his first and only goal for his country. However, the Irish lost the game 6–1 at Dalymount Park, Dublin. Then on 29 April 1912, Hamill scored the first of his two goals for United in their 3–1 Division One victory over Blackburn Rovers at Old Trafford. Hamill's only other goal for United was on 18 January 1913 in a 4–1 defeat to Everton at Goodison Park in Division One.

Following United's 4–1 win over Bolton Wanderers in the final of the Manchester FA Senior Cup on 21 April 1913, an opposing player congratulated Hamill and told him how wonderful the United side was. The cheeky Belfast boy replied: 'Oh, you should see us when we are really trying.' Following a disagreement in the summer of 1914 with United over his request for a written guarantee from United's board of directors of a benefit match, Hamill returned home and re-joined Belfast Celtic, although his registration with United had not been cancelled. Some reporters claimed that Hamill left Manchester only to avoid conscription when the First World War commenced in July 1914, as he returned to the city six years later, some while after the hostilities with Germany ceased.

During the Great War, Hamill played for Belfast Celtic and won his first Irish Cup winners' medal on 4 April 1918, when they beat Linfield in the final played at Grosvenor Park, Belfast. On 22 March 1919, Hamill played for Ireland against Scotland in a victory international at Ibrox Park, the home of Glasgow Rangers. When the ball went out of play, he would yell 'Celtic's ball', much to the amusement of many in the crowd.

In 1914 he captained Ireland to their first ever Home International Championship crown. Making only his second appearance for his country, he gave a virtuoso performance in a 3–0 win over England on 14 February at Ayresome Park, Middlesbrough, his only victory in seven appearances for his country. It is considered by many to be Hamill's greatest performance and it was also the first time Ireland had defeated England on English soil.

In September 1920, he signed for Manchester City, with United receiving the sum of £1,000, because they still held his registration, thanks to the agreement struck up by the FA and IFA. He stayed with City for four seasons making 118 league appearances. The Manchester press loved him, and labelled him the 'world's greatest centre-half'.

In October 1926, he re-joined Belfast Celtic after a brief spell in the USA. His move there had coincided with his marriage to Genevieve in 1925, and during his short career in the United States he became a sports icon and was even invited to the White House to meet President Calvin Coolidge. The Belfast Hamill returned to in 1926 was a completely different city to the one he left behind in 1920, with sectarianism rife. At the end of the 1929–30 season, at the age of 45, he finally retired from playing and ran his own pub, the Centre Half Bar, on the corner of Paton Street on the Falls Road, Belfast. Then, in July 1934, he accepted the offer to become the manager of Distillery. He was just 58 years old when he died, his drowned body being pulled out of the River Lagan at Lisburn on 23 July 1943, with no verdict as to the cause of death ever being returned.

Hamill's first season at Old Trafford turned out to be his boss's last, as in September 1912, Mangnall stepped down as the manager of Manchester United. Controversially, he moved across the city to become the new manager of Manchester City and was succeeded at Old Trafford by J.J. Bentley. Under their new manager, United finished fourth in Division One in 1912–13 and 14th in 1913–14, but in the final season before competitive football was suspended for the duration of the First World War, United slumped to 18th, only just avoiding relegation. When official football started again in the 1919–20 season, it would be a much different world – especially in Ireland.

Chapter 3

Difficult Times

After the success had by Manchester United in the decade before the First World War, the period after it was a difficult one, when the team regularly bounced between the First and Second Divisions and, crippled by the outstanding debts from building Old Trafford and poor attendances, nearly went bankrupt in late 1931. Happily, they were bailed out by local businessman James Gibson. It wasn't the end of United's troubles, however, as the club was almost relegated to the Third Division in 1934. But, from that low point, things gradually started to improve until the outbreak of the Second World War put everything on hold.

United's Irish connection during this period hadn't developed the strength that would come later, but then United weren't really a top team at this time – even in Manchester they were often largely ignored, with City having much more success. However, the arrival of Tommy Breen, Henry Baird and finally Johnny Carey in November 1936 marked the beginning of a revived Irish influx, as the club became one of the first to focus its attentions across the Irish Sea, developing an excellent scouting network there. Carey would go on to be the most significant Irishman at

Old Trafford to date and is still recognised as one of the greatest full-backs in football history.

But at the start of this period, during the First World War, the role of the Irish at United was fairly limited, partly because domestic football in Ireland was quite strong at the time and the vast majority of top Irish footballers played at home. Furthermore, by staying in Ireland, players who wanted to were able to stay out of the war, which became an increasingly important consideration when the full horrors of that conflict were understood. This exemption was made possible because of the political situation in Ireland, where the splits between those loyal to the British crown and the nationalists who wanted Ireland to control its own affairs, meant that conscription was politically impossible. Despite this, some 210,000 Irishmen (the vast majority of them as volunteers) fought against Germany. Whatever the players' politics, they knew that if they played their football in England, there was every chance they would find themselves called up to the British Army.

That said, just before the outbreak of war, United did make one hefty venture into the transfer market as secretary-manager J.J. Bentley broke the club's transfer record and signed Dubliner Patrick O'Connell from Hull City for £1,000 in May 1914. Bentley was attracted to O'Connell after the Irish half-back played well in all three of Ireland's Home International Championship games in 1913–14, captaining his country against Scotland as they went on to win the competition for the first time in their history. Ironically, the player he replaced at Old Trafford, Mickey Hamill, played alongside him in the Irish jersey.

Bentley made O'Connell captain for the 1914–15 season, the first Irish captain in the history of the club. He was born in Dublin in March 1887 and as a teenager he played locally. After working for a while in Boland Mills, Dublin, he moved to the Falls Road, Belfast and joined Belfast Celtic, before leaving them to sign for The Wednesday in 1909 (as Sheffield Wednesday were known until 1929). O'Connell then joined Hull City in 1912. At

5ft 11in and weighing just over 12st, he was a rock in the centre of the Hull City defence and, just like their nickname, he was as ferocious as a tiger in the tackle. On the opening day of the 1914–15 Division One season, he made his debut for Manchester United at centre-half in a 3–1 home defeat to Oldham Athletic, scoring United's goal. Throughout his first season at Old Trafford, he put in commanding performances in the heart of the United defence, missing just four games and even slotted in at right-half when called upon to do so.

In December 1914, J.J. Bentley stepped down as manager and made way for John Robson, who joined United from Brighton & Hove Albion. O'Connell retained his position as club captain and was the outstanding player in the Manchester United team, as the *Manchester Football Chronicle* commented: 'O'Connell, the captain, always sets a good example. He is ever on the move and can withstand the most gruelling day. Big and strong fellow as he is, he always looks as though he carries not an ounce of unwanted flesh, and reaps the benefit when the heavy grounds come along.'

O'Connell played his last game for the club on 2 December 1916 during the war, but didn't leave until early August 1919, moving north of the border to Dumbarton. His story has an interesting postscript, as he went on to become a hugely successful manager. In 1922, leaving his family behind him, he set sail for Spain, where he took charge of Racing de Santander. He stayed with the club for seven years, revolutionising their coaching methods and tactics, winning the regional competition five times before La Liga was inaugurated in 1928–29, with Racing as a founder member of the new league. In 1929–30, he took charge of Real Oviedo before moving on soon after to Real Betis, where he led them to the title in 1934–35 – the only time in the club's history that it has won La Liga. Given his excellent track record, it was not surprising that one of the big teams should come calling, and for the next campaign he was in charge of Barcelona. After he'd been there for just a year, the Spanish Civil

War meant that La Liga was suspended from the start of 1936–37 for three seasons.

Facing mounting debts because of their huge overheads, O'Connell decided to take Barcelona on a tour of Mexico and the USA in 1937. He was a huge hit with the New York media, where his Irish brogue ensured he and his team received a very warm welcome, given the huge Irish-American population in that city. The club made $15,000 on their trip, but he returned with only a few of his players, as many decided not to return to their wartorn country. The money from the tour arguably saved the club from going under, and if you visit the Nou Camp today you will see a bust of O'Connell in the club museum in recognition of his efforts.

Season 1942–43 saw O'Connell in charge of his fourth Spanish club, Sevilla, and that season he guided them to runners-up spot in La Liga before leaving them in 1945. In 1947 he returned to Racing de Santander for two more years. It is unclear what became of him after that, but it is known that he spent his last years in London living in run-down accommodation near St Pancras railway station. On 27 February 1959, despite such a successful football career both as a player and as a manager, O'Connell died in London, aged 71, destitute. He was simply known as 'Don Patricio' by the Spanish football press.

After O'Connell had left United in 1919, the club signed an Irish striker named Billy Toms from local side Eccles Borough. Toms made his debut for United in a First Division game against Middlesbrough on 4 October 1919 at Old Trafford, the game ending 1–1. Born in Curragh, County Kildare on 19 May 1895, he scored his first goal for United away to Port Vale on 10 January 1920 when they won 1–0 in the first round of the FA Cup. In April 1920, he scored in three successive league games for United, but after playing for United against Arsenal on 30 August at the beginning of the 1920–21 season, he was transferred to Plymouth Argyle for a fee of £500. He had made 14 appearances for United, scoring four goals in that time.

James Robinson, who had previously played junior football in Belfast, was also signed by United in 1919. He was born on 8 January 1898 in Belfast and came to Old Trafford as an understudy to outside-left Fred Hopkin, having won junior international honours for Ireland. On 3 January 1920, with Hopkin injured, he was given his Manchester United debut against Chelsea in a First Division game at Old Trafford. United lost the game 2–0 and it appears that Robinson did not make the best of starts to his professional career, with one local reporter writing: 'Robinson, who filled the outside-left berth, has still a lot to learn.'

Hopkin regained his place in the side for the next game and Robinson made just one more appearance in a United shirt in season 1919–20. At the start of the 1920–21 season, he knew he had to work hard to get in the United line-up and was content to play reserve team football, hoping to impress Robson and get another shot at making the big time. However, he had a long wait until 20 February 1921 before he had his chance, against Sunderland in what was also goalkeeper Jack Mew's benefit match. United won 3–0 and Robinson scored the opening goal of the game, his first for the club, and laid on the third for striker William Harrison. His performance on the wing impressed Robson and he retained his place in the team for the next four games, scoring against Bradford City in that run. A report in the local press described his goal as follows: 'At the end of 28 minutes, Manchester United took the lead, Robinson scoring a really great goal for the team. Robinson began his run just over the halfway line and, beating Potts, he cleverly closed in on the Bradford goal and drove the ball into the far corner of the net.'

He played just two more league games that season, as United finished 13th in Division One, slipping a place from their 1919–20 finish. In 1921–22, Robinson made 12 appearances, scoring in United's first home game of the campaign. But it was his fellow goalscorer that day, Edward Partridge, who went on to command the outside-left spot in the team. John Robson stepped down as Manchester United manager in October 1921 and was replaced by John Chapman. But the change of manager did not result in an improvement in Robinson's prospects, and on 17 April 1922, he played his 21st and last game for United, a 3–2 home win over Sheffield United. But by then, United were doomed to relegation, and in June 1922 Robinson signed for Tranmere Rovers on a free transfer.

When David Lyner arrived at Old Trafford in August 1922, Manchester United were about to start the 1922–23 season as a Second Division outfit. Lyner was born in Belfast on 9 January 1893 and the talented two-footed winger was signed up by Distillery. A short time later, he moved across Belfast to join Glentoran in 1912. Lyner played for the Glens for ten years and won two Irish League winners' medals and two Irish Cups with the Belfast outfit. On 25 October 1919, he won the first of his six Irish caps when he played at outside-left against England. By the time the 29-year-old Lyner was brought to Manchester by manager John Chapman, he had already been capped four times by his country.

He made his debut for Manchester United on 23 September 1922 in a 2–0 defeat to Coventry City at Highfield Road. Lyner retained his place in the side for United's next league game a week later, which was also against Coventry City, but this time United beat the Sky Blues 2–1 at Old Trafford. His third consecutive game for United, a 2–1 home loss to Port Vale on 7 October, also marked the end of his time in the first team at Old Trafford. Sixteen days after the Port Vale defeat, Lyner won his fifth cap for his country in their 2–0 loss to England at Roker Park, Sunderland. By the time he was awarded his sixth and final cap by Ireland on 14 April 1923, he was a Kilmarnock player, having signed for the Scottish club in December 1922. And so, after just three games for United and no goals, his brief stint as a professional footballer in England came to an abrupt end. Meanwhile, Manchester United went on to finish in fourth position in the Second Division, having chopped and changed their side frequently during the campaign. Lyner passed away on 5 December 1973 at home in Belfast.

After Lyner left the club in December 1922, it would be more than a decade before another Irish accent would be heard from a Manchester United player. However, in between Lyner moving north of the border to play for Kilmarnock and Walter McMillen travelling across the Irish Sea from his home in Belfast to join Manchester United, the club would be promoted to Division One in 1925 and relegated back to Division Two in 1931. The 1920s and 1930s were dubbed the 'Yo-Yo Years' in the club's history, given the team's inconsistent form throughout the period. Season 1926–27 witnessed no fewer than three different men sitting in the United hot seat of manager: in October 1926, secretary-manager John Chapman was suspended from his managerial role by the Football Association for the rest of the season and was replaced by Clarence Hilditch, the club's only ever player-manager, who then handed over the management reins to Herbert Bamlett in April 1927.

Having ended the 1930–31 season with relegation, Bamlett lost his job and Walter Crickmer succeeded him as secretary-manager of United on a temporary basis until Scott Duncan was brought in to help the club climb out of Division Two in 1932.

Although at first glance it may not have been a great surprise that United failed to attract many Irish players during this difficult period in its history, there are reasons why one might have expected them to do so. In 1924, the United States government introduced the Immigration Act, which greatly reduced the number of Irish people who could emigrate there. As a direct result of this act, the UK again became the primary destination for those Irishmen, women and children who wanted to get away from Ireland and seek a new life elsewhere, with approximately four out of every five migrants who left independent Ireland from the mid-1920s to the 1930s coming to Great Britain. Manchester remained one of their prime destinations, so at least the club could continue to rely on their Irish supporters living in the city, even if there were no Irish players to cheer on.

There was another reason why some people decided to leave Ireland in the period after the end of the First World War, and that was due to the upheaval caused by partition in 1921, when the country split in two. The north-eastern part of the country became Northern Ireland, while the rest of the island became an independent British dominion initially known as the Irish Free State, before eventually becoming the Republic of Ireland. This book is not the place to go into the complicated events and reasons behind what happened, though they did have their impact on football, as from 1926 the new country would begin playing international matches, starting with a game against Italy on 21 March. Meanwhile, the Belfast-based Irish Football Association continued to field a national team in the Home Internationals. They insisted on using 'Ireland' as the name of their team and on choosing players from the entire island of Ireland. This meant there was a possibility for some players to play for both countries until some time after the Second World War when the anomaly was finally resolved.

Bill Clarkson recalls this period: 'When I was growing up in Manchester during the 1930s most of the Irish families lived in North Manchester. You only have to look at the names of some of the pubs in the Ancoats area such as The Exile of Erin, The Daniel O'Connell and The Harp & Shamrock, with them all located within five hundred yards of each other. Most of the Irishmen at the time worked on the Manchester Ship Canal and on the construction of roads. As the years went by, a lot of the Irish could be found working on the construction of the third Woodhead Tunnel (a three-mile-long railway tunnel across the Pennines linking Manchester to Sheffield), which was opened in 1954, and the M60, which was opened in 1960.'

Having spent the previous two seasons in Division Two, Manchester United decided to strengthen their team for the 1933–34 campaign in the hope that they could return to the top flight. Secretary-manager Scott Duncan splashed out in the transfer market and brought in a total of 14 new players, including three Irishmen: half-back Walter McMillen, striker David Byrne and goalkeeper Billy Behan. The club they joined was a very different one from the one that Lyner had been a part of a decade before.

By the end of 1931, the club was again heading for bankruptcy, the fans were protesting about mismanagement and disaster loomed. At this stage, in stepped local businessman James Gibson, who put up the money to save the club from collapse, and took charge of the board early in 1932. He made funds available to invest in new players, and while the turnround was not immediate, at least there was stability and hope for the future. With the club having finished in sixth place in 1932–33, it was hoped that this new batch of signings would make the difference and push United out of the Second Division. They nearly did – but not in the way intended.

Of the three Irishmen signed, it was Walter McMillen who had the largest impact. A cultured half-back who possessed excellent ball control, he was a superb passer, had excellent timing and, standing 6ft tall and weighing 12st 4lb, he was not a man who could be pushed off the ball easily. He crossed the Irish Sea in August 1933 and joined United from the Belfast-based Cliftonville. Born in Belfast on 24 November 1913, he began his footballing career with local side Albert Foundry, then joined West End United, followed by Carrickfergus, before plying his skills at Solitude for Cliftonville. McMillen was handed his United debut on 16 September 1933 for their Division Two away fixture at Brentford. Although a natural half-back, he played at centre-half against the London club and impressed in the team's 4–3 victory. He retained his place in the side for the next three league games and went on to make a total of 23 league appearances that season, scoring one goal versus Port Vale at Old Trafford in a vital 2–0 win on 14 April 1934. Despite having played in the previous five games, he was not selected for the final fixture of the season on 5 May, against Millwall, where United went into the game at the Den knowing that only a win would guarantee they avoided the unthinkable, a drop to the Third Division for the first time in United's illustrious history. Happily, they won 2–0 and finished 20th in the Second Division, their lowest ever position.

He might have been playing in a struggling Second Division outfit, but McMillen's form was sufficient for him to win the first of seven international caps for (Northern) Ireland on 14 October 1933, when he played at right-half in their 3–0 defeat to England at Windsor Park, Belfast. His second game for Ireland was notable for two reasons. No one gave the Irish any chance of beating a strong Scotland team at Windsor Park on 20 October 1934. A hand injury to Elisha Scott, Ireland's legendary goalkeeper, meant that the Irish were reduced to ten men. McMillen went in goal for Ireland as his side trailed 1–0 at half time. In the second half, he made a number of crucial saves to help the Irish to an unlikely 2–1 victory over the Scots. A report on the game in a Belfast newspaper commented on McMillen's heroics: 'McMillen did great work in Scott's place, saving splendidly when called upon with an inspired second-half fight by ten men that brought Ireland a deserved victory.'

In his second season with United, 1934–35, McMillen made just four appearances, three of them at outside-left. On 27 March 1935, he played his 29th and final game in a Manchester United shirt when Burnley visited Old Trafford for a Division Two encounter. Although United went down 4–3, McMillen marked his final appearance for the club with a goal. That season United finished fifth in Division Two, and over the following two campaigns he had to make do with reserve team appearances before Chesterfield called upon his services and signed him for £200 in December 1936.

However, before he left Old Trafford he collected his third Irish cap as a Manchester United player in Ireland's 3–1 home loss to Scotland at Windsor Park on 31 October 1936. He went on to win four more caps for his country without ever finding the back of the net, becoming Chesterfield's first player to win international recognition. On 13 November 1937, McMillen played for Chesterfield against United and the inevitable law of the ex struck, as he scored the only goal for the Spireites. Fortunately, United hit seven at Saltergate to record their fourth biggest away win in history. He died at home in Belfast on 11 May 1987, aged 73.

The second of the new Irish contingent to arrive at Old Trafford that summer of 1933 was David Byrne, who joined United from Shamrock Rovers. Byrne was born in Ringsend, Dublin, on 28 April 1905, the youngest of 11 children, and began his junior career as a striker for St Brendan's in Dublin. In August 1926, he signed for Shamrock Rovers and won a League of Ireland Championship winners' medal and a League of Ireland Shield winners' medal in his first season at Glenmalure Park. His performances in the famous green and white hooped shirt attracted the interest of several English league sides, and in November 1927 he joined Bradford City. However, even though he scored on his debut, he failed to settle in England, and he returned to Dublin in 1928, signing for Shelbourne, winning a second League of Ireland Championship winners' medal, before re-joining Shamrock Rovers in 1929.

After winning more honours with Shamrock Rovers, Byrne then decided to give professional football a second try and moved to Sheffield United in October 1932, but was soon back home in Dublin for his third spell with Shamrock Rovers. Despite missing the early part of that season playing in England, Byrne scored 33 goals to help Shamrock Rovers to another trophy-winning campaign.

Scott Duncan was anxious to bring a proven goalscorer to the club and persuaded the 27-year-old Irish international to move to Old Trafford, agreeing to pay him £5 per week. It was clearly a gamble, given Byrne's track record in England. But, prior to joining United, Byrne had been capped twice at international level by the Republic of Ireland (scoring on his international debut versus

Belgium in a 4–0 friendly win on 20 April 1929 at Dalymount Park and appearing against Spain in a 5–0 friendly defeat on 13 December 1931 at the same ground), so it seemed a risk worth taking.

On 21 October 1933, Byrne made his United debut and immediately made an impact by scoring in a 2–1 Second Division defeat to Bury at Gigg Lane. Byrne's debut saw him line up alongside McMillen; it was the first time in the club's history that two Irishmen had played together in the same team. Despite his goalscoring debut, Byrne made only three more league appearances for United during the 1933–34 season, including a 7–3 mauling at Grimsby Town on Boxing Day in which he scored twice to spare some of United's blushes. His fourth and last game for the Reds came four days later, resulting in a 3–0 home defeat by Plymouth Argyle.

In February 1934, Byrne made his way back across the Irish Sea and signed for Coleraine, after the Irish side agreed to meet his weekly wage at Old Trafford of £5. Shortly after moving to Coleraine he won a third cap for the Free State in a 1934 World Cup qualifying game against Belgium. Byrne did not stay long at Coleraine after they encountered financial problems and could no longer afford his wages. He then joined Larne and moved on again to Shamrock Rovers in 1935. He died in May 1990, aged 85.

Duncan's third Irish recruit, Billy Behan, was born on 8 August 1911 in Dublin. Aged 19, he made his debut for Shamrock Rovers in goal on 8 February 1931. After just three months with the Dublin outfit, he helped them to victory in the Football Association of Ireland Cup, along with Byrne. He then moved across the city and joined Shelbourne. Scott Duncan brought 22-year-old Behan across the Irish Sea to Old Trafford in September 1933 a month after his first-choice goalkeeper, John Moody, left the club to sign for Chesterfield. However, Behan was not signed as Moody's replacement, but was recruited to provide cover at goalkeeper during the 1933–34 season, when United fielded four different goalkeepers.

On 3 March 1934, following three successive league defeats and with United languishing dangerously close to the relegation zone, Duncan gave Behan his big chance and handed him his debut for a home Division Two encounter against Bury, which United won 2–1. He thus became the first Irish goalkeeper to play for United. Even though he conceded a goal in the opening minute of the game, he went on to put in a solid performance, but was dropped for United's next game. When Duncan signed Jack Hacking from Oldham Athletic at the end of March 1934, Behan knew he was fourth-choice goalkeeper at Old Trafford and quickly made up his mind that he wanted first team action. In July 1934, Behan returned home to Dublin and re-joined Shelbourne and played one season for them before signing for a second time for Shamrock Rovers in the summer of 1935. At the end of the 1935–36 season, aged just 24, he hung up his boots and went on to become a highly respected referee in the League of Ireland.

But Behan's association with Manchester United was far greater than his solitary league game, as he went on to serve the club for more than 50 years as their chief scout in Ireland. He had a keen eye when it came to spotting young and talented footballers, and after being handed the role of scout by United in the summer of 1936, he set about scouring the country for the best talent available. His first, and perhaps his most important find, was Johnny Carey. Other notable finds credited to the astute eye of Behan include Liam Whelan, Johnny Giles, Don Givens, Tony Dunne, Gerry Daly, Kevin Moran and Paul McGrath, but more about these Irish Manchester United legends later. In September 1983, United presented Behan with an inscribed watch to commemorate his 50 years of service to the club. In 1987, he decided to retire and sadly passed away on 12 November 1991, aged 80, at his home in Dublin.

Behan was part of a much larger trend. From the mid-1930s onwards, United were one of the first English clubs actively to scout in Ireland and recognise it as a fertile recruiting ground. Indeed, one former United scout who travelled regularly between

Ireland and England used to joke about the tariffs Ireland and England put on goods imported from one country to another in those days. Chief scout Louis Rocca had close connections to the Manchester Catholic Sportsman's Club, and through them he appointed a network of scouts from the Catholic Church. Even the manager, Scott Duncan, paid regular scouting visits to Ireland, which was how McMillen had been signed. Because of limited travel opportunities in those days, these links may not have encouraged masses of people to take the ferry across from Ireland to watch United in action, but they were creating a level of interest and affection that would have to wait many years fully to spark into life.

Meanwhile, having narrowly avoided relegation the previous campaign, in 1934–35 United bounced back to finish fifth in Division Two and were then crowned Second Division champions in 1935–36, clinching the title by a single point over the surprise challengers, Charlton Athletic. Sadly, United struggled in the top flight, and soon Scott Duncan was looking for new recruits. The Belfast-born Tommy Breen arrived at Old Trafford from Belfast Celtic in a transfer deal worth £2,500. Following a 6–2 defeat at Grimsby Town and a 5–2 home loss to Liverpool, Duncan decided to rush Breen, already an Irish international, into the side. He was the sixth goalkeeper signed by United in as many seasons, a reflection of the club's inability to maintain stability at this time.

Tommy Breen was born in Belfast on 27 April 1917 and surprisingly began his football career as a striker with Drogheda United. During one game their goalkeeper got injured and Breen was called upon to play in goal for the remainder of the game. He did so well that his manager asked him to continue in the role and soon Belfast Celtic came calling and signed him up. Prior to joining United he represented an Irish League side on two occasions and on 6 February 1935, he won the first of his nine Ireland caps when he made his debut for his country against England at the age of just 17 (he also made five appearances for the Republic between 1937 and 1947). On 28 November 1936, Breen made his debut in goal for Manchester United in their 2–1 loss away to Leeds United. Like his Irish predecessor, he made an inauspicious start to his United career, having to pick the ball out of the back of his net within a minute of the kick-off. However, he played in 25 of United's remaining 26 league games as they battled unsuccessfully to avoid relegation back to the Second Division.

The following campaign, Breen was United's regular goalkeeper and appeared in 33 of their 42 league games, helping the side to runners-up place behind Division Two champions Aston Villa and earning an immediate return to Division One, though Walter Crickmer had taken over from Duncan as manager during the season. However, Breen had a major embarrassment in the FA Cup fourth round at Barnsley on 22 January 1938 when he failed to prevent a throw-in from a team-mate from rolling over the goal-line and into the back of the net, helping the home side to a 2–2 draw. It was the first time a goal had been scored directly from a throw-in. In the 1938–39 season, Breen lost his place in goal to Jack Breedon, making only six appearances for United. When the Second World War broke out in September 1939, Breen returned home to Ireland and re-joined Belfast Celtic.

He subsequently joined Linfield, and after the war Matt Busby tried to re-sign him for United, but the clubs could not agree on a fee. He eventually signed for Shamrock Rovers on a free transfer and then went on to play for Newry Town and Glentoran, but dislocated the cartilage in his knee soon after joining the Glens, which brought his career to a premature end.

Breen wasn't alone in making the journey to Old Trafford at this time. Later in the 1936–37 season striker Henry Baird joined United. He was born in Belfast on 17 August 1913 and, after starring for Bangor and Dunmurry, he joined Linfield where his form earned him a place in the Irish League XI. He quickly established a reputation for himself as one of the best strikers on the island of Ireland, which attracted the interest of United manager Scott Duncan, but his attempts to sign the talented player were dismissed. However, when United continued to struggle, they contacted Linfield once again in early January 1937, and this time the Belfast-based club did not refuse United's £3,500 offer for his services.

On 23 January 1937, Baird made his United debut in a 1–0 First Division defeat to Sheffield Wednesday at Hillsborough. He went on to play 13 more league games in the second half of the season, scoring three times; his first United goal coming three weeks after his debut when he scored the only goal of the game in a 1–0 victory over Brentford at Old Trafford. The following season, Baird's 12 league goals in his 35 appearances helped United finish runners-up to Aston Villa in Division Two and so make an instant return to the top flight. He also scored three times in four FA Cup ties that campaign. However, the Belfast man did not enjoy the fruits of his efforts with United as he was transferred to Huddersfield Town in September 1938 after playing 53 times for the Reds and scoring 18 goals.

His move to Huddersfield brought with it international recognition when he won his only cap for Ireland against England on 16 November 1938 when he lined up alongside former United player Walter McMillen. In June 1946, Baird moved to Ipswich Town after appearing as a guest for the East Anglia club during the war. He played more than 200 times for Ipswich Town, mainly at wing-half, before becoming a reserve team coach at Portman Road until 1953. He passed away on 22 May 1973.

That final season before the outbreak of war created a moment of history at Old Trafford that didn't involve United, but did involve an Irishman, when the ground hosted the 1939 FA Cup semi-final between Wolverhampton Wanderers and Grimsby Town on Saturday 25 March 1939 that attracted a record crowd of 76,962. As Ed O'Riordan from Skeheenarinky, County Tipperary, recorded in an article for *Avondhu* newspaper in January 2010: 'Unfortunately, during a Wolves attack on the Grimsby goal, [their keeper] Moulson committed himself to a save and received a kick in the head from the Wolves forward Dickie Dorsett that caused him to be taken to the local hospital for treatment . . . Clogheen-born George Bernard Moulson played an important part on that record-setting day. Moulson was also part of another piece of soccer history that day at Old Trafford; that was the first time that the players all wore numbered jerseys.'

But while the signings of Breen and Baird were important ones, there is no doubt that the most significant recruit from Ireland during that 1936–37 season was also one of the bargain buys of the 20th century. John Joseph Carey was playing at inside-left for his local side, St James's Gate in Dublin, when Billy Behan spotted him and immediately recommended him to United's chief scout, Louis Rocca. Within hours Rocca was on his way over to Dublin to see this young talent play. Behan's words were as true as gold and Rocca had no hesitation in parting with a mere £200 to snap him up.

Carey crossed the Irish Sea with his father and when the pair got off the train at Piccadilly Station in Manchester, Carey spotted a newspaper stand with a poster that read: 'United's Big Signing.' Johnny nudged his dad and urged him to buy a copy of the paper. However, much to their disappointment, they opened the pages to find a story about Ernie Thompson, a prolific centre-forward who had just signed for United from Blackburn Rovers in a transfer deal worth £4,500, more than 20 times the fee United paid for Carey. His father chuckled as Carey handed him the newspaper and walked away. Just two lines of the newspaper story touched on the acquisition of Carey, and yet it was he, not Thompson (who played only three games for United), who went on to become one of the most accomplished footballers in Europe.

Carey was born on 23 February 1919 in Dublin and played for local side Home Farm while still at school. He loved playing football, but also played Gaelic football and was selected to represent Dublin at minor level before being banned by the Gaelic Athletic Association (GAA) because of his links with football. However, the GAA's loss was football's considerable gain, as Carey went on to become one of the greatest players not only in the history of

Manchester United, but at international level for Ireland (North and South) too.

Duncan gave him his Manchester United debut at inside-left against Southampton in a Second Division game at Old Trafford on 25 September 1937. United lost the game 2–1, but he kept his place for the next match and within a few weeks, on 7 November, Carey won the first of his 29 caps for the Republic of Ireland, against Norway at Dalymount Park in a qualifying game for the 1938 World Cup finals in France.

Carey did not play again for United until they visited Nottingham Forest on 28 December 1937, by which time Crickmer was in charge. He scored his first goal for the club in United's 3–2 victory that day, and his performance was good enough to see him go on a run of eight consecutive league games and he played in three of United's four FA Cup games in that season as well. That campaign Carey appeared in 16 league games, scoring three goals, to help United to win promotion. The teenager had already impressed many, so a number of the top clubs in England contacted Crickmer to enquire about Carey's availability, but all advances were rebuffed. With United back in the top flight in 1938–39, Carey played in 32 of United's 42 First Division games, scoring six times, to help the Reds to a respectable 14th place in the table.

The recent increase in the numbers of Irish recruits at Old Trafford was clearly having an impact by now. When Cliftonville came over to England on their annual outing to see the Grand National at Aintree, the club traditionally organised a few friendly games. Given the good relationship they enjoyed with Manchester United, a friendly took place between the two teams at Old Trafford on Monday 13 March 1939. Carey played and scored in the game for a rampant United who hammered their Irish visitors 9–1.

The outbreak of the Second World War interrupted Carey's Manchester United career from 1939 to 1945. He could have taken the easy option and returned to neutral Ireland until the end of the hostilities. However, despite being a patriotic Irishman, in 1943 he volunteered for service stating at the time: 'A country that gives me my living is worth fighting for.' He served in the Queen's Royal Hussars and was stationed in North Africa and Italy. During the war, the affable Irishman managed to make in excess of 100 wartime appearances for United and also made a number of guest appearances for several English league clubs. When peace was restored in 1945, he was asked to stay in Italy and play his club football there, but luckily for United and Ireland, he opted to return to the Reds.

Author Iain McCartney, who has written many books on United, has this to say about United's Irish links and support up to the outbreak of the Second World War: 'The flame of that support [that has grown so big now] had to be ignited at some point, and many of those early sparks came from the Irishmen who had crossed the water in search of employment and a better life, heading for the industrial sprawl of Manchester. A considerable number of them found work within the shadows of Old Trafford in the docks of Salford Quays. Some would obviously fall by the wayside in their search for recreation within their new, adopted home town, giving their support to Manchester City (perhaps Maine Road was closer to their lodgings), but for the majority, it was United that captured their attention. It is perhaps because of the influx of this early Irish support that United is perceived to be a Catholic club. This belief has, in my opinion, little or indeed no foundation whatsoever. In England, unlike north of Hadrian's Wall, religion is a totally irrelevant subject where football is concerned.

'The steady influx of players from both sides of the Irish border to United will certainly have added to the interest in the club from Ireland, with the inhabitants of whatever city, town or village that a certain player came from, showing great interest in their progress. Again, such support would undoubtedly be passed down, keeping that eternal flame burning. Johnny Carey, to a certain extent, would have done much to cement the love for

Manchester United into the hearts of the Irish, but his contribution to the story would be minimal compared to that of Munich
and the genius that was George Best.'

But for everyone during this period, the big question was not so
much about football, but about what sort of world would emerge
from the horrors of the war. In Manchester, they were about to
find out, and Johnny Carey would have his part to play in the
transformation of United, who would rise from the ashes of a
bombed-out stadium to become one of the most famous names in
the sporting world.

Chapter 4

Gentleman John

As the Second World War drew to a close, Manchester City were considered to be Manchester's premier team. Between the wars they had won the league title in 1936–37 and the FA Cup in 1934, and were runners-up in both competitions at least once. United, by contrast, had won nothing major, and had spent much of the period struggling on and off the pitch. During the war, things got even worse for United when Old Trafford's Main Stand was destroyed in a German bombing raid in March 1941. With their stadium out of action, and unable to be repaired because of the wartime (and then post-war) priorities of rebuilding factories and homes, United were forced to use Maine Road as their home ground. Homeless and almost penniless, the club was hardly an appealing prospect.

Yet one man saw things differently, and believed he could rebuild the club – but he was going to do it on his terms. That man, of course, was Matt Busby. The ex-Manchester City, Liverpool and Scotland international was just 36 at the time he became manager of United, having been recommended to the board by Louis Rocca, who had been an influential figure at the club for more than 40 years. Busby had an offer from Liverpool as well, but chose United partly because of family reasons, but also because he was given complete control to do things the way he wanted to. On taking up his post in October 1945 after he was demobilised, having been appointed in February, Busby knew the two men he wanted to build his team around. The first of them would be by his side throughout his time at the club: Jimmy Murphy.

As the war drew to a close, Busby took an Army team to Italy to play several friendlies. While he was there, he had seen Murphy making a speech to a group of soldiers. Busby stood in the crowd and listened intently. He was so impressed with Murphy's words that when he finished he walked over to him and introduced himself. The pair bonded immediately, with the Scot persuading the Welshman to join him at Old Trafford as his assistant when the fighting in Europe had ceased for good. Murphy accepted the offer.

Busby's second key man was Johnny Carey. On 13 October 1945, much to the delight of the United supporters and the fans back home in Ireland, Carey appeared in a United shirt in a Football League North 3–0 loss at Everton. Busby knew that in Carey he had a natural leader at his disposal, a player highly respected by his team-mates, someone he could ask to play anywhere and who would never disappoint him, but above all else a man who could be his general on the pitch. Not surprisingly, Busby decided to appoint Carey the captain of Manchester United.

Carey was himself immediately impressed by his new manager. On his first day taking training at United, Busby did something very few other football managers of the day did. He took to the pitch wearing a tracksuit, adopting a more hands-on approach to the management and coaching of his players. When asked about Busby's managerial style, Carey said: 'When I joined United, Scott Duncan, with spats and a red rose in his buttonhole, typified a football manager. But here was the new boss playing with his team in training, showing what he wanted and how to do it. He was ahead of his time.'

Therefore, not only was Carey the club's first post-war captain, but he was also the first player from outside the United Kingdom to lead Manchester United on the field of play. Busby decided to try Carey out at half-back and played him in this position at home to Blackburn Rovers on 9 March 1946, a game United won 6–2. After five consecutive games at half-back, Busby and Murphy asked Carey to play at full-back away to Manchester City on 13 April. He put in an impressive performance in his new role to ensure United won the derby 3–1. Both Busby and Murphy had seen enough from Carey that day to continue playing him at full-back for the rest of the season.

It wasn't until the following campaign, however, that normal league football resumed, and somehow Busby, Murphy and Carey led United to the runners-up spot, finishing a point behind champions Liverpool. It was their best league position in more than 35 years, and the team played a brand of attacking football that would become Busby's hallmark throughout his time at the club.

For Carey, there was personal honour, too. On 28 September 1946, he won the first of his seven caps for Northern Ireland, England running out 7–2 winners at Windsor Park, Belfast, in a Home International game (he was eligible to play because he had served in the British Army). Two days later, he was playing for the Republic of Ireland against the same opposition at Dalymount Park in Dublin, losing 1–0. In total, he won 29 caps for the Republic between 1937 and 1953, scoring three goals, and seven for Northern Ireland between 1946 and 1949. Uniquely, Carey captained both Irish international teams, but without question his greatest moment in an Irish jersey came on 21 September 1949 when he captained the Republic of Ireland in a friendly against England at Goodison Park, Liverpool. The Irish won 2–0 to inflict the first home defeat on England by a 'foreign' side.

On 10 May 1947, although the club was fighting for the title and had a game that day, Carey was released by United to travel to

Glasgow, where he was given the honour of captaining a Rest of Europe side against Great Britain in an exhibition match played at Hampden Park. Can you imagine the same thing happening today! A bumper crowd of 137,000 fans poured in to the stadium, paying a world record £31,000 in gate receipts, and were treated to a magnificent game of football, celebrating Great Britain's return to FIFA, an organisation they had left in 1920. Great Britain won the game easily 6–1.

Bill Clarkson remembers a visit Carey paid to his school soon after that game: 'He spoke to us about all aspects of football and warned us all that, despite the fact that his side had been well beaten, within the following ten years teams in Europe would become very dominant at both international and club level. Johnny told us that he visited coaching camps in Europe quite a lot and had taken note of how the game was developing there. None of us believed him, but how right he proved to be because within seven years Hungary had beaten England 6–3 at Wembley Stadium and 7–1 in Budapest, while Real Madrid dominated the early years of the European Cup.'

Carey wasn't Busby's only Irish connection at this time. Busby's parish priest at St John's Roman Catholic Church in Chorlton-cum-Hardy was Monsignor William Sewell from Killarney. Busby attended mass almost every day of the week and he always sat in the same place in the church. In return, there was a special seat reserved for Monsignor Sewell at United's home games. The priest was a regular visitor to Killarney for his summer holidays and doubtless spread the word about United to any decent young footballer he encountered.

Sometimes, in those days when information on players was scarce, United picked up Irish fans in the most curious of ways. Walter Donaldson is now in his eighties, and began following football before the war through collecting cigarette cards. The first one he ever got was the United player George Vose. But it wasn't that that made him a Red. In September 1944, he went to a game at Windsor Park between Ireland and the Combined

Services. He recalls: 'Listed in the Ireland team was a player called Peter Doherty, who actually played for Manchester City, but in the programme he was listed as Manchester United. I was unaware of this error at the time, because information about players was very restricted and limited because of the war. Peter Doherty, the Irish captain, was to be a player that stuck in my mind from that day because he was almost a one-man team, scoring all four Ireland goals in a brilliant spectacle for my football-watching debut.

'It was due to this baptism of goals that I would then listen intensely to the radio for any results coming through and news of goalscorers, with my ear cocked for any news of Manchester United. This was how I discovered that Peter Doherty was playing for Manchester City, not United as I had thought. The seed had been sown though, and my interest in Manchester United has remained from that time to the present day.'

United went into the 1947–48 season with high hopes of going one better and claiming their first title since 1910–11, with players including Carey, Stan Pearson, Charlie Mitten, John Aston, Allenby Chilton, Henry Cockburn, Jack Rowley and Jimmy Delaney, the latter being Busby's first signing in February 1946. However, they were simply no match for a well-drilled Arsenal team, who won the title by seven points from United.

But the season did produce a memorable high point when United won the FA Cup for the second time, defeating a strong Blackpool team that included the legendary Stanley Matthews at Wembley Stadium. In the final, United trailed the Seasiders 2–1 at half time, and when the players returned to the changing rooms it was Carey who spoke to them, encouraging them to express themselves more in the second half. His words of wisdom did the trick, as United ended up 4–2 winners. And so on 24 April 1948, Johnny Carey became the first Irishman to captain an FA Cup-winning team in the 76-year history of the world's most famous cup competition.

A few days after the season ended, United travelled to Ireland to play three friendlies and, at the same time, have a look at several players their main Irish scout, Billy Behan, had been keeping a watchful eye on. Their journey to the Irish capital was made all the easier from a travel perspective as the Irish airline, Aer Lingus, had just commenced operating a regular scheduled service from Dublin to Manchester. The latter service was not only good news for the players and staff, but paved the way for Irish Reds to start planning journeys to Old Trafford to watch their team play. This was the beginning of a new Irish invasion to the UK mainland, driven by football not hunger as so often in the past. Prior to Aer Lingus establishing the Dublin to Manchester route, the journey to Old Trafford meant a long and sometimes very choppy sailing from Dublin to Liverpool, followed by a train journey to Manchester Central Railway Station and finally a bus journey out to the ground.

On 6 May 1948, United were in Dublin for their friendly against a Bohemians Select XI. A crowd of 37,000 poured in to Dalymount Park to watch five Irish players and six guest players from the Football League take on United, captained by local hero Carey. Four of the six guest stars for the Irish side that day were Blackpool players who had played against United in the FA Cup final 12 days earlier. United lost the game 2–1 and never looked comfortable playing on a rock-hard pitch. Carey was given a standing ovation by the home support as he walked off the pitch.

Six days later, United played a Shelbourne Select XI at Dalymount Park, who included seven guest players from the English Football League. On this occasion, United adapted much better to the playing conditions and ran out 4–3 winners to send the 25,000 fans home happy after an attacking game of football. Again the vast majority of the cheers at the end of the game were in honour of Johnny Carey who, alongside Allenby Chilton, had a superb game.

The last of United's three Irish friendlies saw them travel north of the border to face a Linfield Select XI at their Windsor Park home in South Belfast. Again led by Carey, United tasted victory, winning 3–2 in front of 30,000 fans. The Irish football public, who previously had read about Manchester United only in the sports pages of a newspaper or had tuned in to BBC radio to listen to the 1948 FA Cup final, could now see these players in the flesh and embraced them as Ireland's other team. If there was a moment when you could say that the Irish love affair with Manchester United really began, it is arguable that it was now. United had just won the world's most famous cup competition, they were captained by an Irishman, there was a relatively easy way to get to visit the stadium – and what's more they had taken the trouble to come to Ireland to show everyone what they could do.

To cement the relationship, Busby took the players back to Ireland to play two friendlies after the end of the following season. The Irish fans, smitten by United 12 months earlier, continued to show their support. On 29 May 1949 a huge crowd had been expected at Glenmalure Park to watch a Shamrock Rovers side entertain the giants of English football. However, it was a dismal day in Dublin, with constant rain falling on the capital, resulting in just 18,000 fans braving the elements to cheer on both teams – actually an excellent turnout in the circumstances. The home team, with a sprinkling of guest players, led 2–0 at half time, but United turned things around in the second half and entertained the fans with their swashbuckling style of play and pulled two goals back to earn a 2–2 draw. Three days later, United beat a Bohemians Select XI 3–1 at Dalymount Park in front of 22,000 ecstatic fans.

During this time, 'Gentleman John' Carey continued to captain the United team with distinction, a model professional both on and off the pitch. For the third successive year in a row, United finished the 1948–49 season in second place in the First Division, this time behind Portsmouth. That season also witnessed Carey receiving an individual award when he was voted the Football

Writers' Association Footballer of the Year, following in the footsteps of Stanley Matthews, who was the inaugural winner of this most prestigious award the previous campaign.

In those days, although footballers were relatively well paid, many would have some alternative form of employment. In the late 1940s, Carey would coach at St Bede's College, Manchester. The pupils knew all about him as he was the captain of Manchester United and, although he would not become a manager until August 1953, he displayed at this early stage how good a manager he would go on to become. He earned the respect of all of the boys under his charge with his quiet and gentle approach to training. One ex-pupil recalled that Carey's most famous advice to them was: 'Go to meet the ball.' Matt Busby's son, Sandy, was at St Bede's College then, and Carey spent many extra hours at the end of the school day coaching the young Busby to become a centre-half.

Father David McGarry (parish priest of Church of St Catherine of Siena, Didsbury) recalls Carey's time there: 'Johnny Carey used to call in and see us on games afternoon at St Bede's College, where his son Michael went to school. Johnny helped coach the football team and on one afternoon he took five of the Under-14s team to one side, including me, and confided in us that United's first team were having some trouble with missed penalties and the club needed our help. As young lads, this statement made us feel very important.

'He wanted us to try out a method of taking a penalty in a way he had been thinking about. Naturally, we were all very flattered and were all ears. The Manchester United captain demonstrated to us the following method. Assuming the penalty taker is right footed, he placed the ball on the penalty spot. He then turned his back on the ball and walked back slowly before turning very quickly and smacked the ball very hard making sure that his left foot was placed right next to the ball. The ball flew into the net past a shell-shocked classmate, but Johnny pointed out to us: "No method is fireproof, but this method at least has the advantage of approaching the penalty with a simple plan.'"

Carey did not remain the sole Irish voice at United for long after the war. Perhaps as a result of United's tour of Ireland earlier that year, in November 1948 Manchester United signed goalkeeper John Ignatius 'Sonny' Feehan from Waterford. He was born in Dublin on 17 September 1926 and chose soccer over Gaelic football. He joined his local team, Bohemians, as an amateur in 1942, before moving to play in goal for Waterford in 1944. He worked as a motorcycle repairman while playing part-time football in the League of Ireland. Feehan spent his first season at Old Trafford playing for United's reserves, with Jack Crompton being Busby's first-choice goalkeeper. But when Crompton suffered an injury in a 0–0 draw away to Portsmouth on 29 October 1949, Busby had no hesitation in calling up the 23-year-old Feehan for United's next game.

On 5 November 1949, he made his United debut in a 6–0 romp against Huddersfield Town at Old Trafford. Feehan had little to do in the game, but when called upon to act he dealt with the situation calmly. Crompton returned for the following two matches before injury ruled him out again, with Feehan again deputising for him. Ray Wood, a recent £5,000 signing from Darlington, was then handed his debut for the club in United's next game, before Busby decided to recall Feehan, this time allowing him a run of six games to show his manager what he could do. After that, he made just four more league appearances in United's goal that season and played in two FA Cup ties.

When Busby bought Reg Allen from Queens Park Rangers in June 1950 for £11,000, a world record fee for a goalkeeper at the time, Feehan knew his time was up at United as he was fourth in the pecking order behind Allen, Crompton and Wood. With Busby clearly looking to improve on United's fourth position that season, the writing was on the wall for Feehan. Within two months of Allen's arrival, Feehan packed his bags at Old Trafford and joined Northampton Town for a fee of £520. He spent five seasons with the Cobblers before moving to Brentford, where he ended his career after playing five seasons for them. He died on 11 March 1995.

Busby craved for his team to be the champions, and at the end of the season he realised some of his older players would have to be moved on. Busby's youth policy was starting to reap its rewards, with players from the junior ranks starting to stake claims for a senior appearance. In season 1950–51 United were runners-up yet again, with Tottenham Hotspur claiming the title.

Finally, in season 1951–52, Carey led Manchester United to the club's third First Division title success. In the process, Carey also became the first Irishman to captain a team to the First Division Championship (and the first non-Englishman to captain an FA Cup-winning team and a Division One Championship-winning team). That season he played in 38 of United's 42 league games (scoring three goals), many of them at half-back to accommodate Roger Byrne, who made his United debut at Liverpool on 24 November 1951.

During the 1952–53 season, Carey continued to play at half-back, occasionally reverting to full-back, but it marked the 34-year-old Irish international's last full season as the captain of Manchester United, with the team finishing in a disappointing eighth position in the First Division. On 18 February 1953, however, he got to play a very different role when Busby called upon him to help out the team, following an injury to goal-keeper Ray Wood. At this stage, any other fit keepers on United's books must have realised they were never going to get picked! Carey obliged and donned the United No.1 jersey for a tricky First Division away game to Sunderland at Roker Park. United drew 2–2, with Carey performing admirably as the United custodian in goal.

With a group of young players coming through the ranks at United, Carey realised that it was time to move on, having spent almost 17 years with the club, and in August 1953 accepted an offer to become the new manager of Blackburn Rovers. Amazingly, in his 344 appearances for Manchester United, Carey had played in every position on the pitch except outside-left.

In his first managerial role, Carey eventually guided Blackburn Rovers to promotion to the First Division at the end of the 1957–58 season, but then accepted Everton's invitation to become their new manager. However, things did not work out well for him at Goodison Park, although he did take the Toffees to fifth place in Division One in season 1960–61, two places above United. Before the 1961–62 season could get under way, Carey was sacked by the Everton chairman, John Moores, in the back of a London taxi while en route to the annual general meeting of the Football League.

Carey then moved on to Leyton Orient in August 1961 before managing Nottingham Forest from July 1963 to December 1968. Forest were runners-up in the league in 1966–67, behind United. For much of this time, between 1955 and 1967, he also served as team manager of the Republic of Ireland. However, Carey had very little say in the composition of the team, as a selection committee decided which players were chosen to play. In January 1969, he returned to Ewood Park and was made co-manager of Blackburn Rovers with Eddie Quigley before leaving the Lancashire outfit in June 1971.

Johnny Carey was, above all else, a true gentleman, both on and off the pitch, but on 22 January 1995 Manchester United and Ireland had to mourn the passing of one of the greatest captains and full-backs the club or country have ever had.

But while Carey was at United, he was a figurehead who helped draw in other players from across the Irish Sea. The earliest of them was 16-year-old Belfast-born John 'Jackie' Blanchflower. In May 1949 he made his way to join Matt Busby's band of talented young players, scoured from every corner of the United Kingdom and Ireland, who were making their way through the ranks. Soon, there was a torrent of young

Irish talent making its way to United, lured by the club's excellent links, the manager's enthusiasm for blooding young talent and an excellent scouting network to help the Old Trafford outfit scoop up the best players. For United, the post-war era of players who had fought in the war was coming to an end. Now was the time for youth to have its say.

Chapter 5

Irish Babes

Jackie Blanchflower was born in the Bloomfield area of East Belfast on 7 March 1933 and was the younger brother of Danny Blanchflower, who was at Aston Villa at the time of his arrival in 1949 and who would famously go on to captain Tottenham Hotspur to Double glory in 1960–61. The Blanchflower brothers had both attended Elmgrove Primary School, Beersbridge Road, Belfast. Prior to accepting Manchester United's invitation to join their youth ranks, Jackie played for Orangefield Star, a team managed by his mother, and Pitt Street Mission in the Belfast Boys' League before moving on to Boyland FC.

Jim Rodgers, Lord Mayor of Belfast in 2001–02, grew up in this area and recalls: 'Boyland was situated in Lomond Avenue just off the Holywood Road in the heart of East Belfast, and the club was to prove a great recruiting ground for many English clubs – especially United. They played under the name Lomond Star and participated in many of the big tournaments that were organised at junior level in Belfast. United's Belfast scout Bob Bishop lived in nearby Laburnum Street and regularly watched their games, hoping to discover a new football star. A lot of the boys from the youth club would gather around Irvine's Shoe Shop, on the corner of Bloomfield Avenue where it met the Newtownards Road. Bishop would often take an evening stroll, making sure he walked by Irvine's Shoe Shop to stop and chat to the boys. He would invite the most talented boys away to attend the football training camps he held at Helen's Bay, County Down. For many of them, those weekends at his football camps were a stepping stone to a better life as a professional footballer.'

In this case, however, it was not Bishop but his colleague Bob Harpur who spotted Blanchflower while playing as a schoolboy international for Ireland. Harpur immediately recommended him to Busby. With Bishop and Behan, he was one of a number of scouts who searched Ireland looking for the next Johnny Carey.

Another of their discoveries around this period was Jackie Scott. He was born in Belfast on 22 December 1933 and, like Blanchflower, played youth football for Boyland in Belfast, the two future United players appearing in the same side, even though Blanchflower was nine months older. It was Bishop who spotted him, and Scott became his first referral to Matt Busby. Scott signed amateur forms upon his arrival at Old Trafford, before signing as a professional in October 1951. He set about impressing Busby and Murphy, playing as a striker for United's youth sides.

Scott's big moment arrived on 4 October 1952 when he was called up to the first team to stand in for the injured Roger Byrne on United's left wing. However, his debut was one he would rather forget as United were mauled 6–2 in a First Division game away to Wolverhampton Wanderers at Molineux. He played in United's next game, a 2–0 home defeat to Stoke City, but the fight for first team places was fierce as so many good young players had joined the club. Scott made only one further appearance for United, on 21 January 1956, in a 3–1 First Division defeat to Preston North End at Deepdale. After making just three appearances in almost five years as a professional, he joined Grimsby Town in June 1956. Former United hero Allenby Chilton was in charge of the Mariners at the time and hoped Scott would boost Grimsby Town's chances of pushing for promotion to Division One. Scott's time at Blundell Park proved to be much more successful, as he made 240 league appearances, scoring 51 goals, for them.

He was in Northern Ireland's 1958 World Cup squad in Sweden, even though he was yet to be capped. He won his first cap appearing in Northern Ireland's vital Group 1 play-off encounter with Czechoslovakia in Malmö on 17 June 1958. They won 2–1 after extra-time, and progressed to the World Cup quarter-finals, where they were paired against a strong French team. His second and final appearance for his country came in that game, which France won by the convincing margin of 4–0.

During the summer of 1963, after seven years at Grimsby, he moved on to Fourth Division York City, where he played 21 league games in 1963–64, before ending his career at Southern League side Margate. After hanging up his boots, he took a job working on a building site and died in an accident at work in June 1978, aged just 44.

Meanwhile, Billy Behan discovered another young Irish talent playing for Eire Schoolboys: Patrick Anthony 'Paddy' Kennedy. He was born in Dublin on 9 October 1934 and played at centre-half for local side Johnville, before Behan sent him over to Old Trafford in February 1952. He signed amateur forms for United before turning professional in February 1953. However, the United coaching staff switched him from centre-half to full-back where he played a number of games for the Manchester United youth team. Busby saw Kennedy as an understudy to Roger Byrne, but it was always going to be a difficult task to oust Byrne from the left-back slot in the United first team.

Just three months after becoming a professional, however, Kennedy played in the first leg of the inaugural FA Youth Cup final versus Wolverhampton Wanderers at Old Trafford. The young Irishman helped keep the Wolves attack relatively at bay as

United romped to a 7–1 win. Five days later, he played in the second leg at Molineux, which ended 2–2. The United youth team, captained by Duncan Edwards, had recorded an impressive 9–3 aggregate win. Kennedy was, as we will see, one of three Irishmen to play in that famous team that personified Busby's faith in young players. It was the first of five successive wins for the youth team in the competition and proved that United had the best youth system in the country. So renowned were they that crowds of 30,000-plus would turn up to watch the stars of the future play.

Kennedy eventually made his first team debut in place of Byrne (who, with Ray Wood and Bill Foulkes, was away on England duty) for United's First Division game at Wolves on 2 October 1954. Wolves won the game 4–2 in what proved to be Kennedy's solitary first team appearance for the club. Realising his chances of making it at Old Trafford were slim, he moved to Blackburn Rovers in August 1956 before joining Southampton in July 1959 and ended his career back in Lancashire with Oldham Athletic in 1960–61. Kennedy was quite simply unlucky to be at Manchester United at a time when there was a plethora of outstanding young talent on the club's books. He died on 18 March 2007, aged 72.

The second Irishman to play in that inaugural FA Youth Cup final was Noel William McFarlane, also spotted by Behan. Born in Bray, County Wicklow, on 20 December 1934, McFarlane started his career with his hometown club, Bray Wanderers. Like Kennedy, he came to Behan's attention when playing for Eire Schoolboys and was persuaded to move to Old Trafford in April 1952. The Irish contingent at the club seemed to be growing by the season. Despite his relatively small physique for an outside-left, he stood 5ft 8in and weighed 10st 4lb, he impressed Busby and Murphy and gradually worked his way through the United reserve teams. The coaching staff saw enough talent and ability from him that he was selected for the 1953 Youth Cup final. For many, the young Irishman was the star of the game, constantly menacing the Wolves defence, and scored twice in United's 7–1 victory. He deservedly retained his place for the second leg at Molineux and celebrated the team's success by having a pint with his fellow Irishmen – a pint of cold milk, that is!

But McFarlane was vying with Johnny Berry for a place in the senior side, and Berry's consistent form and fitness meant McFarlane was always struggling to make his mark. Finally, on 13 February 1954, he made his debut in a home game against Tottenham Hotspur, helping his side to a 2–0 victory. However, Berry returned for the following game, and after that McFarlane never had a look-in. So, after spending four years in the shadows of the first team, he decided the time was right to return home to Ireland and signed for Waterford.

The third Irishman to play in the first FA Youth Cup final would have a much more successful career than either Kennedy or McFarlane: he was William Augustine Whelan, better known as Billy or Liam. Whelan was born on 1 April 1935 in Cabra on the north side of Dublin. He was a devout Roman Catholic who came from a very large family and had to overcome the tragic loss of his father when he was just eight. The young Whelan was a prodigious talent, something that was evident from the moment he kicked a football in the playground of St Peter's School, Phibsboro, Dublin. From the window of his classroom, Whelan could see Dalymount Park, where the Republic of Ireland played their home international matches. Whelan would often stare out of the window dreaming that one day he would follow in the footsteps of his hero, Johnny Carey, and run out in the famous green national jersey.

Whelan started his football career at Dublin's famous football nursery, Home Farm. Like so many wonderfully gifted footballers to play for United over the years, he was spotted by Behan. He was the star performer in an Eire Schoolboys side that defeated England Schoolboys 8–4 in Dublin. Behan sent a telegram to Matt Busby in which he raved about the young Irish kid he had just seen in action. Busby was intrigued and sent first team coach Bert Whalley to Dublin for a closer look. Four days after Whalley arrived in Dublin, the 18-year-old was put on a boat and sent to Old Trafford to sign as an amateur for United.

Although he was not blessed with lightning pace for an inside-right, he possessed other skills in abundance: he was athletic, a quick thinker, a magnificent dribbler and he could ghost past defenders with a deft shimmy. Three days after he arrived in Manchester, Busby was so impressed with the young Irishman in training that he handed him a place in the first leg of the FA Youth Cup final, replacing the injured John Doherty. He scored that day and was such an instant success that he had signed professional terms within a fortnight of arriving in Manchester. Whelan scored again in the second leg. Not many players can lay claim to making their first appearance for their club in a cup final and scoring in it to help win the trophy. Not a bad start to what promised to be a glittering career for this affable yet very shy young Dubliner.

When he arrived at Old Trafford, the soon-to-retire Johnny Carey told the young Whelan to hold on to his Irish name, as the people in Manchester were unaccustomed to Irish names such as Augustine or Liam. However, in the end, he had no say in it, as his team-mates started to call him Billy and it stuck with him until he went home for the occasional visit when his family and friends called him Liam.

While Kennedy and McFarlane were to wear the red shirt of United only briefly, things were different for Jackie Blanchflower and Whelan. Blanchflower had signed amateur forms with United upon his arrival in Manchester in 1949 and a year later he turned professional. The young Irishman was well liked at Old Trafford, for United had finally returned to their home ground at the start of the 1949–50 season, and team captain Carey was always there to offer the kid from Belfast any advice he needed. After all, Carey knew what it was like to be a teenager so far away from home with no family or close friends around you to pick you up when you were down or to celebrate moments of happiness with you. Blanchflower was a very versatile player who was comfortable in most positions on the pitch and, although he initially played up front as an inside-forward for the team, Busby decided half-back was his strongest position.

On 24 November 1951, 18-year-old Blanchflower, along with fellow 'Babe' Roger Byrne (aged 20), was handed his senior debut for the club in a tough First Division game at Liverpool. Busby was increasingly beginning to look at the younger players on United's books as the way forward. Partly this was due to circumstance (the club still didn't have the money to pay big transfer fees) and partly it was because he liked to educate and mould players in the United way; established stars were often harder to control, as he had found out with the 'Bogotá Bandit' Charlie Mitten, who had left the club in search of the fortunes supposedly on offer in Latin America.

That day, Blanchflower played at half-back in place of Thomas Gibson, while Byrne played at left-back deputising for William Redman. Both debutants impressed, helping United to a well-earned point from a 0–0 draw. However, while Byrne retained his place in the side for the rest of the season, Blanchflower lost out to Carey, who had played at right-back in the Liverpool match, but was switched to half-back for the rest of the 1951–52 title-winning campaign.

It was 17 months before Blanchflower made his second senior appearance for the team, replacing Henry Cockburn in United's 2–2 draw at Charlton Athletic on 3 April 1953. It was his only first team game of the season, as his place was taken by an even younger player, a 16-year-old debutant called Duncan Edwards. Edwards would then himself lose out to Jeff Whitefoot, a former youth prodigy, for the rest of the campaign.

For the first third of the 1953–54 season, various players donned the No. 8 jersey before Blanchflower did enough in training to prove to Busby that he was the man to command the shirt, and he did. He played in all 27 of United's remaining league fixtures to help the team to fourth in Division One, netting an impressive 13 times. He also appeared in United's solitary FA Cup game of the season, scoring in a 5–3 away defeat at Barnsley in the third round; it was the only goal he ever scored in the cup. He also made his international debut for Northern Ireland on 21 March 1954 (alongside elder brother Danny) away to Wales in a qualifying game for the 1954 World Cup finals.

Meanwhile, Whelan was still playing in the junior ranks that season, and was part of the side that made the trip to Europe's premier youth competition, the Zurich Blue Star Tournament. He was in mesmerising form and helped United win the trophy. Busby gave an interview to the *Manchester Evening Chronicle* and said: 'I wish you could have been there to see some of Whelan's five goals in our 9–2 win over Bienne on Saturday. For three of his goals, he dribbled through the entire defence and rounded the goalkeeper too!'

Unknown to Busby, the Brazilian national team were in the crowd watching the game on a day off from preparing for the 1954 World Cup finals, which were also being hosted by the Swiss. They were so impressed with the skinny kid from Dublin that United received enquiries from Santos of São Paulo as to whether they would release him and allow him to play for them. The young Irishman was very flattered but politely declined the invitation, much to the relief of Matt Busby who held high hopes for his as yet uncut Irish diamond.

In 1954–55, Blanchflower scored 10 league goals in his 29 league games, but United could manage only a final placing of fifth in Division One. Increasing numbers of the Busby Babes were now playing their part for United, but at this stage they did not yet have sufficient experience to avoid making costly mistakes. Looking to change things round, on 26 March 1955, Whelan made his senior debut for United in their First Division game at home to Preston North End. The young man from Dublin knew he had to seize the moment and impress his manager. Things went well for him on his debut, as he helped the team to a 2–0 victory and he kept his place for the following Saturday's visit to Sheffield United. Whelan was magnificent at Bramall Lane, scoring in the game and helping his strikers to four more goals for an impressive 5–0 win. He played for the next five games, before Busby reinstated Blanchflower for the last three fixtures of the season.

This young side of Busby's was beginning to capture the imagination of those beyond the outer reaches of Manchester. As Colm Devine, who was growing up in Aghyaran, County Tyrone, at this time recalls: 'My love for Manchester United goes back more than half a century ago, to 1955 to be precise. I became aware of United mainly because of my brother Johnny, and to a lesser extent my brother Eddie. They were a bit older than me, and I used to listen to the stories they relayed to one another. Johnny was, and still is, full of talk about United, but at that time they were always referred to as "Manchester United" and the name had a ring to it and denoted something special like Rocky Marciano. It may have been the way it was pronounced, but it just had that tone of difference to it and signified something to take note of.

'Eddie, in particular, was often to be found with his ear to the radio on a Saturday afternoon listening to the football scores. Johnny would just say "United won/lost today" and a few words commenting on how great a team United were. When we used to have a kick around or a mini match in one of the fields, it was always names like Blanchflower, Foulkes or Edwards that Johnny would be shouting, and to me these names were not names that I'd heard before, and they were not names we'd hear in our part of Northern Ireland, so they stuck in my mind and had a sort of special tone like Manchester United. Names and how they sound to young people can have a lasting effect.

'In those days it was also the norm for whole families to follow the same team, unlike today where it is not uncommon for four members of one family to support four different teams. This may have been a factor in my support for Manchester United in those days, and in fact we all still follow United. This has been the case with my children as well as my brothers' children.'

Of course, Devine did not have the opportunity to see the Babes in action himself, but when he moved to England (he now lives in Rochdale), he quizzed those who had watched them to find out more. 'When I later moved to Manchester to work, I met many people who were regulars at Old Trafford during the Babes era. Jimmy Wilson from Stretford gladly painted a picture of the famous Busby Babes for me many times over a pint. He was a tough old guy, but you could see in his face and hear in his voice the effect the Munich Air Disaster had on him. He could hardly bring himself to go back to Old Trafford after the Babes had gone and in fact he returned only once. He used to give us a running commentary of how they all played, but when he came to "Big Dunc" he would just stop and he'd apologise and say that he couldn't do the "big fella" justice and would drift off silently to his own memories.'

With so many talented youngsters gaining such valuable early experience, hopes were high that the club could once again challenge for honours in 1955–56. Blanchflower started 16 of United's 17 opening league games of the 1955–56 season but made only two more appearances in the rest of the campaign, scoring three goals in all, to help the club to a fourth league title. Whelan appeared in 13 league games, scoring four times, as the two men battled with John Doherty to get a regular slot at inside-right. During that early part of the season, Blanchflower scored the only goal of his 12-cap international career, in a 2–1 win over Scotland at Windsor Park on 8 October 1955.

United's team that season had an average age of 21 and were widely known by now as the Busby Babes. They won the title by an astonishing 11 points from runners-up Blackpool, a record margin in the 20th century, and were unbeaten at home. The two Irishmen were surely only going to play a greater part in the club's success in the future.

Just two days after being crowned champions of England,

United were in Dublin on 23 April 1956 to face a Home Farm Select XI, Whelan's former club. He enjoyed his trip, especially as the game was played at Dalymount Park, close to his family home. He opened the scoring for the visitors after a shot from Blanchflower rebounded off the crossbar and fell at his feet. Even though they had Bolton Wanderers, England international striker Nat Lofthouse in their side, the home team played poorly. United won comfortably in the end, 4–0, with further goals from Blanchflower (two) and Johnny Berry. Whelan's display was enough to convince the Irish selectors to call him up to win his first international cap. He made his Ireland debut on 10 May 1956, in a friendly against the Netherlands at Feyenoord, and helped his side win 4–1. For United, however, the trip was further confirmation of the importance of Ireland in the club's thoughts.

Having achieved success at home, Busby was adamant that his young team should be allowed to show what they could do against the best sides Europe had to offer. Whereas the previous season, champions Chelsea had been forbidden from entering the newly created competition for champion clubs across Europe, the European Cup, Busby insisted that United must take part. He had observed the success of Hungary in beating England in 1953, and had entered his youth teams in various continental tournaments, so he knew that United could only learn from the experience. He persuaded club chairman Harold Hardman that European football would be both profitable and beneficial, and together they worked on Stanley Rous of the FA to overcome the objections of the Football League, who feared that their competition would be diminished by the distractions in Europe.

For the start of 1956–57, Busby made his decision as to which of his two talented young Irishmen should be his first choice at inside-right – and Whelan got his vote. His career at Old Trafford really took off, as he played in all bar three of United's league games, scoring 26 goals, to ensure United retained their title. In September and October, he was in sensational form, scoring in eight consecutive league games. Blanchflower, however, pulled on the United shirt just 11 times in defence of their crown, with Mark Jones usually keeping him out of the side, as the adaptable Irishman was now more often used as a half-back. However, this was still enough to give him his second championship winners' medal.

But everyone's attention was on the European Cup. United played their first game in the competition on 12 September 1956 in Belgium against champions RSC Anderlecht and came home with a 2–0 win in the first leg. Both Blanchflower and Whelan played in that match but neither scored. In the return leg, played at Maine Road because Old Trafford did not yet have any flood-lights, Whelan was on target twice as United won 10–0, the club's biggest victory in all competitions.

A snapshot of just how well Whelan played that season came in the European Cup quarter-finals when United took on reigning Spanish champions Athletic Bilbao. The first leg was played before 60,000 boisterous Basques at Spain's oldest stadium, Estadio San Mamés, on 16 January 1957. The pitch was rock hard and covered in snow, with the match played in extremely cold conditions. The partisan home crowd were baying for United's blood and Bilbao powered their way to a 3–0 half-time lead. Talk among the fans on the terraces was of yet more goals in the second half. How right the fans were, with first Tommy Taylor and then Dennis Viollet netting for the visitors within ten minutes of the restart. Suddenly the stadium took on an eerie, almost spooky, silence as attack after attack rained down on the Spanish goal. Fear spread throughout the ground before the home fans' prayers were finally answered as Bilbao scored twice more. Even Busby and Murphy knew that United would have a mountain to climb to turn around a three-goal deficit in the home leg. But up stepped Whelan. The Irishman collected the ball deep in his own half, dribbled his way up the pitch leaving five defenders in his wake and scored with an unerring, precise finish.

The Savoy Cinema in Dublin showed Whelan's goal on Pathe

News and the whole audience erupted, clapping with delight as
they got to their feet. All of Dublin was proud of his achievements
in the famous red jersey of Manchester United. His goal was to
prove crucial, for in the return leg United won 3–0 to qualify for
the semi-finals. In those days, of course, few people had television
sets and, in any case, the stations showed little football. One programme sports fans could watch was *Sports Report* on RTE
Television on a Saturday evening at 5.00pm.

At this time, Whelan used to write home to tell his family
about another teenage star, Bobby Charlton, and how it would
not be long before he would have the football world at his feet.
On his rare trips back home to Dublin, Whelan would sit with
his family for ages and tell them about the famous Busby Babes
and the superb skills of Byrne, Charlton, Colman and Edwards,
in awe of their ability but overlooking his own skills. With 33
goals in 54 appearances that season, Whelan was becoming a
United superstar, idolised on the streets of Dublin. Charlton
once remarked that he always wanted to be the best player in the
world, but knew that as long as Whelan was at United that particular dream would never come true. This was high praise
indeed from one of the greatest footballers that has ever graced
the beautiful game.

Bill Clarkson recalls watching him play, and has this to say
about Whelan's style: 'Liam Whelan was a player who did things
at his own pace and often gave the impression that he was slow,
but of course he wasn't as he was very difficult to get the ball off.
He would shield the ball and then when he moved, he moved
with artistry and purpose. In many ways Dimitar Berbatov
reminds me of Liam, both appearing quite languid at times and
then they would do something magical which often took your
breath away.'

During that season Whelan won three more caps for his coun-
try, including two against England, all in World Cup qualifiers.
His Manchester United team-mates Roger Byrne, Duncan
Edwards, David Pegg and Tommy Taylor were all in the England

team for his final game in an Ireland shirt, in Dublin on 19 May 1957, when the two sides drew 1–1.

Blanchflower returned to European action on 11 April 1957 when United faced the reigning champions of Europe, Real Madrid, in the semi-finals. Busby's gamble that his young United side could cope with the pressures of Europe while remaining just as strong at home had proved to be the case. However, at the Bernabeu, United met their match as a side containing Alfredo Di Stéfano, Francisco Gento and Raymond Kopa were simply too strong for them on the night and deservedly took a 3–1 lead to Old Trafford for the second leg.

With United finally having installed floodlights, Old Trafford hosted its first European match in the return. An expectant crowd of 65,000 crammed into the stadium on 25 April hoping their heroes could again turn around a two-goal deficit against a Spanish side and ensure that a new name would be engraved on the trophy. Alas, the task presented to Whelan, Blanchflower and their team-mates was simply too much for them, as they could manage only a 2–2 draw, losing 5–3 on aggregate. Real Madrid went on to retain the European Cup and would win the trophy five years in succession. However, Busby now had a taste for European football and was far from finished in his ambitions to claim European football's most coveted prize.

With the title won, there was just one trophy left: the FA Cup, where United faced Aston Villa in the final, as they sought to become the first side in the 20th century to complete the Double. Whelan had played in every round of the FA Cup for United, hitting the target four times in their run to Wembley, while Blanchflower had played only in the semi-final. Both men were called upon by Busby in the final. In the sixth minute of the game, the United goalkeeper, Ray Wood, collected a cross, but Villa striker Peter McParland forcefully barged into him, knocking Wood unconscious and breaking his cheekbone.

Blanchflower's versatility was put to the sternest of tests when he took over in goal for his injured team-mate, as he became the second Irish outfield player that decade to keep goal for the Reds. It wasn't the first time he'd played in goal for United, having done so for a full 90 minutes during their tour of Scandinavia the previous May when they beat Helsingborg 5–1. Blanchflower made a number of fine saves from the Villa players before finally conceding the opening goal of the game in the 68th minute, when McParland found the back of the United net.

Wood, still somewhat dazed, came back on merely as nuisance value. McParland added a second goal in the 73rd minute, but when Tommy Taylor pulled a goal back for United with only seven minutes remaining, Wood went back into goal allowing a fresh Blanchflower to try to help United grab the equaliser. As pointed out by Iain McCartney in his book *Irish Reds*, Blanchflower's stint in goal has thrown up a trivia question that has left many a Manchester United fan baffled: 'Who is the only outfield player to wear a cap during a competitive game for Manchester United?' For Blanchflower not only wore Ray Wood's goalkeeper's jersey during the final but also wore his cap to keep the sun out of his eyes.

As United sought to make it a hat-trick of league titles, Blanchflower was a regular first choice in the early part of 1957–58, partnering the magnificent Duncan Edwards at centre-half. But he played his last game for United on 30 November against Spurs at Old Trafford. In all he played 117 times for United and scored 27 goals.

Bill Clarkson was watching that game and recalls what happened: 'Jackie partnered Duncan Edwards at centre-half. He was just so creative that he forgot about his defensive duties that day and would spread the ball around as he pushed upfield. However, he made three mistakes and United trailed 3–0 at half time, with all three goals coming from Bobby Smith. In the end United lost 4–3 and after that Busby dropped him in favour of Mark Jones.'

Meanwhile, Whelan faced a new rival for his position at United, as he vied with Bobby Charlton for the inside-right jersey. The season could not have started any better for Whelan, who scored a hat-trick on the opening day as United beat Leicester City 3–0 away at Filbert Street. But, before Christmas, he lost his place to the younger man, playing his last game for United on 14 December in a 1–0 home defeat to Chelsea. In 98 appearances for the club, he had scored an astonishing 52 goals. The following game, on 21 December, marked the United debut of the Northern Ireland goalkeeper Harry Gregg, signed from Doncaster Rovers, who would preserve the Reds' Irish connection.

Before then, however, there was a special moment for Whelan when he returned home to Dublin to play against League of Ireland champions Shamrock Rovers in the preliminary round of the European Cup. It was the first time teams from Ireland were permitted to take part in the competition, and so United had the privilege of playing the first ever 'official' fixture between an English and an Irish team. In the weeks before the match, Dublin was buzzing with excitement. The Whelan family were inundated with requests for tickets for the game, while the kids in Cabra had already played the match on the streets a dozen times before the two teams even met.

United were hot favourites and won the game 6–0 at Dalymount Park (Blanchflower also played) on 25 September. The vast majority of the 45,000 in attendance that day just turned up to see their fellow Dubliner play and he did not disappoint them, scoring twice. Standing on the terraces that day were hundreds of young Irish boys who were all sharing the same wish that one day they too could pull on the famous red jersey of Manchester United. One 12-year-old boy in particular that evening watched in awe, transfixed by Whelan. His name was Eamonn Dunphy, a highly promising young midfielder, who grew up in Drumcondra on the north side of Dublin. Within five years Dunphy found himself at Old Trafford as an apprentice, but never fulfilled his dream of playing for United as he left in May 1965 to join Millwall without making it to the first team.

This was another crucial moment when Ireland, or Dublin

anyway, became United-mad and adopted the team from across the Irish Sea as their own. Jimmy McCann played for Shamrock Rovers in both legs (scoring in Rovers' 3–2 loss at Old Trafford) and recalled: 'I can remember the crowds trying to get up the lane at Dalymount to get into the changing rooms. You had to almost beat your way up. The whole country went bananas when Shamrock Rovers were drawn to play Manchester United. They had lots of great players such as David Pegg, Johnny Berry, and, of course, Duncan Edwards and Liam.'

He added that all of the Shamrock Rovers players knew Whelan from his Home Farm days, and were shocked by his death at Munich a few months later: 'Liam used to come up to train at Milltown because he was a friend of Tommy Hamilton [a former United trainee, who had returned to Ireland to play for Shamrock after failing to win a place in the side]. He became a friend of all the Shamrock Rovers players then. They had a TV in the bar at Milltown and most of the squad went up to watch the news on the BBC. It was a terrible blow. It was like losing one of your own family. Liam was a really lovely guy.'

Blanchflower won his last cap for Northern Ireland against Italy on 15 January 1958 in a World Cup qualifier. The game was at Windsor Park and the Irish won 2–1, a crucial victory that helped them secure their long-awaited first appearance at a World Cup finals tournament. The Blanchflower brothers celebrated the team's victory well into the night, but unknown to them it was not only the last time they ever played together, it was also Jackie's last competitive game of football.

The following month, both Blanchflower and Whelan flew out with the United team to face Red Star Belgrade in the second leg of the European Cup quarter-final on 5 February 1958. United took a slender 2–1 lead to Yugoslavia, and when they held on for a 3–3 draw they knew that they were through to a second successive semi-final. Whelan had made the trip as cover for Charlton, while Blanchflower was in reserve. Fellow Irishman Harry Gregg was also in the party, and kept goal in the match.

Flying back to England the following day, the team stopped off in Munich, where the weather conditions were appalling. At one stage, it seemed as though they would be stranded overnight in Germany, but the pilots made a third attempt to take off. Whelan, always a nervous traveller, feared the worst and as they set off was heard to say: 'If the worst happens I am ready for death. I hope we all are.' Tragically, he was proved right, and he perished on the runway.

When Whelan's body returned home from Munich, it was briefly placed in the gymnasium at Old Trafford and lay alongside those of his team-mates whose lives were also so cruelly ended. In all, 23 people died in the accident, among them eight Busby Babes and three other club employees, eight journalists, two of the crew, plus a travel agent and a supporter. Whelan's funeral took place at Glasnevin Cemetery in Dublin. The cortège left the Christ the King Church on Offaly Road, Cabra, close to his parents' home and slowly made its way through the streets of the north side of Dublin, with thousands of fans lining the route to pay tribute to one of their own. As the funeral procession passed St Peter's School, hundreds of pupils stood with their heads bowed.

His coffin was covered in wreaths including one of a miniature Old Trafford sent by his former team-mates, the management and directors of United. At one point the hearse carrying his coffin had to wait until the police moved mourners off the road as they were blocking its path. Many Irish fans still visit his grave today, placing red, white and black wreaths on the grave as a mark of respect to a footballer who quite possibly could have even rivalled George Best for the title of Ireland's greatest ever player. The vast majority of visitors to his grave never saw him play for United, yet because of the everlasting legacy he left behind, still regard him as one of the best footballers to play for Manchester United and Ireland.

On 8 December 2006, the railway bridge on the Faussagh Road/Dowth Avenue junction in Cabra was renamed in his honour. As a young boy, Whelan had had to cross this bridge to go to school and to play at Home Farm. Fittingly, the unveiling ceremony was performed by Whelan's close friend and Manchester United team-mate Sir Bobby Charlton. Sir Bobby said: 'Billy had brilliant close control and was a natural goalscorer. His forte was to scheme, to shape possibilities with his skill and excellent vision. He scored so many goals from midfield, he would be a wonder of today's game.'

Father David McGarry, who was coached by Johnny Carey as a boy, remembers the artistry of Whelan: 'Billy Whelan was a very unusual player. One day, I was watching him from the Scoreboard End at Old Trafford and I saw him walk up to a full-back with his knees in a high step with the ball at his feet. He mesmerised the poor chap as he walked along the dead-ball line. In many games there are certain magic moments that capture the beauty of football. I'll never forget the grace of Billy Whelan and I bet those standing beside me in the Scoreboard End that afternoon will never forget him either.'

Fifty years after the tragedy, *taoiseach* Bertie Ahern led a memorial service at Liam Whelan Bridge and the Irish national postal body issued a 55 cent postage stamp to commemorate the anniversary of the Munich Air Disaster, which showed a photo of Whelan. On 6 February 2008, exactly 50 years to the day after the disaster occurred, the Republic of Ireland played an international friendly against Brazil at Croke Park and marked the occasion with a minute's silence in memory of those who lost their lives in the Munich Air Disaster. Manchester United's John O'Shea played in the game, as did former United player Liam Miller.

Amazingly, Blanchflower fought back from the terrible injuries he sustained in the disaster, including a fractured pelvis, broken ribs, severe kidney damage, a severed arm and many other fractures, and held hopes of making a return when medical specialists broke the news to him that his body was simply incapable of coping with the pressures of competitive football. In June 1959, aged only 26, he was forced to retire. And so we will never know just how good a footballer he would have become, or what other glories he would have achieved with a United team that could have gone on to even greater things.

When he realised that he would no longer be able to earn a living as a professional footballer, Blanchflower took on a succession of jobs in the Manchester area, but these occupations were a long way from replacing the excitement he felt running out at Old Trafford before an adoring crowd.

However, things at long last seemed to turn around for the better for Blanchflower after his wife, Jean, decided to resume her singing career in the late 1980s and he went along to introduce her. He proved a natural with a mic and the crowd loved his soft Irish brogue and humour. It wasn't long before he carved out a new career for himself as a successful after-dinner speaker. Not long before his death, he spoke about his Manchester United career saying: 'Life has been full of ups and downs, but without pathos there can be no comedy. The bitterness goes eventually and you start remembering the good times. I loved it at United. From this distance, even going through the accident was worth it for those years at Old Trafford. I feel happy and at ease now.'

Sadly, Blanchflower lost his battle with cancer on 2 September 1998 and died aged 65. Tributes poured in following his death, with former team-mate Bill Foulkes saying: 'Jackie was a brilliant footballer, capable of filling in for Duncan Edwards in midfield and Tommy Taylor in attack. He was a fun-loving character, a little bit more outgoing than his brother Danny. He was a first-class man and footballer. He will be sadly missed.'

The third member of the Irish contingent on the plane that fateful day, Harry Gregg, not only survived but was the hero of the day. Almost miraculously, he emerged from the crash largely unscathed, and would continue to play for United for many years to come and would form an important part in the next chapter of the club's story, as they tried to rebuild United in the aftermath of Munich.

Matt Busby said of the young side he had built: 'In all modesty, my summing up of 1955–56 and 1956–57 must be that no club in the country could live with Manchester United.' No one can really say just how good the Busby Babes would have become. But in the short time they were together, they had become a team that had attracted fans not just from all over England, but from around the world. Because of the strong Irish links with the club, the Irish players who joined United in the decade or so after the war, the frequent friendlies the Reds played in Ireland, and the fact that they had played an Irish team in the European Cup, this sense of loss was felt as keenly in Ireland as anywhere else. United were already becoming Ireland's favourite team before Munich; after it, that bond would become unbreakable.

Chapter 6

The Phoenix Rises

There is little doubt that the Munich Air Disaster, and the tragic loss of so many of the Busby Babes, transformed the way in which United was viewed in Ireland and elsewhere. Colm Devine, who grew up in Aghyaran, County Tyrone, gives one example of how the legacy of the Babes continues even to this day, even among those you would not expect to feel it so strongly. He was watching a game at home in Rochdale in 2011 with 84-year-old Manchester City season-ticket holder Harold Thomas. He explains what happened next: 'I made a rather silly suggestion that Steven Gerrard of Liverpool might resemble the great Duncan Edwards in stature. Harold nearly exploded: "Duncan Edwards was a man like no other you'll ever see. He was the nearest thing to a superman the football world has ever seen. Don't even mention him and Steven Gerrard in the same breath." Harold paused for a moment, gave me an ice-cold stare and continued: "I saw him close-up when he was playing and I can assure you there are none of today's players in the same mould." I must admit that I was more than a little embarrassed having just been chastised by my friend, who was a dyed-in-the-wool Man City stalwart.'

John Conran is the chairman and a co-founder member of Clonmel Manchester United Supporters' Club in South Tipperary. He remembers how as a child, back in the 1950s, long before they had a television, his father, a Manchester United fan, would stand in front of the old Pye radio listening to the football results on the BBC's *Sports Report* programme every Saturday. 'The radio was operated by battery and it was my job to take it to the local Post Office each Friday to have it charged. The radio valves took about five minutes to warm up, and the reception was totally dependent on weather conditions. I can still remember the music played just before the radio announcer's voice was heard reading out the football results from the four English leagues at five o'clock. That was my introduction to United. My friends supported Liverpool, Leeds United and Nottingham Forest, but I was a United man just like my dad. The Munich Air Disaster caused widespread shock at the time in Clonmel and all across County Tipperary, and got widespread coverage in the papers and on the radio. The only other event in my lifetime that caused the same shock and received similar coverage was the assassination of President John F. Kennedy in Dallas.'

William John Pollock Angus, one of the oldest members of the George Best Carryduff MUSC, also remembers that day: 'I was in the store room of the gas works [in Bangor] when the news of the air disaster came in. I could not believe what I was hearing at first, but then the news on the radio and in the newspapers the following day told us all what we did not want to hear: a number of the famous Busby Babes had lost their lives in a plane crash at Munich Airport. I was absolutely devastated and in many ways I was in total disbelief. I still regard Duncan Edwards as one of the greatest players I have ever seen. Duncan was so powerful and he played the game as if he was having a kick-about with his mates in someone's back garden. Although I have always supported Bangor FC, I was also a very keen follower of Manchester United from an early age. I still remember reading in the local newspaper about Harry Gregg, that famous Northern Ireland international goalkeeper, joining Manchester United from Doncaster Rovers in December 1957. He was a great goalkeeper.'

Chris Ryder, a former journalist with the *Sunday Times*, also remembers those times: 'I first got interested in football when I was eight or nine, from listening to the radio and reading the newspapers. Then I began to get *Charles Buchan's Football Monthly*. I was really proud to see that Northern Ireland-born players were doing well in England, and I wrote to Harry Gregg at Doncaster Rovers asking for an autograph and enclosing a stamped addressed envelope. A few days later the envelope and signature arrived at my then home in Banbridge and I was completely delighted. Within a short time, Harry moved to Manchester United, so from that point on I was hooked on United and remain so steadfastly to this day.

'Not long after, I recall arriving home from school and hearing on the radio that the United plane had crashed at Munich. I waited anxiously for the main news at six o'clock for more details. There were still only sketchy details later and so I recall getting up very early the next morning and cycling to Adair's news agency in Church Square, Banbridge, to get the morning papers which were, of course, filled with detail about the incident. I started a scrapbook and over the succeeding days remember waiting for news of the injured players and about Matt Busby's fight for life. I also remember Jimmy Murphy's efforts to rebuild a team and play in the emotion-laden matches that followed, which I recall were televised. The fact that Harry Gregg had survived and was being praised for his heroism thrilled and moved me greatly. My support for United was cemented even more by the events that followed.'

At that time a certain 11-year-old boy was usually to be found playing football on a pitch near his family home in Burren Way, Castlereagh, Belfast. He wrote about the disaster in his autobiography: 'The crash had happened in the middle of the afternoon and I remember people talking about it as I came home from school on the bus. I then turned on the radio when I got home and heard all the details. The whole thing had an air of unreality about it because for most normal people then, flying was a fantasy in itself.' We will hear a lot more of his story in the next chapter.

Indeed, the power of those events in Munich could influence people many years later, as Noel Flannery, who was born in January 1974 and grew up in the Moyard area of West Belfast, reveals: 'When I was a young boy, Glasgow Celtic and Liverpool were the teams everyone in my street supported. I knew, after reading up on Manchester United and watching videos of the team playing, there was only one team for me. I even managed to turn a friend of mine, who was a Liverpool supporter, into a devoted United fan. My friend, like me aged eleven years old, came into my house one day and my father had just bought the history of Manchester United on video. After watching the tape, and in particular the section on the Munich Air Disaster and George Best, my friend immediately changed from being a Scouse Red to a United Red.'

As we have seen, only one of United's three Irishmen caught up in Munich played for the club after the disaster. Henry 'Harry' Gregg was born on 25 October 1932 in Magherafelt, County Londonderry, Northern Ireland. He played for Linfield Rangers, Linfield Swifts (also known as Windsor Park Swifts) and Irish League side Coleraine before he accepted an offer to sign for Second Division Doncaster Rovers just before his 20th birthday.

He was delighted to sign for a club whose player-manager was a Northern Ireland legend, Peter Doherty. Coleraine received £2,000 for releasing him. Gregg played a total of 92 Division Two games for Rovers before United approached his club to sign him up. While Gregg was at Doncaster, Doherty was also in charge of Northern Ireland and awarded him his first international cap in a 2–1 away win over Wales in Wrexham on 21 March 1954 in a World Cup qualifying game.

United's offer of £22,000 was instantly dismissed, so Matt Busby and Jimmy Murphy drove to Doncaster to ask Gregg in person to join United. By then, he had gone on to win nine caps for Northern Ireland and was changing the way goalkeepers operated, as he was one of the first to venture out of his box to shout encouragement to his team-mates in front of him. At the time, most goalkeepers rarely left the goal line, but the innovative Gregg liked to bark orders to his defenders if he saw one or two of them out of position.

The Old Trafford pair duly turned up at Doherty's home just six days before Christmas to meet Gregg and discuss the terms of the transfer with Doherty and his player. Gregg liked what he heard and without a moment's hesitation the big Irishman agreed to move to United. A fee of £23,500 was agreed, the second time the club had broken the world record fee for a goalkeeper. Gregg received a paltry £30 from the transfer fee, but as he said himself he would have gone to United for nothing. However, Busby had the utmost faith that the young Irish international goalkeeper would be worth every penny, and Gregg did not let him down.

Two days after signing Gregg, Busby gave him his debut and he put in a commanding, almost flawless, performance as United ran out 4–0 victors over Leicester City at Old Trafford in Division One on 21 December 1957. His attitude to training and dedication to the task in hand were exactly what Busby was looking for and he retained his place in the team, playing in 18 of United's remaining 20 league games that season, which saw them finish ninth in the table.

By the time of Munich, United had not lost one of the ten games since Gregg's arrival, and everyone was in buoyant mood having qualified for the semi-finals of the European Cup the previous evening. Gregg, who had been reading *The Whip* by Roger MacDonald, put the book down and gazed out the window as the third attempt to take off got underway. The plane crashed into a building at the end of the runway and burst into flames. Amid the wreckage and pandemonium, he clambered out of a hole in the fuselage, repeatedly returned to the burning aircraft to rescue the survivors, despite the danger that the plane might explode at any stage.

In an interview with *The Times* some time after the disaster

Gregg said he could still remember how dark and silent it was after the plane crashed: 'I thought I was dead until I felt the blood running down my face. I didn't want to feel my head because I thought the top had been taken off like a hard-boiled egg. I was so confused. It was total darkness yet it was only three in the afternoon – it was hard to reconcile. The first dead person I saw, did not have a mark on him. It was Bert Whalley, the chief coach, who'd been taken with us as a bonus for developing all those great young players. At first I thought I was the only one left alive. In the distance I noticed five people running away, they shouted at me to run. At that moment, the aircraft captain came around from what had been the nose of the aircraft carrying a little fire extinguisher. When he saw me he shouted in his best pukka English accent: "Run, you stupid bastard, it's going to explode."'

Then Gregg heard a baby crying: 'The crying seemed to bring me back to reality and I shouted at the people running away to come back. But they were still shouting at me to run. I could hear the child crying and felt angry they were running away, so I shouted again, "Come back, you bastards, there's people alive in here." For me to shout that was difficult because, at that time, I was a God-fearing man and wouldn't normally have cursed. But the people just kept running away.'

So he climbed back into the burning aircraft and found the baby: 'She was beneath a pile of debris and, remarkably, she only had a cut over her eye. I scrabbled back to the hole with her and got her out.'

After Gregg handed the baby to someone close by, he returned to the smouldering wreck and pulled the baby's mother, Vera Lukič, out of a hole in the fuselage. He then made a third trip back to the plane, ignoring cries for him not to given the likelihood that a further explosion could occur at any time. 'I began to search for Jackie Blanchflower and I shouted out his name. Blanchy and I had been friends since we played together for Ireland Schoolboys as fourteen-year-olds and I was desperate to find him.'

But in his frantic search for Blanchflower, he soon came across Bobby Charlton and Dennis Viollet, both of whom were unconscious. Gregg dragged his two team-mates out of the plane and laid them on the snow a short distance from the plane before resuming his search for Blanchflower and, much to his utter relief and joy, he finally found him. 'When I found Blanchy, the lower part of his right arm had been almost completely severed. It was horrendous, a scene of utter devastation.'

Quite amazingly, Gregg overcame the shock and horror of what he had seen and played in United's next match, on 19 February, a fifth-round FA Cup tie against Sheffield Wednesday at Old Trafford. Famously, the section in the match programme where you would normally see the United team was left completely blank, while Jimmy Murphy had the task of trying to find 11 players to wear the famous red shirt of United. He had missed the trip to Belgrade as he was in Cardiff at the time, coaching the Welsh national team for an important 1958 World Cup play-off game against Israel.

Gregg told Murphy he wanted to play, as did fellow Munich survivor Bill Foulkes, and on a solemn night under floodlights at Old Trafford a young and inexperienced Manchester United side beat their opponents 3–0. Gregg wasn't the only player with Irish connections in the United side, for the game marked the debut of Seamus Anthony 'Shay' Brennan. The Sheffield Wednesday players had no chance of winning the game, such was the emotion of the occasion. In the lead-up to the tie, football fans everywhere, regardless of their club affiliation, were so overcome with grief at the terrible loss of so many innocent lives in Munich that it seemed like everyone, including fans from the Steel City, was willing United on to win.

Players from both sides, as well as many fans at Old Trafford that night, wore black armbands in memory of those who had died. For Brennan, it was an astonishing occasion on which to make his debut. He had not been born in Ireland but in Wythenshawe, South Manchester, to Irish parents on 6 May 1937 and played his early football as an inside-forward for Manchester Schools. He left school when he was 16 and began an apprenticeship as a joiner, but continued to play football at the weekend for St John's Old Boys in the South Manchester & Wythenshawe League. During a game for his league against a Manchester Catholic League XI in late March 1955, he put in a performance that did not go unnoticed. This sort of game always attracted the scouts, and that day scouts from both United and City were stood on the touchlines. Brennan heard they were there, and hoped it would be United who came calling as they were the team he supported.

However, somewhat to his disappointment, it was City who contacted him first and offered him a job on the groundstaff. He turned down their advances, but a few days later his dreams came true when United called and he signed as a professional in early April 1955. After making a few outings in the United youth set-up, he played in the first leg of the 1954–55 FA Youth Cup final and helped the team to a 4–1 win over West Bromwich Albion at Old Trafford on 27 April. Three days later, United won the second leg at the Hawthorns 3–0 to claim the Youth Cup with a convincing 7–1 aggregate victory, the third consecutive season Busby's exciting young team proved themselves the best in the country. Given that he lined up alongside the likes of Eddie Colman, Wilf McGuinness, Duncan Edwards and Bobby Charlton, perhaps the result wasn't such a surprise.

He had then made gradual progress through the ranks at Old Trafford, but nothing he had ever done before could have prepared him for what had happened in Munich. Brennan was still only 20 years old and on his way home from training at Old Trafford when the news started to trickle down the wires about the crash. Like everyone else in Manchester at the time, Brennan huddled around a radio and listened intently to the numerous broadcasts as they came in. Some of the boys with whom he had won the 1955 Youth Cup were on that flight. As the bodies of some of the players were laid out in the Old Trafford gymnasium, Brennan could only look on in disbelief.

Like many others at the club, he attended the funerals of his fallen comrades.

Although he had been playing well in the Central League for the Reserves, when he set off for Old Trafford that day, he thought he was merely going to watch United play. On his way into the ground, he was told that Murphy wanted to see him, and a mixture of shock and excitement filled his body when he was told that he was going to be playing in the game at inside-forward, replacing David Pegg, who lost his life in Munich.

Astonishingly, Brennan scored twice in United's 3–0 victory (Alex Dawson scored the other goal). He kept his place in the side for the next game, making his league debut against Nottingham Forest at Old Trafford three days later in a 1–1 draw. However, as new players were signed and others recovered from their injuries, he did not play again until late March.

During this period, Murphy remained in charge of the team and began the impossible task of replacing those Busby Babes whose careers ended on a snowy runway in Munich. He signed numerous players, including the Scot Tommy Heron from Portadown in March 1958. In the circumstances, it was not surprising that United's league form was poor (they finished ninth), but somehow the team continued their run in the FA Cup, the players putting everything into getting United to Wembley in honour of their team-mates. Having seen off Sheffield Wednesday, West Bromwich Albion were next, beaten 1–0 in a replay at Old Trafford in the quarter-finals. Then only Fulham now stood between United and the final. After another replay, when Brennan returned to the side, the Reds won through to the final, with the young Irishman again scoring in the 5–3 victory.

By this time, Busby had returned home to Manchester after a period of recuperation in Interlaken in Switzerland. But despite being ordered to stay at home and take things easy, nothing was going to keep Busby away from the final against Bolton Wanderers on 3 May. A frail Busby made his way to the United bench with the aid of a walking stick, while Murphy proudly led the team out on to the pitch. Despite his goal in the semi-final, Brennan was not among them. They wore red shirts with a crest depicting a phoenix rising out of the ashes in memory of their fallen comrades. Sadly, Bolton won the game 2–0, with England's prolific international centre-forward Nat Lofthouse scoring both goals, including one where he barged Gregg over the goal line and into the back of the net.

For Gregg, the routine of playing football was vital at this time, so he was fortunate that the season did not end there. That summer he played in four of Northern Ireland's six games at the 1958 World Cup finals in Sweden, where he was voted the tournament's best goalkeeper. After drawing 2–2 with West Germany in Malmö on 15 June, Gregg played so magnificently in the game that the Germans, who needed a late equaliser from Uwe Seeler to save the game, lined up and applauded him and his team-mates off the pitch.

However, Gregg twisted an ankle against the Germans and after the game it blew up like a balloon, swelling to three times its normal size. He bathed it for a few hours in the cold sea water near the team's hotel, but it was of no use and he hobbled to the next game, against the Czechs, aided by a stick. When the All-Star team from the tournament was voted on by the journalists covering the finals, Gregg received 478 votes, almost four times more than his closest competitor, the great Russian goalkeeper Lev Yashin, who received only 122 votes. His last appearance in the green of Northern Ireland was on 20 November 1963 at Wembley Stadium. Unfortunately, for him it was an embarrassing 8–3 defeat at the hands of England.

The season after Munich, 1958–59, Gregg missed just one of United's league games and played a pivotal role in the team's comeback, when they finished runners-up to Wolves in the First Division. But things did not go as well for Brennan, who had held high hopes that he could establish himself in the first team during this campaign. However, he did not get a game until the final day of the season, at centre-half.

But that season saw the emergence of another Irish player in the United ranks – though it had seemed a long time in coming, not least to the man himself. Joseph 'Joe' Carolan was born in Dublin on 8 September 1937 and, like Johnny Carey and Liam Whelan before him, began his playing career at Home Farm, which was slowly becoming the team in Ireland for up-and-coming young players. He played schoolboy football for the Republic of Ireland and put in a superb performance at full-back against a Liverpool County FA XI at Goodison Park in 1955. The game was attended by numerous scouts, and Carolan's performance was the talk of the terraces. Liverpool made the first approach to sign him, but he was working as an apprentice cabinet-maker in Dublin at the time, and his father refused to let his son accept the Anfield club's invitation. So Carolan continued his apprenticeship while still turning out for Home Farm at the weekends.

Carolan's father knew that his son had his heart set on becoming a professional footballer and when Billy Behan came calling, he knew he could not hold back his son any longer and agreed to let Behan take Carolan for a trial to see if he was good enough to join the famous Busby Babes. It was February 1956 and United were well on their way to clinching the title. The fact that his father was a United fan probably helped matters, too. Carolan was 18 years old when he left his Home Farm team-mates behind, although one of them would follow him across the Irish Sea to United just five months later.

He was placed in digs supplied by the club and had a week's trial at Old Trafford, where he impressed Murphy and Busby sufficiently to be offered a contract as a part-time professional; he accepted immediately. Like many of the young apprentices at the club, he managed to stave off homesickness by staying in regular contact with his family back home thanks to the players' telephone box. The players had a dedicated telephone for their use situated beside the treatment room.

Carolan performed solidly for the junior teams, and three months after arriving at Old Trafford he collected a winners' medal after helping United to FA Youth Cup success over Chesterfield. Joe played in both legs of the final, a 3–2 win at Old Trafford and a 1–1 draw away, which saw United win the trophy 4–3 on aggregate, to retain it for the fourth year in a row.

The young full-back could not break through into the senior side during 1956–57, as the full-back partnership of Bill Foulkes and Roger Byrne was Busby's first choice. The following season had become a mirror image of the previous campaign, with Foulkes and Byrne again working in tandem. Then came Munich and while Foulkes survived, Byrne was lost forever. Ian Greaves returned to the left-back role vacated by Byrne, while Carolan and the rest of his team-mates could only mourn the loss of their friends.

Finally, on 21 November 1958, Carolan was probably amazed as anyone when he walked down the corridor that led to the Old Trafford changing rooms and glanced up at the team sheet to face Luton Town at home the next day and saw his name on it beside the No. 3 jersey. Greaves had picked up an injury in the previous game, which meant he would miss the match against the Hatters. United beat the visitors 2–1 and Carolan seemed at ease despite the huge step-up in class he had just made. Busby played him in United's next five games, which all ended in wins, before Greaves was recalled to the side for one game. Carolan didn't miss another game for United that season, playing in a total of 24 matches.

Next year, 1959–60, United finished seventh as the rebuilding work continued. And by now the Irish contingent was playing a major part in things. Carolan played so consistently well that he was a guaranteed Busby pick all season. He also won his two international caps for the Republic of Ireland at this time, making his debut against Sweden at Dalymount Park on 1 November. Things went considerably better for Brennan that season, too, as he made 29 league appearances, while Gregg played all but nine games.

The three of them were joined by another Irish recruit, and it was someone very well known to Carolan: Johnny Giles. Michael John 'Johnny' Giles was born in Ormond Square, Dublin, on 6 November 1940. His father, Christy, had played for Bohemians in

Dublin during the 1920s, and when his career came to an end he managed Drumcondra in the 1940s. Incredibly, Giles was just nine years old when he made the Dublin City Under-14 team and once scored four goals for the Republic of Ireland Schools side against their English hosts, who had gone unbeaten for two years. Giles played for a number of clubs in Dublin before he joined Home Farm. United scout Billy Behan was keeping a constant watchful eye on his progress and in July 1956, when Giles was 15, sent him over to Manchester for Busby and Murphy to assess.

It was a daunting journey for the young Irish kid. His father took Giles to the North Quay at Dublin docks and put him on the Leinster and Munster ferry to England. His mother, too emotional to see her son to the docks, stitched a one-pound note into the lining of his jacket just in case of an emergency. When he arrived in Liverpool, he had to make his way to Lime Street Station where he boarded a train to take him to Central Station in Manchester. Giles knew he would be meeting Manchester United's chief scout, Joe Armstrong, when he got there, but he did not know what he looked like, while Armstrong had never cast eyes on Giles before.

At the end of his long journey, he got off the train in Manchester and slowly walked down the platform carrying a little suitcase wondering what would happen next. Luckily for Giles, Armstrong could tell this was who he was waiting for and introduced himself. He stayed in Armstrong's house in Stockport for the weekend and then on the Monday morning he went to his digs where he would spend the next fortnight. He travelled to Old Trafford by bus, and when he arrived at the ground the first person he met was Duncan Edwards, who was sitting on top of a post box waiting for a bus.

Giles could not believe his luck. Here he was at Old Trafford, having just been introduced to Edwards, and about to play in a trial game for the famous Manchester United, the team he had supported with a passion because of his hero Johnny Carey. It did not take the Old Trafford management team long to make their minds up to sign him for the club, with Home Farm receiving just £20 for his services. With fellow Irishmen Jackie Scott and Liam Whelan there, not to mention former team-mate Carolan, any chance of homesickness was reduced.

In his first season at the club, 1956–57, Giles was making steady progress through the junior ranks, until a broken leg almost brought his promising career to a premature end, but he soon recovered. The following campaign, on his 17th birthday, he signed professional terms after starring at both inside-forward and outside-right in the youth teams. He was still only 18 when, on 12 September 1959, he was given the opportunity to show that he could carry his tricky footwork and close ball control into the first team. Things did not go well for United that day, as Tottenham Hotspur were the visitors and defeated the Reds 5–1. However, despite the humiliating home defeat, the local press praised his performance and commented that he just needed a good run of games in the side to gain experience. He played nine more times that season, scoring twice.

A few weeks after his club debut, Giles collected the first of his 59 caps for the Republic of Ireland (he would score five goals for them) in the same match as Carolan made his debut. They found out that they had been called up to the national side only when Carolan bought a newspaper while United were on a team break in Blackpool and read their names in the sports section. No one had contacted them. The Swedes had arrived in Dublin in confident mood, having just beaten England 3–2 at Wembley four days earlier and soon took a 2–0 lead. Giles put his lack of international experience to one side and inspired the Irish to a 3–2 victory, scoring their first goal in the dramatic comeback.

Carolan's second game for Ireland, against Chile in a friendly, caused him to miss a United match for the only time in the entire 1959–60 campaign. The Irish won the game 2–0 and again Giles also played, but so did West Ham United's Noel Cantwell, who was the captain of his country but who would soon have a major impact on Carolan's future.

Carolan started as left-back in the opening two league games of 1960–61, but after two defeats, and seven goals conceded, Busby decided to ring the changes. Carolan was dropped and replaced by Brennan, with Bill Foulkes moving from centre-half to right-back. He never regained his place in the first team again, with the exception of a 4–1 victory over Exeter City in a League Cup first round replay at Old Trafford on 26 October (Giles scored one of United's goals). It marked Carolan's 71st and last game for the Reds. That month a 19-year-old Dubliner signed from Shelbourne earlier in the year, Tony Dunne, had made his debut, while in November, Busby paid West Ham United £29,500 for Cantwell, a world record transfer fee at the time for a full-back. Carolan knew his days at the club were numbered. Four Irishmen into two full-back positions simply would not go, and so the following month he was sold to Brighton & Hove Albion for £8,000, before eventually moving into non-league football in 1962.

Although Brennan had played in the opening game of that season at left-half, he was then switched to full-back, because Busby thought his pace and ability to get up and down the pitch would best suit the manager's style of free-flowing attacking football. It proved to be one of many masterstrokes by Busby. In 40 of the remaining 41 league games, Brennan alternated between right-back and left-back, while Bill Foulkes was moved back to centre-half after the arrival of Cantwell.

Meanwhile, Giles had very mixed fortunes that year. Although his name was one of the first on the team sheet at the start of the campaign, he broke his leg against Birmingham City in a 3–1 loss at St Andrew's on 12 November. It would be five months before he returned to action on 1 April 1961, and he held on to his place until the end of the season as the club ended up in seventh place for the second successive year.

That season also saw the debut of two other Irishmen: Jimmy Nicholson and Ronnie Briggs, neither of whom made a particularly big impact at Old Trafford. James Joseph 'Jimmy' Nicholson was born in Belfast on 27 February 1943, and he attended

Methody College in his home city. They played rugby at his school, so he played rugby for Methody on Saturday mornings and football in the afternoon for Boyland, a club that had already supplied United with first-teamers Jackie Blanchflower, Jackie Scott and Ronnie Briggs. The midfielder was spotted in action for Boyland by one of United's Irish scouts, Bob Harpur. On his 15th birthday Nicholson joined the groundstaff at Old Trafford and he then turned professional on his 17th birthday. He didn't have to wait long before he got his big chance.

On 24 August 1960, he was given his first team debut by Busby when he played in United's First Division game at Everton. United had lost the season opener 3–1 four days earlier and Nicholson came in for right-back Ronald Cope. However, Busby moved Brennan to cover Cope's slot, while Nicholson took over Brennan's No. 6 jersey and played at half-back. Sadly, things didn't go well as United lost 4–0. He was clearly not to blame, and retained his place in the side for the return fixture at Old Trafford a week later. In a complete reversal of fortunes, the Toffees came unstuck and United romped to a 4–0 victory, with the teenager finding the net in only his second game for the club.

Nicholson then played in every game for United until mid-February and the way the 17-year-old settled into his role had some sports writers, and indeed some United fans at the time, thinking that they were watching the progress of an Irish Duncan Edwards. Such a daunting comparison was highly unfair on the young player. However, Gregg, who often seemed to take United's new Irish recruits under his wing, felt that the comparison might not turn out to be entirely outlandish. Less than three months after making his United debut, Nicholson lined up for Northern Ireland on 9 November 1960 in a 5–2 loss to Scotland at Hampden Park in the British Home International Championship. It was a meteoric rise to prominence.

A back injury forced him to miss United's 3–1 Division One win over Bolton Wanderers at Old Trafford on 18 February 1961, but he made an immediate return to the side the following week before injury once again curtailed his progress. It wasn't just the niggling back injury either, the boy from Belfast was also feeling the heat of competition for his position from a tenacious little teenage half-back who had made his debut on 1 October 1960, a certain Nobby Stiles. When Stiles made his senior debut, he played alongside Nicholson, while Busby moved his normal half-back partner, Maurice Setters, to right-back. So Busby had a gifted triumvirate of half-backs to choose two from; it was quite a dilemma. After 37 appearances in his first season, the football world was at his feet – or so it must have seemed in the summer of 1961 for the 18-year-old Nicholson.

But Nicholson's first full season as a regular in the United team proved to be the highlight of his Old Trafford career. In 1961–62, Busby decided that Setters and Stiles were his preferred half-back pairing, with Nicholson left to make sporadic appearances for the Reds (just 21 in total). His 68th and final outing for United came in their 3–0 defeat away to West Bromwich Albion on 15 December 1962. A few weeks later, Paddy Crerand joined the Reds, and thereafter there were no more opportunities for him. He bided his time in the reserves, but in late December 1964 was transferred to Second Division Huddersfield Town for £7,500. He played almost 300 games for the Leeds Road outfit before moving to Bury in 1973–74, where he finished his career a couple of seasons later after making a further 83 appearances. He eventually won 41 caps for his country between 1960 and 1971, scoring six goals, the first ten coming while he was at United. While never rising quite to the heights that some had predicted for him – and who could live up to being 'the next Duncan Edwards'? – it was still a fine and distinguished career.

William Ronald 'Ronnie' Briggs was born in Castlereagh, Belfast, on 29 March 1943, almost exactly a month after Nicholson and like him played for Boyland. Shortly after playing for his country at international youth level, he was spotted by an Irish scout and recommended to Busby. Aged 15, he headed across to Manchester and was immediately signed on as an apprentice, signing professional terms on his 17th birthday. Standing an impressive 6ft 2in and weighing 13st 3lb, the ginger-haired keeper made his United debut on 21 January 1961. Harry Gregg had been injured the previous Saturday and with David Gaskell also injured, Busby decided to give Gregg's fellow countryman his chance in goal.

If he was reassured by seeing Nicholson in the line-up ahead of him, it didn't show. Briggs's inexperience was clear to see and he had a nightmare start to his United career, conceding six goals against Leicester City at Filbert Street. Busby gave the teenager another chance the following Saturday, when United took on Sheffield Wednesday in the fourth round of the FA Cup. Briggs played well in the cup tie at Hillsborough which ended 1–1, Cantwell scoring United's goal. Four days later he was still in goal for the replay. But it was a night he would want to forget, as the visitors inflicted a humiliating 7–2 defeat on the home side. Newspaper reports state that the young Irishman walked off the pitch with his head in his hands, too embarrassed to make eye contact with the fans. It was a crushing blow to his confidence. However, undeterred, and to his credit, Briggs put the recent disappointments behind him and ploughed everything into training in an effort to become a better goalkeeper.

Perhaps he was thrust into the Old Trafford spotlight too soon at the beginning of his young career, as he played only eight more games for Manchester United, all in season 1961–62, and was sold to Swansea Town in May 1964 after spending the remainder of his Old Trafford career in the Reserves. He then moved on to Bristol Rovers, before playing non-league football. Briggs did win international honours for Northern Ireland, making his debut on 11 April 1962 in a 4–0 loss to Wales at Ninian Park, Cardiff, while his second and last cap came on 17 March 1965 at Windsor Park. It was a St Patrick's Day for the Irish to celebrate in style as they defeated Netherlands 2–1 in a World Cup qualifier. He died aged 65 on 28 August 2008 at St Peter's Hospice, Bristol.

Samuel Thomas 'Sammy' McMillan was yet another recruit

from Boyland. Born on 20 September 1941 in Belfast, he was almost 18 months older than Nicholson and Briggs, but took longer to reach the United first team. He was a promising left-winger and it came as no surprise to his manager in East Belfast when he was approached by United in late 1957 and asked to allow the 16-year-old to go to Old Trafford for a trial. Bob Bishop, United's chief scout in Belfast, was a regular spectator and liked what he saw. After his parents agreed, Boyland reluctantly permitted McMillan to go. He arrived in Manchester in December 1957, around the time his fellow Ulsterman Gregg was joining from Doncaster and just a couple of months before Nicholson. Not only did United have a great record in finding Irish players, thanks to Bishop and Harpur, but the image of Busby as a caring, paternalistic figure who would set up young players in digs with respectable families reassured many parents and encouraged them to allow their children to go to United above other rival clubs.

Busby liked what he saw and offered McMillan an amateur contract, which he duly accepted. Like all the promising young players, McMillan had to impress his coaches if he was to earn a call-up to the first team. With competition so tough, opportunities to impress were severely limited, and it wasn't until November 1959 that he signed as a professional – once more just before his fellow Boyland recruit Nicholson.

Despite this crucial sign of progress, it would be a further two years before he was given his debut, against Sheffield Wednesday at Hillsborough on 4 November 1961. United lost 3–1 on the day, but McMillan had done enough at outside-left in the United attack alongside Bobby Charlton and Dennis Viollet to keep the No. 11 shirt for the next two fixtures, with McMillan scoring the United goal in the latter game, a 4–1 defeat against Ipswich at Portman Road. He went on to make 11 appearances in the league for United that season, scoring six goals in total. In only three of them did he line up alongside Nicholson, but on the first two occasions (against Leicester City on 4 April and Sheffield United on 24 April) he scored twice in each game. The shrewd Busby used McMillan's incredible speed to alternate the Irishman from his favoured inside-forward role to outside-left and centre-forward.

Such a promising start to his career brought him to the attention of the Northern Ireland manager, Bertie Peacock. McMillan won his first cap standing in for Derek Dougan in a 3–1 defeat to England at Windsor Park on 20 October 1962. He won his second and final cap in Glasgow just over a fortnight later, on 7 November, this time at inside-right. The Scots won 5–1 at Hampden Park, with four of their goals coming from his United team-mate, the irrepressible Denis Law.

McMillan found himself frozen out of the starting line-up in 1962–63, with Ian Moir and then Bobby Charlton occupying the No. 11 jersey for much of the campaign. He did manage four appearances (without scoring), all before Christmas and three of them alongside Nicholson, but soon realised that his number was up at Old Trafford. Despite being offered a new contract by Busby to stay at United, the Ulsterman eventually moved to Third Division Wrexham on Christmas Eve 1963 in an £8,000 transfer. He made 149 appearances for the Welsh club, scoring an impressive 52 goals, before moving to Southend in 1967–68. The goals increasingly dried up and he went on to Chester and then finished his career at Stockport County at the end of the 1971–72 season, when he top-scored with 13 league goals in 36 appearances for the struggling Fourth Division outfit.

Colm Devine remembers this early 1960s period well, for this was the dawn of regular TV coverage of English football in Ireland, as well as additional media reporting: 'When we moved into the TV era around 1961 it was fantastic, as we got to see the odd bits of matches on Saturday night. Around this time Northern Ireland had an evening sports paper giving reports on all Irish League matches as well as the cross-channel football. As far as I can remember it was simply called *The Saturday Night*. It did not reach Castlederg until around eleven o'clock and we used to pick one up after the cinema.'

They may have been getting more attention across the Irish Sea, but things did not go as well for United in 1961–62, when the prolific forward Dennis Viollet was sold and David Herd was signed by Busby. Rebuilding the club was taking time, and United would finish the 1961–62 season in 15th place – the worst since 1938. Gregg was in and out of the United team, sometimes forced to the sidelines by an injury and sometimes for disciplinary reasons. Like Cantwell, he played in roughly a third of United's games. Giles played in 30 league games, but scored only twice – a disappointing return for an inside-forward.

However, for Brennan, who was very popular at the club, both in the changing room and with the fans on the terraces, it was another good campaign. He was confident on the ball, a strong tackler who never shirked a challenge and was rarely caught out of position, despite regularly supporting United's marauding midfield players further up the pitch. His willingness to run all day for the team and attack at every opportunity earned him the nickname from his team-mates of 'The Bomber'. All-in-all he was a highly skilled player and just loved to be able to play football for a living for his boyhood team. The ever-reliable Irish local boy missed just two league and cup games all campaign.

In the 1962–63 season, the long-serving Irish trio of Brennan, Giles and Gregg still had Noel Cantwell for company (not to mention Nicholson and McMillan), while Tony Dunne was becoming an increasingly regular pick at full-back. At the start of the season, they were joined by Denis Law, and then Paddy Crerand would arrive from Celtic midway through the campaign. The core of the side that would do so well throughout the rest of the 1960s was there – all it needed was a spark of inspiration, but that would not be long in coming, either.

Somewhat surprisingly, United found themselves in a relegation battle, eventually finishing in 19th place, just three points above the drop. Fortunately, there was a cup run to cheer the fans. Brennan did not miss a game for the Reds all season until the day of the semi-final, when Dunne took his right-back slot in the 1–0 defeat of Southampton. It was a cruel blow to the popular Irishman to miss out on United's first final since 1958.

Having missed the first ten games of the season, Gregg helped United to the semi-finals of the FA Cup in 1962–63, but lost the keeper's jersey to David Gaskell shortly before the semi due to injury, and by the time he had recovered, Busby decided to stick with Gaskell for the final.

Gregg and Gaskell battled for the No.1 shirt during the next campaign, but by 1964–65, Gregg faced further competition for the goalkeeper's jersey when new signing Pat Dunne arrived, and he didn't play once in that title-winning campaign. Although he was back in goal for 26 of United's 42 league games in 1965–66, helping them to fourth spot in the table, he knew his time at Old Trafford was coming to an end.

Gregg was a no-nonsense goalkeeper who could more than handle himself in a crowded penalty area at a time when referees offered them very little protection. He used his 6ft frame and weight of 12st 8lb to barge defenders out of his way. Put simply, he was not a man to mess about with, and this was proven when Blackburn Rovers visited Old Trafford on 6 November 1965. The Rovers players tried to bully Gregg at every corner and each time a ball was floated high into the United goalmouth. But he was having none of it and, to the amazement of most of his team-mates further up the pitch who were totally unaware of what had happened behind them, the referee sent Gregg off for allegedly kicking Rovers defender Mike England.

Gregg played in the first seven league games of 1966–67, but made his 247th and last appearance for United on 7 September 1966, against Stoke City at home. While at United, he kept 48 clean sheets. Busby had just paid Chelsea £55,000 for goalkeeper Alex Stepney, who was immediately handed the No. 1 jersey upon his arrival at Old Trafford, which effectively ended Gregg's career at United.

In December 1966, Gregg moved to Stoke City, but he played

only two games for them before retiring. And so the career of undoubtedly the greatest Irish goalkeeper in the history of Manchester United came to an end, just before United would go on to win the 1966–67 title, meaning that he yet again missed out on winning a major honour at the club.

In 1968, Gregg moved into management, taking charge of Shrewsbury Town, handing future United centre-half Jim Holton his league debut at the Shrews. After four years with Shrewsbury, he moved on to manage Swansea City (November 1972–January 1975), Crewe Alexandra (1975–78) and Kitan Sports Club, Kuwait (August–November 1978) before returning to United as their goalkeeping coach under Dave Sexton. He left the club in June 1981 soon after the arrival of new manager Ron Atkinson, before taking up a coaching position at Swansea City (1982), then he became Swindon Town assistant manager (July 1984–April 1985) and finally manager of Carlisle United (May 1986–87). When Gregg left football for good, he owned a hotel in Portstewart on the north Antrim coast which was appropriately called the Windsor Hotel, as he had begun his football journey at Windsor Park, Belfast.

Gregg was awarded an MBE in 1995 and in the summer of 2008 he was made an Honorary Graduate of the University of Ulster and awarded a Doctor of the University (DUniv) in recognition of his contribution to football. Earlier in the year, he had made a very emotional return to Munich airport for a BBC documentary entitled *One Life: Munich Air Disaster*, and stood at the scene of the crash that cruelly claimed the lives of eight of his team-mates 50 years earlier. It was the first time he had been back to Munich, and during the filming of the documentary he met the son of Mrs Lukič, who had been in his mother's womb at the time of the disaster. Zoran Lukič said to him: 'I have always wanted this moment, to look into your face and say to you, "Thank you". I was the third passenger you saved, but, at the time, you were not to know that.'

Gregg blushed slightly before responding: 'You've nothing to thank me for. I did what had to be done without thinking about it. I've lived with being called a hero, but I'm not really a hero. Heroes are people who do brave things knowing the consequences of their actions. That day, I had no idea what I was doing.'

In an interview with the BBC prior to the television documentary being shown on the channel, Gregg looked back at Munich and said: 'I don't want my life to be remembered for what happened on a runway. I don't need the sheriff's badge and I don't want to play the hero. The wonderful thing to me about that period of time was the freshness of youth and the free spirit, the manner in which we played. I'm not a poet, but I always think "They laughed, they loved, they played the game together, they played the game and gave it every ounce of life and the crowds – they thronged to see such free, young spirits." To me, that's what I want to remember, that was the wonderful thing.'

As for Giles in the 1962–63 season, he missed just six games in all competitions in the run to the final, but unlike Brennan and Gregg, he was a part of the side that took on favourites Leicester City, who had finished fourth in the league. Captained by full-back Noel Cantwell, who thus became United's second Irishman to lift the trophy (after Johnny Carey) and with Tony Dunne also at full-back, Giles joined in the celebrations as United lifted the FA Cup for only the third time in their history, after they beat the Foxes 3–1 at Wembley on 25 May 1963, with David Herd (2) and Denis Law the goalscorers. It was a first winners' medal at United for all three Irishmen.

Little did he know it at the time, but the 1963 FA Cup final proved to be almost Giles's last game in a United shirt. In August 1963, after losing the Charity Shield 4–0 to Everton, he was dropped. Busby had occasionally played him on the right-wing, but Giles believed his best position was at inside-forward, and the two men differed over these issues. He was soon on his way across the Pennines to join Don Revie's Second Division Leeds United team in a £37,500 transfer. He helped them to win the Division Two title in his first season, and the following campaign they would be one of United's closest rivals in the title race. Indeed, Giles played a pivotal role for Leeds for more than a decade, commanding the midfield along with his team-mate Billy Bremner, and would go on to play in the European Cup final in 1975. At Leeds, he won two league titles, the FA Cup, the League Cup and the Fairs Cup twice. No wonder Busby later commented: 'Selling him to Leeds, not seeing his potential as a midfield player, was my greatest mistake in football.'

In 1966, he married Ann Stiles, sister of his ex-Manchester United team-mate Nobby Stiles, and the couple had four sons and two daughters. In 2004, the Football Association of Ireland (FAI) voted Giles the Greatest Republic of Ireland international footballer of the last 50 years. In 2006, a plaque was also erected in his honour at his birthplace in Ormond Square in Dublin.

Giles was a magnificent footballer who could split a defence with a pass for one of his strikers to latch on to without even looking up. England manager Sir Alf Ramsey rated Giles as one of the most influential players British football had ever seen, saying: 'As I look at all the talent and character at my disposal today, my one regret is that John Giles wasn't born an Englishman.'

When he left Leeds United in June 1975, after making 521 appearances and scoring 115 goals, he accepted an offer to become the player-manager of West Bromwich Albion, even though he was at the time the player-manager of the Republic of Ireland. Giles managed the Irish international team from 1973–80. In his first season at the Hawthorns, he guided the club into the First Division and then steered them to a highly respectable seventh place in 1976–77. Having done so, he resigned and returned home to Dublin to become player-manager of Shamrock Rovers, where he remained in charge until 1983. After a brief spell in the United States, he returned to West Brom in 1983–84, but he left the club early in the 1985–86 season, handing over charge to his brother-in-law, Nobby Stiles. In 1986, he joined RTÉ's expert panel for the World Cup finals in Mexico and ever since then he has been a regular football pundit on the Irish TV station.

But while the departure of Giles from United brought to an end one chapter in the story of United's Irish Reds, another chapter was about to begin. And this one would change the history of football in Ireland and Manchester, and arguably around the world.

Chapter 7

The Best Years

In June 1945 Dickie Best married his sweetheart Anne Withers and 11 months later, on Wednesday 22 May 1946, a baby boy was born in Belfast who would change the face of football forever. The couple named him George, after Anne's father. Has any footballer ever been born with a more suitable name than George Best?

Dickie was a hugely respected figure in the local community of Castlereagh in East Belfast where the Best family lived at Burren Way. He worked at an iron turner's lathe at the Harland & Wolff shipyard at Queen's Island, Belfast. Anne worked on the production line at Gallaher's tobacco factory in North Belfast. Dickie was 26 years old when Geordie, as the family called him, was born and played amateur football until he was 36, while Anne was an outstanding hockey player. From the moment he could walk, all Geordie ever did was play football and it was Granda George who would play with him. On the other side of the family, Granda James 'Scottie' Best took him to his first football match, to see Glentoran play at The Oval in East Belfast.

The young George attended Nettlefield Primary School in Radnor Street, and on his way to and from school he would dribble a tennis ball along the pavement, throwing his hips from side to side as he weaved in and out of the other pedestrians. At play times during school and after school, he played football and it was usually quite dark by the time he got home, perhaps having kicked a ball around for four hours at the end of the school day. When all the other kids had been dragged home by their parents, he improvised and kicked his tennis ball against the kerb so it would bounce back to him, then he could control it and pass it against the kerb again. He would practise his shooting by aiming for the handle of a garage door.

However, despite football taking up all of his spare time, George was an excellent pupil and a very quick learner. He passed the 11-plus and went to Grosvenor Grammar School on the Grosvenor Road, Belfast. He hated the school because none of his mates were there, but worse than that: his school played rugby. He gave rugby a go and was a half-decent fly-half. Soon he started to 'go on the beak' (Belfast slang for playing truant) and after a year his parents moved him to Lisnasharragh High School in Stirling Avenue in September 1958 where he could play football and be reunited with his friends. He thrived and became a school prefect in 1959, remaining so until he left in June 1961. In those days, he supported his local team, Glentoran, and an English side: Wolverhampton Wanderers.

At 13, George began to play for his local youth club, Cregagh Boys. The team was run by Bud McFarlane (a close friend of Dickie's), who was also reserve team coach at Glentoran. McFarlane knew from the first moment he saw him play that George had what it took to become a footballer and mentored the young Best. When he suggested George was concentrating too much on playing with his right foot, Best took Bud's advice on board and over the following week he never touched the ball with his right foot. When he turned up for Cregagh Boys' next match, he brought only one football boot with him, his left one. George put the boot on and wore a 'guddy' (Belfast slang for a plimsole) on his right foot. He scored 12 goals in the game and never once used his right foot to kick the ball.

Quite amazingly someone, somewhere decided that George was not good enough to represent Northern Ireland at Schoolboy level. And this unbelievable decision was actually taken after George dominated a game for Cregagh Boys against a Possibles Northern Ireland Schoolboys XI. No one really knows why he didn't make it into the side, but perhaps his frail-looking 5ft, 8st frame was the main reason. Despite McFarlane's support, even Glentoran thought he was too small and too light to be a footballer.

But McFarlane was good friends with Bob Bishop, United's chief scout in Northern Ireland from 1950 to 1987. He persuaded Bishop to take George away for the weekend to one of his training camps at Helen's Bay, County Down. Bishop liked what he saw and decided to keep an eye on him. Meanwhile, a Leeds United scout decided George was far too skinny to cope with the demands of life in the English leagues.

To prove that Best could cope with professional football, McFarlane asked Bishop to organise a friendly match between Boyland and his Cregagh Boys Under-16 team. At McFarlane's request, the Boyland team was made up of their best 17- and 18-year-olds. Bishop stood on the sidelines watching the 15-year old Best weave his magic on the pitch, scoring twice in a 4–2 win against the much bigger and stronger boys. It was at that moment that Bishop realised McFarlane had been right: Best had what it takes. So he sent his now famous telegram to Matt Busby with the message reading: 'I think I've found you a genius.' How right he was.

Best was invited over to Old Trafford for a trial in the summer of 1961. He travelled with another young player who Bishop thought could make the grade at United, Eric McMordie, and they boarded the Belfast to Liverpool ferry in June 1961. George wore his best clothes for the journey, his school uniform. Speaking shortly after Best died in 2005, McMordie fondly recalled that journey to Manchester: 'George became one of the first to go to United who didn't play for Boyland. Bob Bishop's eye for talent was equal to none – he was a very special man. But a match between us and Cregagh Boys, who George played for, was set up. I've never seen a player with so many bruises on his body as George. He was picked on not just because he was wee, but because he was so talented. But he fought back and that's what made George the great player he was.'

The entire journey was a terrifying ordeal for two kids from the streets of Belfast. When they arrived in Manchester, there was nobody holding a sign with their names on it, so they jumped in a taxi, as they had been told to do, and asked the driver to take them to Old Trafford. However, as it was the cricket season, the driver took them to the cricket ground instead.

When the pair finally made it to United's stadium, they were met by the club's chief scout, Joe Armstrong, who took them to the Cliff training ground. At the Cliff they met a number of the first-team players, including Northern Ireland's Harry Gregg and Jimmy Nicholson, before being taken on to their digs. Armstrong drove the two bewildered young boys to a terraced house in nearby Chorlton-cum-Hardy, and introduced them to Mrs Fullaway. Little did Best know it at the time, but Mrs Fullaway's house would be his home on and off for the next ten years. The Belfast boys were homesick on their first night away from their families, and when Armstrong called at Mrs Fullaway's house early the next morning to pick them up, Best told him that both he and Eric wanted to go home. So the boys made their way back across the Irish Sea to their Belfast homes.

Speaking many years later McMordie, who went on to play for Middlesbrough (1964–75) and winning 21 caps for his country, recalled the journey: 'It was an incredible time. There was George in his Lisnasharragh school uniform with his prefect's badge and me. We were just a pair of kids who had never been out of Belfast. It was like another world. But it all became too much and we ended up back home in less than a couple of days. We were both overawed. A short while later George went back and the rest is history.'

Best's father telephoned Busby to find out what had gone on and Busby persuaded him to send his boy back over again to see if he possessed the necessary talent and ability to become a professional footballer. Best had planned to take up an apprenticeship as a printer in Belfast when he left school, but thankfully Busby persuaded him to sign amateur forms at United in August 1961 and he ended up keeping printers all over the country busy for the rest of his life.

It took the young Best a while to get over the homesickness, so to keep him occupied after training United got him a job as a clerk at the Manchester Ship Canal. He hated the job, having to make countless cups of tea all day long. But on 22 May 1963, the day of his 17th birthday, he signed professional forms with Manchester United. Three days after celebrating his birthday and becoming a professional footballer, he was sitting in the stands at Wembley Stadium, a member of United's non-playing party at the 1963 FA Cup final. Harry Gregg was sitting beside him and recalls: 'Goodness knows how many United fans brushed past George that day without even knowing who the skinny dark-haired kid was.' They would soon know all about him.

Best made his first team debut on 14 September 1963, when he replaced Ian Moir in the No. 7 shirt. Busby had decided that the time was right to blood his teenage prodigy, after he had demoralised the defences of every Reserve team he faced in the Central League. The truth is, Busby could not delay his progress any longer as it was clear to see that he had a very special talent on his hands, a player who had exceptional speed, perfect balance, bewildering close ball control, a sublime feather-like touch, was courageous and brave as any in the tackle.

United defeated West Brom 1–0 at Old Trafford that day in the First Division, and for those among the 50,453 crowd who were privileged to see the game, they witnessed the debut of a teenager who would not only go on to change the game but also how the media followed it. Having given him his debut, it was an agonising three-month wait before his next competitive game for United. On 28 December 1963, United welcomed Burnley to Old Trafford and this time Best wore the No. 11 shirt. He was magnificent, teasing the Burnley players at every opportunity, constantly driving at the heart of their defence and helping United to a 5–1 victory by grabbing the first of his 179 goals for the club.

This time, he kept his place and on 18 January 1964, as United took on West Bromwich Albion at the Hawthorns in the league, for the first time he lined up alongside both Bobby Charlton and Denis Law. The trio clicked instantly, with the young Irishman and Law seeming to be able to read one another's minds, such was the telepathy between the pair. The Baggies stood no chance, with United easing to a 4–1 win and the trio took all of the plaudits that afternoon, with Law scoring twice, while Charlton and Best also found the net.

From having been relegation candidates the previous season, this year United were title challengers, but despite the brilliance of this sensational triumvirate, the Reds finished runners-up to Liverpool in the title race. In the FA Cup, although Law missed the third-round tie, the trio were together for the rest of an impressive cup run, as they tried to retain their hold on the trophy. In the end, United got knocked out in the semi-finals by West Ham United. Best was also handed his European debut when United beat Sporting Lisbon 4–1 at Old Trafford in the first leg of their European Cup-Winners' Cup quarter-final tie. But United were trounced 5–0 in the return in one of the worst-ever performances from the club in Europe.

Before the season was over, Best was called up to the Northern Ireland squad by Bertie Peacock and won the first of his 37 caps for his country, against Wales on 15 April 1964, but lost 3–2 at Vetch Field. At the end of the season, Best starred in the first leg of the 1963–64 FA Youth Cup final against Swindon Town on 27 April. A crowd of 17,000 poured in to the County Ground and saw Best score United's goal in a 1–1 draw. Three days later, United won the second leg 4–1 at Old Trafford in front of a crowd of 25,563, giving him his first winners' medal with the Reds.

After dazzling opponents, fans and reporters alike the previous season, Best was a marked man going into the 1964–65 season. Many defenders had his name in their little black books, all out for revenge after having been embarrassed, on more than one occasion, by the youngster the previous campaign. But Best was almost unstoppable, impossible for defences to control, as he helped Manchester United claim their sixth First Division title that year. It was a long, hard season, with the battle for the championship coming down to a three-way tussle between United, Leeds United and Chelsea. But in the end it was United who came out top, beating Leeds to the title on goal average, after the pair finished on 61 points apiece, while Chelsea ended up five points adrift.

Those managers who gave their full-backs seek-and-destroy orders to eliminate the threat Best posed were disappointed. He had learned his game playing against much older, bigger and physically stronger players in Belfast. So resilient was he that he missed only one of United's 60 games that season. This was despite the fact that he was kidnapped in February 1965, as part of the Manchester College of Commerce students' rag stunt (which rival manager put them up to it has never been discovered!). During the season George also scored his first goal for his country in a 2–1 loss away to Switzerland in a qualifying game for the 1966 World Cup, played on 14 November 1964.

The following season, 1965–66, a few niggling injuries meant Best missed 11 league games, but he still managed to find the net nine times as well as setting up countless other goals. He missed the 1–0 FA Cup semi-final defeat to Everton. But it was United's two tussles with Benfica in the quarter-finals of the European Cup that would transform him from a local hero into an international phenomenon.

The Portuguese champions had an excellent track record in the tournament, having reached three finals in the previous five seasons, winning it twice. Unsurprisingly, they arrived at Old Trafford for the first leg in confident mood on 2 February 1966. United drew first blood, winning 3–2 in front of a packed audience of 64,035, with goals from David Herd, Denis Law and Bill Foulkes. It was a slender one-goal advantage to take to Lisbon on 9 March, and the Portuguese giants were probably the favourites to progress to the semi-finals, especially after the 5–0 hammering United had been given by Sporting Lisbon just two years earlier. Indeed, Benfica had never lost a European Cup tie at home. But this was a different United team: they were the reigning English champions, and in George Best they possessed a player who could win a game on his own if he was in the mood.

He terrorised the Eagles' defence, and within 13 minutes put United in the driving seat in the tie having scored two magnificent goals. In the sixth minute, Best headed past Costa Pereira. Less than seven minutes later, he collected a pass from Herd just inside the Benfica half. He looked up and saw six white shirts in front of him blocking his way to goal. For some people their future is defined by a certain moment in time, their chance to show what they can do, and this was most definitely Best's moment. With the ball at his feet, he took off and headed straight for the goal. For those watching inside the Stadium of Light and on TV at home, it must have looked like time stood still for everyone on the pitch, except Best. He raced through the Portuguese defence to fire into the net and put United 2–0 up on the night and 5–2 ahead on aggregate.

Soon after, United were 3–0 up when John Connelly hammered a pass from Best beyond a well-beaten Pereira. By now 75,000 voices had fallen silent, dumbstruck by what was unfolding on the pitch before their very eyes. Half time could not have come too soon for the home side, who left the field to a chorus of boos. United then put through their own goal, past Best's international team-mate Harry Gregg. But United had not finished and added two late goals through Paddy Crerand and Bobby Charlton to complete an 8–3 aggregate victory. When the final whistle sounded the Benfica fans hurled cushions down on the home players as they trudged off the pitch. It was one of the greatest away performances in the history of European competition, and it was Best, not Eusébio, who looked the best player in Europe on the night.

At the end of the game, a fan ran on to the pitch with a knife and made his way towards Best. Thankfully, he was brought to the ground before he could get anywhere near United's hero and afterwards it was discovered that he had intended to claim a lock of his hair. It was a sign of things to come for Best.

When Busby was interviewed afterwards, he was asked what his plans had been going into the game trying to protect United's slender one-goal advantage and answered: 'Our plan was to be cautious, but thankfully somebody must have stuffed cotton wool in George's ears.'

After the game, Best was photographed wearing a huge sombrero and was dubbed the 'Fifth Beatle' by the local press, and when the team arrived back home in Manchester the following day he donned the sombrero again for the British press and the tag of *El Beatle* stuck. For Best, it was the moment he began to move away from the back pages of the papers to the front.

But for all the attention that came Best's way after that match, it must not be forgotten that he was far from being the only Irishman on the pitch. As we have seen, Harry Gregg was in goal that night, though his United career would come to an end within a few months. In front of him, Gregg had two Irish full-backs in Shay Brennan and Tony Dunne. In season 1964–65, Brennan had been so indispensable that he played in every one of United's 60 games, as did Dunne. For Brennan, who had made his debut immediately after Munich, winning a league title was a fitting reward for his long service.

Anthony Peter 'Tony' Dunne was born in Dublin on 24 July 1941. While still at school he began his career at the Stella Maris Boys' club, alongside Johnny Giles. He also played for junior sides St Finbar and Tara United. When Gerry Doyle was appointed manager of Shelbourne at the start of the 1956–57 season he began searching for the best talent available in Dublin to challenge the dominance of Shamrock Rovers and St Patrick's Athletic. Dunne was recruited the following year, and Shelbourne went on to win the FAI Youth Cup in 1959. Doyle then promoted six of that side into the senior team, including Dunne, for season 1959–60, and the young side went on to win the FAI Cup. It was only the second time in the history of the club that they won the trophy. Dunne's performances attracted the interests of a number of English league scouts, not least United's Billy Behan, who persuaded Busby to travel to Dublin on two separate occasions to watch Dunne play.

No sooner had he won the FAI Cup than Dunne was on his way to Manchester United in a bargain £5,000 transfer. He arrived at Old Trafford in April 1960 and six months later, on 15 October, he made his league debut at Burnley, when he replaced Brennan, but couldn't prevent the Reds from losing 5–3. He played only three further games for United that season, as Brennan and Noel Cantwell were the regular full-backs.

Little changed at the start of the next campaign, but in September 1961 Cantwell picked up an injury that presented Dunne with a golden opportunity to impress Busby. Happy in either full-back role, he started in United's next two games until Cantwell's return. He won back his place on 18 November at Ipswich Town and then did not miss a game until mid-April. He probably needed the break by then, as he'd played for United on 4 and 7 April, then nipped across to Dublin to make his international debut on 8 April (a 3–2 defeat against Austria) before lining up again for United on 10 April – four games in under a week.

In season 1962–63, Dunne and Cantwell had a ding-dong battle to partner Brennan at full-back, both making 25 league appearances (though not always at full-back). With Brennan out of action, it was Dunne and captain Cantwell who filled the full-back slots in the 1963 FA Cup final victory over Leicester City. For

Dunne, it was his first winners' medal with United and the moment his Old Trafford career really took off – he would miss just four games in all competitions over the next three seasons, though an injury to Cantwell in 1963–64 meant there was somewhat less competition for places.

Just before the 1964–65 season began, United made the short trip across to Dublin to take on Shamrock Rovers at Dalymount Park on 14 August. With the Irish trio of Dunne, Brennan and Best in the team, not to mention Charlton and Law, the Irish side lost 4–2. But it was a reflection of the club's understanding of the growing importance of its Irish following and cemented the relationship that had been so visible with the number of recruits that had come from all parts of Ireland.

Two other Irish players were nearing the end of their United careers by the end of 1965–66: Noel Cantwell and Pat Dunne. Neither of them played in that game against Benfica, but both were key members of the squad. However, Cantwell's path to United was very unusual.

Born Noel Euchuria Cornelius Cantwell on 28 February 1932 in the Mardyke area of Cork, he was educated at St Joseph's Primary School and later at the Roman Catholic Presentation Brothers College in his home city. He was a talented footballer, an excellent cricketer, a good rugby player and an all-round athlete. Whatever the sport, he was a handful for most opponents, standing 6ft tall and weighing 13st 3lb. He started his football career with local side Western Rovers before moving to Cork Athletic. Although his favourite team was United, because of Johnny Carey, the club's scouts didn't get there in time.

His lucky break came because of Frank O'Farrell, who was born in Cork, but joined West Ham United in January 1948. During the summer months, O'Farrell would return home and often make guest appearances for Cork Athletic alongside his Hammers team-mate Tommy Moroney, who was also from Cork. Moroney and O'Farrell suggested to their manager, Ted Fenton, that the club should take a look at Cantwell. After Fenton had persuaded

Cantwell's father to let him make the journey to London, Cork Athletic sold him for £750 in September 1952, with Cantwell receiving £150 from the transfer.

Moroney took Cantwell under his wing and helped the 20-year-old Irishman settle in at Upton Park. His new team-mates included not only O'Farrell and Moroney, but also Malcolm Allison, John Bond, Malcolm Musgrove and Dave Sexton. All of these players except Moroney and Musgrove went on to manage a club in the First Division, while O'Farrell and Sexton would of course go on to manage United, while Allison and Bond would manage Manchester City.

Cantwell made his international debut for the Republic of Ireland on 28 October 1953 against Luxembourg at Dalymount Park, and scored his first goal for Ireland against the reigning world champions West Germany in a memorable 3–0 win in Dublin on 25 November 1956. In 1957–58, he captained the Hammers to promotion to Division One and the following year he was voted the Irish Footballer of the Year.

Whereas most professional footballers went on holiday during the close season, Cantwell liked nothing better than playing cricket. When the football season ended, he turned out for Cork Bohemians. He was a fine all-round cricketer, good enough to play for Ireland five times between 1956 and 1959, making him a dual international.

After making 248 appearances for West Ham United, scoring 11 goals, Matt Busby paid a world-record fee for a full-back, £29,500, to bring Cantwell to Old Trafford in November 1960. He was 28 years old when he joined Manchester United and so became Busby's oldest signing in his entire period in charge after Munich. He bought him not only for his outstanding ability, but because he was also very well respected by his fellow professionals. He was a gentleman on and off the pitch, in the same mould as boyhood hero Johnny Carey, and was just what United needed in the post-Munich years. He made his debut for United at left-back on 26 November 1960 in a 3–0 First Division away defeat at

Cardiff City, with Shay Brennan switched to right-back and Bill Foulkes moved to centre-half.

In 1961–62, he wasn't a regular starter, appearing in just 19 games, scoring twice – one of the goals coming when he was played at centre-forward for three games near the end of the season. He was appointed team captain for the 1962–63 season, but it was an up and down campaign for both Cantwell and United, not helped by the Big Freeze that winter. But he did have the honour of following in his hero's footsteps, becoming the second Irishman to lift the FA Cup for the Reds.

Two-thirds of the way through season 1963–64, Cantwell suffered an injury which not only cost him his place for the rest of the season, but also meant he played only two league games in the title-winning season in 1964–65, both outings at centre-forward, as Brennan and Dunne were ever-present in the full-back slots. With time on his hands, in February 1965, he joined the management committee of the Professional Footballers' Association (PFA), and the following year became its chairman, a sign of the respect in which he was held by his peers.

Although he managed 29 appearances for United in all competitions in 1965–66, he turned out just four times for United in the following campaign (like Harry Gregg, he failed to win a league title medal, despite his long career at United), and at the age of 35 realised that his playing days were coming to an end, after making 146 United appearances and scoring eight goals. He had won 36 caps for Ireland (22 as captain), the last of them in February 1967, scoring an impressive 14 goals – a national record at the time, helped by the fact that five of them were penalties. So in October 1967, he moved into management and took over the reins from Jimmy Hill at Coventry City. Briefly, that season, he was in charge of the Ireland team, too.

He remained at Coventry until 1972, before having two spells as manager of Peterborough United, the last of which finished in 1988, as well as two periods working in the USA. At Peterborough, he remains something of a legendary figure for the club's fans. Some had wondered if he might go on to succeed Busby as United manager, and felt that he was being groomed for the position, but his managerial career was not quite as successful as his playing career had been. Cantwell died aged 73 on 8 September 2005, after a long battle against cancer.

He was the first player from United's triumphant 1963 FA Cup-winning side to die. His funeral at Peterborough Cathedral was attended by some 1,500 people, a reflection of the high esteem he enjoyed in the game and in his adopted home city. Writing in his autobiography, Sir Bobby Charlton gives an idea of the role he played at Old Trafford: 'I liked him as a man and, if there was such a thing, I thought he was a United type. I also admired him as a player . . . sometimes the quality of his playing ability was overlooked, but he was a defender of considerable class, strong on the left side and with a very nice touch. When he led us out for the 1963 Cup final, I thought, "This is good – we have a real captain."'

Patrick 'Pat' Anthony Joseph Dunne was another player whose path to United was not entirely smooth. He was born on 9 February 1943 in Dublin and, like his namesake Tony, began his career at Stella Maris. In 1958, he was invited to Old Trafford to have a trial for United. However, Busby elected to sign Belfast-born goalkeeper Ronnie Briggs instead, leaving the dispirited Dunne to return home in October. Just a few months later, he had a successful trial at Everton and in May 1960, he signed as a professional for the club. But that summer he tripped and landed on a broken bottle, which ripped into his arm and he had to have several operations to repair the damage. By the time he returned to action for Everton, Andy Rankin had replaced him in the pecking order at Goodison Park to be understudy to Gordon West in the Everton goal.

So in the summer of 1962, he joined Shamrock Rovers and in 1963–64 helped them win almost every domestic honour in the Republic of Ireland (League of Ireland Championship, FAI Cup, League of Ireland Shield and the Leinster Cup).

Furthermore, they were only narrowly defeated by Valencia, the holders and eventual finalists of the Inter-Cities' Fairs Cup. Billy Behan alerted Busby to come and watch him play in the FAI Cup final.

Busby quickly realised that he had made a mistake by letting Dunne slip through his fingers five years earlier and wasted no time in persuading him to join United in a £10,500 transfer deal. On 8 September 1964 at Everton, Busby handed Dunne his United debut as a replacement for David Gaskell. With Gregg injured and out of action for the entire season, Busby needed the 21-year-old Dubliner. Dunne's debut coincided with a welcome return to form for United, as he was inspirational in goal helping the team win 13 of their next 14 league games. Busby had seen enough in those games for Dunne to retain the No. 1 jersey for the rest of the season, and the young Irishman was rewarded with a league-winners' medal at the end of the campaign.

Just when he thought things could not get any better, exactly one week after celebrating the title success with his team-mates, he made his debut for the Republic of Ireland in a World Cup qualifier on 5 May 1965. He marked his international debut by keeping a clean sheet for his country as they beat Spain 1 0. Shay Brennan also made his long-awaited international debut in that match, while Tony Dunne played alongside him at full-back and Noel Cantwell played centre-forward; former United star Johnny Giles was also in the team.

Despite his record in helping United to the title, Dunne still had his doubters. Some critics said that his bravery, good reflexes and shot-stopping ability were outweighed by his inability to dominate his area and to deal with crosses. With Gregg fit again, there was a three-way tussle for the goalkeeper's jersey, and for the majority of the season it was Gregg who won through. Dunne made just 11 appearances in 1965–66, the last of them at Sunderland on 11 December. After 67 games for United, he did not play again for the Reds, and when United signed Alex Stepney from Chelsea in late September 1966, Dunne (like Gregg) knew his time at Old Trafford was up, and in February 1967 he signed for Plymouth Argyle in a £5,000 transfer.

He played for Argyle until 1971, making 152 appearances in front of the Home Park faithful, who always rated him very highly, before returning to Ireland, initially at Shamrock Rovers. He was capped just five times by his country, the last of them in November 1966. He played on into his forties, and also took up management in Ireland.

Although there were rare occasions when United were fielding five Irishmen in their line-up (on 19 April 1965, for example, when Pat Dunne, Brennan, Tony Dunne, Cantwell and Best were all in the side), there was little doubt who it was that was most capturing the imagination of fans in Ireland – and elsewhere – George Best.

By the age of 20, he was the first footballer to gain pop-star fame. The British game had never before witnessed anything close to the adulation and media coverage the young Belfast Boy attracted from all corners. Certainly, the nation had produced some truly magnificent footballers, such as Stanley Matthews and Tom Finney; indeed, England had even won the World Cup that summer, making heroes of Bobby Moore, Geoff Hurst and the rest of the team, but none of their careers was under the spotlight in the way that Best's was. He was the most phtographed footballer of his day, every sports reporter's dream scoop. Boys and girls loved him in equal measure, clamouring for his autograph, swooning girls tried to steal pieces of his hair or rip the clothes off his back. Large companies knocked at his door, lavishing huge sums of money on him to endorse their products, from Stylo football boots to Fore aftershave to Cookstown sausages. Inevitably, he also attracted a string of glamorous girlfriends.

And for those who couldn't get to see him live, there was always *Match of the Day*, which helped bring a new level of interest in football – and in Best. Billy Dickson from Newtownards used to persuade his father to allow him to stay up late to watch United games on TV: 'I grew up in Sandy Row, Belfast, and my mates supported Leeds United and Chelsea. "Here, Da. Are United on TV tonight?" I'd ask him, "Can I stay up and watch?" "Yes they are, and no you cannot, you will be in bed asleep," he replied. It was 1966 and I was eight. We had this conversation every Saturday night. We both knew that if I managed to stay awake, I would be watching TV from the top of the stairs until he called me down to sit beside him and watch the likes of Paddy Crerand, George Best, Bobby Charlton, David Herd, John Aston, Nobby Stiles and Denis Law all weave their magic spell on me, as I watched mesmerised looking at an old black and white television. Then the next day I would be out practising, trying to emulate my heroes.'

Ed O'Riordan from Skeheenarinky, County Tipperary, sees the influence of Best as going beyond what he achieved in football: 'Having an English mother and an Irish father I can say this: there has always been an inferiority complex among us Irish when comparing ourselves to Britain. Not so much nowadays, but certainly in the sixties and seventies. British pop-stars and actors were regarded as more glamorous, exciting and interesting. An Irish band getting a number one hit in the Irish charts was not really as good as number twenty in the British charts. An English accent was always more authoritative than an Irish one. It must follow that English footballers were more glamorous than Irish players.' But Best changed all that.

Best (and United for that matter) also stood for something else in a divided city, as Jim Hunter from Sion Mills, County Tyrone, recalls: 'I started supporting Manchester United on 25 May 1967. How do I know the exact date? I was only an eleven-year-old kid at the time, living on the Rathcoole Estate on the outskirts of North Belfast. I supported Celtic because they were the big name at the time. In Rathcoole, only Scottish football was ever talked about. But I was too young to understand the difference between Celtic and Rangers. My father had no interest in football and all my brothers were younger than me, so they had even less knowledge than me.

'I also followed a lad by the name of George Best. You couldn't help but know about George. Everyone was talking about him. We had no TV, but the *Belfast Telegraph* was always full of reports of how he was winning games for Manchester United almost single-handed. You just couldn't help but love George Best. After all, he was Irish.

'Anyway, on 25 May 1967 Celtic beat Inter Milan 2–1 to win the European Cup. As I said, my father had no idea about football, but as it had been my birthday only a week or so before, he bought me a Celtic jersey. I wore it out into the street on that evening. I never wore it again. I was attacked by grown men, who beat me so badly I was carried, unconscious, into our living room at home. When I came round I couldn't remember what had happened. My Celtic shirt was covered in blood. At that moment, I realised the difference between Celtic and Rangers. I wanted nothing to do with tribalism, so I decided to follow George Best and Manchester United.'

Colm Devine has spent a lifetime following United, and he looks back fondly on watching Best in action: 'The first time I saw George playing was at Windsor Park on 2 October 1965 against Scotland and Northern Ireland beat a very good Scotland team 3–2. George was brilliant as usual, and Paddy Crerand was wing-half for Scotland and Denis Law was inside-forward for the Scots. George always seemed to put on a great show when he played in his home city of Belfast. It was as though he owed it to his home-town fans after leaving the Emerald Isle for England.'

Not long after that Devine moved to England, to work in the construction industry. After a spell living in Croydon, he visited Manchester for his brother Patsy's wedding: 'I was really taken by the city. There were more Irish people knocking around than I found in Croydon. However, that was not necessarily always a good thing. I moved to Manchester after Christmas 1966 and the one saving grace was being able to go to see United play at Old Trafford.

'I lived with Patsy for a time in his home close to Ardwick Green, about a mile or so from the centre of Manchester. He had pictures of United players, and George in particular, all around his house. Manchester United had a huge Irish following, mainly down to George and of course Tony [Dunne] and Noel Cantwell. Patsy and I used to go and watch the United youth team hoping to spot another George, but of course we had a better chance of seeing another Halley's Comet.

'On match days we used to stand in the old Scoreboard End, which was not covered in those days and I can still remember the first time I went in there. It cost four shillings to get into Old Trafford, the programme cost ninepence, sixpence for a pie and threepence for a cup of soup. Altogether it would have come to around 27 pence in today's money and we were watching a fantastic show every time we went. You knew you were going to see something you had not seen before and would probably never see again: George's wizardry, Denis the acrobat, Bobby with the power in his shot, Nobby taking the ball off some of the best players in the game, Paddy driving 40-yard passes with inch-perfect precision, Tony running alongside a flying winger and nicking the ball with the ease of a professional pickpocket.

'George Best always had time for the fans and I remember getting his autograph outside the players' entrance at Old Trafford. It was about 2.45pm, and when I got into the Scoreboard End George was out on the pitch warming up. He used to come out of the tunnel, which was then on the halfway line of the South Stand, with a football in his hands. He would drop the ball on the pitch and shoot for goal at the Stretford End. If he hit the target then he was confident of scoring during the match and most times he did. He could do no wrong as far as I, or any of the other Irish supporters, were concerned. He was our George and that was that. I don't believe he ever realised what he did for the Irish people in Manchester at that time. We could hold our heads up and we knew he was the best and no other nationality could argue otherwise.

'The Irish fans at Old Trafford mainly gathered in the Scoreboard End and a few had seats in the stands. A lot of Irish sub-contractors used to own season tickets and would allow their employees to take full advantage of them for home games. If we were losing, these men would lose whatever little bit of English twang they pretended to have. I remember Alex Stepney letting in a rather soft goal and a guy stood about twenty feet behind him let rip: "Stepney, ya couldn't keep cows in a slap." I recognised this dialect right away and moved closer: I actually knew him as he came from a town quite near my family home in Aghyaran, County Tyrone. A lot of priests were often seen going to matches and some people regarded United as a Catholic club, but I can honestly say that I couldn't find a great deal of truth in that. The majority of Manchester United fans that I have come across had little or no religion to speak of. However, I could of course understand where that story would come from. If you are looking at a crowd of maybe two hundred people and you saw four dog collars, then you could quite conceivably think to yourself that there were a lot of clergymen at the game.'

The 1966–67 season held much promise for Best and United, and it came as no surprise when they were crowned champions for the second time in three years. United were in scintillating form throughout the campaign, with their non-stop attacking football drawing admirers from all corners. United finished the season four points clear of their nearest rivals, Nottingham Forest, who were managed by Johnny Carey, and were the leading goalscorers in the league with 84. Best himself was in fantastic form, and did not miss a game all season, scoring ten goals. Tony Dunne missed just two, though Brennan played in only 16 league games.

This set up United for another crack at the European Cup. There were high hopes at Old Trafford that this would be the year in which Matt Busby would claim the trophy he regarded as his Holy Grail ten years after the Munich Air Disaster. With two former winners of the European Footballer of the Year Award in the side, Denis Law (1964) and Bobby Charlton (1966), plus

Best, the time had surely come for Busby's third great side to conquer Europe.

Going into the 1967–68 season, Best had played for his country on 13 occasions, but according to the Northern Ireland press (and contrary to Colm Devine's recollections) he seemed to be more interested in pleasing the Manchester public than his home fans when he wore the green jersey of Ireland. On 21 October 1967, as he prepared to take on Scotland that day in a Home International game that also doubled up as a qualifier for the 1968 European Championships, he read what they were saying and decided to ram the reporters' claims back down their throats. He ripped the Scots apart almost single-handedly. And this was a Scotland side that had just beaten the world champions, England.

Best was arguably at his peak. He missed just one game all season and scored an astonishing 32 goals in all competitions, including 28 in the league where United just missed out on retaining their title, with Manchester City snatching it from their grasp on the last day of the season. He finished up being the Football Writers' Association Footballer of the Year, and was also the 1968 European Footballer of the Year.

But whatever the personal honours that came Best's way, at United everything was gearing up for Europe. Their path to the final began with relatively straightforward opposition in Hibernians Malta and Sarajevo. In the quarter-finals there was a hard-fought tussle against Górnik Zabrze of Poland, which set up a semi-final encounter with Real Madrid. Best scored the only goal of the game at Old Trafford, but it was a narrow lead to take to the Bernabeu, especially as the game was played just four days after the disappointment of losing the title. But a 3–3 draw was enough to secure for Busby's team their dream final at Wembley.

The first half of the final resembled a game of chess, with each side cancelling out the other's every move. Charlton put United ahead in the 52nd minute, forcing Benfica to attack United in search of an equalising goal. With 15 minutes left to play, the Portuguese side drew level. So far, Best had been relatively quiet, but in extra-time he took charge. In the third minute of extra-time, Best collected a clearance from Benfica just inside the Portuguese half. He set off towards goal with the Eagles captain, Mário Coluna, and a few others in hot pursuit of the slender Irishman. Having outpaced them, he threw one of his famous shimmies and rounded the goalkeeper, José Henrique, and passed the ball into the empty net. Two more goals, from Brian Kidd on his 19th birthday and a second from Bobby Charlton, gave United a stunning 4–1 victory. Best, Brennan and Tony Dunne followed the United captain, Bobby Charlton, up Wembley's famous 39 steps to receive the European Cup. United were finally the champions of Europe; Busby's dream had at last been fulfilled.

David Edwards was born and bred in East Belfast where George Best grew up, and remembers that night vividly: 'I have supported United for as long as I can remember. Growing up as a football-mad young lad in Cregagh Estate, I can clearly remember the buzz going round the school when we heard George was home. The first game I can recall watching on TV was the 1968 European Cup final, and bouncing around the room as George turned away after rolling the ball into the net. I have been totally hooked on United since then. My first visit to Old Trafford was in 1969, and I can still remember sitting in the old stand in the Stretford End when, for no seemingly good reason, everyone just stood up in front of me. Why were they standing I asked myself? The answer was simple – George had the ball at his feet in his own half! Magic!'

Cathal Mullan, who has lived in Belfast since 1984, recalls that night: 'The first match I really remember was the 1968 European Cup final. I was seven and lived in the Creggan Estate in Derry in a row of maisonettes that between the six of them housed forty children! Most of us were very good friends and days were spent basically playing in the streets. Anyway, every boy aged six to sixteen in the street ordered a Manchester United strip from my ma's catalogue [she worked for Kays] in preparation for the big final. The families paid two shillings a week to pay for the kit, which cost two pounds, so it took twenty weeks to pay for it! We wore this strip everywhere, and I have photos of myself and my friends wearing this strip over my school shirt and tie, which was the common dress for boys in the late sixties, even in working-class areas.

'George Best was everyone's hero and we all had the No. 7, made from old bed sheets, stitched onto the back of our shirt. The match itself is still a vivid memory. It was fantastic and I remember, even at seven years old, feeling sick with nerves that United might get beaten. I remember Bobby's first goal, the equaliser by Benfica and the great save by Stepney near the end of the ninety minutes. And then of course genius George's wonder goal in extra-time, followed by Kiddo's header and a great second goal by Bobby that I think has never been fully recognised for how good it was, because the match was sealed by then. As soon as the match was over, I remember everyone pouring onto the streets and singing and roaring United songs. The *craic* was great. I was already a big fan of United before the final, but after this great achievement I was hooked, especially on George.'

For me as well, even though I was too young to have watched the game, the European Cup final was what made me a United fan – and Best was a part of that from the start. We were on holiday in Newcastle, County Down, and we went into a souvenir shop where I saw a huge red football pennant with the words 'Manchester United, European Cup Winners 1968' written on it in white ink. However, there was also a smaller pennant, which was half red and half white and had a black and white image of George Best on it with the words: 'George Best, Manchester United & Northern Ireland'. I was intrigued and my dad went on to tell me all about George Best. That was it for me, I was hooked – without any hesitation I can say it was the moment I became a United fan. My dad bought me that pennant that day, and before we went home at the end of our holiday, he also bought me the other one. Some 43 years later, I still have these two items of United memorabilia at my home in Carryduff.

European Cup success had an impact on another young lad at that time. Jimmy Copeland is a branch secretary of a Manchester United Supporters' Club and began supporting United in 1967 when he was a boy of seven growing up in Ballymurphy, West Belfast: 'My father informed me that the firm he worked for had a sister factory just one mile down the road from Old Trafford. The firm was called Parkinson & Cowan Sheet Metal Works. He said we would be travelling over to Manchester to see the mighty Red Devils play against Leeds United, as Parkinson & Cowan had organised a trip to Old Trafford for all the staff and their friends and family. So on Friday 1 November 1968 we set off on the overnight ferry from Belfast to Liverpool. It was the first time I had ever left Ireland and by this stage I was nine years old.

'Around lunchtime we made the short walk to Old Trafford [from Parky's]. I remember being nervous about the roar and noise of the crowd on the way to the game. I had never experienced anything like this before. I also remember the chip shop at the top of Warwick Road, which today is Lou Macari's Fish & Chip Shop. One thing that really does stick out in my mind is the number of ladies there with no male companions. It was mainly the ladies that were carrying and wearing all the George Best memorabilia. I remember this very well because I was astonished to see so many females go to a football match, which I did not see at home in Belfast. However, the one thing I remember most of all about my Old Trafford debut is a visit to the club's souvenir shop, which was then situated at the East Stand, where the away supporters' entrance is today. My father then bought me a miniature replica of the European Cup, the old traditional red and white scarf and he also purchased a ladies' silk head-scarf for my mother. I still have all three items to this day.

'The next thing I remember is sitting in my seat at the rear of the old Stretford End and being in absolute awe of the whole situation. I enjoyed the records that the disc jockey dished out to us before the match began. Music from Gary Puckett & The Union

Gap with "Lady Willpower" was the song I remember most from that day. What an introduction to live top-flight football in England, with Best, Law, Charlton and Crerand playing for United and Jack Charlton for Leeds, who I remember roughed up his younger brother Bobby a bit on the day. The game ended in a 0–0 draw, but I didn't care as I was just so ecstatic to have been there. So that was me hooked. After our return journey, while trying to copy George Best's silky skills outside our house, no one would believe me when I told them where I had been the previous day. Not too many people from Northern Ireland travelled to England to watch football matches back then. Not even my new United scarf could persuade them initially, but in the end they did believe me.'

Although Best had been the star of the show that Wembley night in 1968, United's unsung hero Dunne had played just as crucial a role at the back. He had played in every round of the European Cup campaign, and many sports writers agreed that he played one of the finest games of his career that night, up against Eusebio. The following year, he was voted the Irish Footballer of the Year, and he continued to be a highly consistent performer for United over the next few seasons, turning out at least 40 times in each campaign to 1971–72.

However, following the appointment of Tommy Docherty in late December 1972, Dunne hardly played again for United. He played his last game for the Reds on 17 February 1973 in a 4–1 defeat at Ipswich Town. Realising that Docherty was looking to bring in his own players, and although he had only just turned 32, on 1 August 1973, the Irishman said farewell to Old Trafford and joined Bolton Wanderers on a free transfer. He had played 535 times for United, more times than any other Irish player in the history of the club and seventh in the all-time list, scoring two goals. He then spent six seasons at Burnden Park, where he went on to play more than 200 matches for the Trotters, helping the Lancashire club gain promotion to Division One in 1977–78, before playing briefly in the USA in 1979.

At international level, he had made his debut for the Republic of Ireland in their 3–2 home defeat by Austria on 8 April 1962, and over the course of his 13 years as an international he won 33 caps, captaining his country on four occasions. His last game for the Republic of Ireland was on 29 October 1975 against Turkey in a European Championship qualifier. The Irish won 4–0 at Dalymount Park, and all four goals were scored by another former United star.

Dunne is unquestionably one of the greatest full-backs in the history of Manchester United, and despite his compact wiry frame (5ft 6½in tall and 10st 9lb), he was a ferocious tackler who possessed great speed and reflexes, and was an excellent distributor of the ball. Today he lives in Sale, near Manchester, and runs a local golf driving range. Bobby Charlton gave this assessment of just how good Dunne was in his autobiography: 'Tony Dunne was possibly the quickest defender I ever saw. His marking ability was brilliant, and I recall telling a journalist who had commented on Tony's great form around the time we won the European Cup, "Well, you know he's been the best left-back in Europe for years. He goes like lightning." . . . He read an opponent so well that, with his speed, he could go out against any winger on earth confident of putting him in his pocket.'

Dunne's regular partner at full-back, Shay Brennan, decided to call time on his playing career at the end of the 1969–70 season. He had played 359 games for United, scoring six goals, and he became the first recipient of a pension from the club. He was a cool, calm and collected player with superb positional sense. He played his last match on 3 January 1970 as United beat Ipswich 3–0 in the FA Cup third round. Although he was born in England, he qualified for selection for the Irish national side as his mother was from County Carlow, and he won 19 caps for the Republic of Ireland, captaining them on five occasions. When he made his debut against Spain on 5 May 1965 in a World Cup qualifier, he became the first player born outside Ireland to be capped by the Republic.

When Brennan left Old Trafford, he took up an offer to become player-manager of Waterford in August 1970 and spent four seasons there, guiding them to the League of Ireland Championship in 1971–72 and 1972–73 and the League of Ireland Cup in 1973–74. He also collected the last three of his international caps while playing for Waterford. Afterwards, he ran a parcel courier business in Waterford.

In 1986, he suffered a heart attack and United sent a team over to Dublin on 14 August 1986 to play a testimonial match for his benefit against a Shamrock Rovers XI. Such was his popularity that a crowd in excess of 10,000 poured into Glenmalure Park to see the home side win 2–0. Sadly, Brennan collapsed and died from another heart attack while playing a round of golf near his Tramore home in County Waterford on 9 June 2000, aged 63. He was the first member of the 1968 European Cup-winning side to die.

Just one week before he died, his close friend Nobby Stiles had visited Waterford and called in to see him. 'He christened me "Happy" because I was anything but that on the pitch – I was a narky little sod, if the truth be told. He was the "quiet man" on the pitch at the time. But Shay was a brilliant full-back, always dependable and consistent. He was very quick on his feet – a thing which he often pointed out to me when I was a yard behind him. Shay had a great understanding of the game – to play with him was a joy. He was one of the greats, everyone loved Shay.'

Brennan was the life and soul of the United dressing room and was renowned for cracking a good joke, as he showed when he was invited on to the *Breakfast* TV programme and sat alongside the Spanish crooner and heart-throb Julio Iglesias. Anne Diamond seemed smitten, and when the Spaniard kept using the term '*mañana*', she asked what it meant. He explained that it meant there was no need to hurry or rush into doing something. Diamond turned to Brennan and asked him if the Irish had a similar word. Brennan looked at her and famously replied that the Irish had no word that matched the same degree of urgency as *mañana*.

The man who scored those four goals for Ireland in 1975 was Daniel Joseph 'Don' Givens. He was born in Limerick on 9 August 1949 and began his career with Dublin Rangers and was a prolific striker for the amateur side. He signed as an amateur for Busby in September 1965 and found himself surrounded by Irish voices at the club and was desperate to join them in the first team. However, he had to wait his turn in the junior sides. He was sufficiently impressive for them that, on 27 May 1969, he was handed his first cap for the Republic of Ireland in their World Cup qualifier against Denmark in Copenhagen, losing 2–0, even though he had still to make his debut for United.

By now the club was managed by former player Wilf McGuinness, after Sir Matt Busby's decision to retire at the end of the 1968–69 season. Busby had hoped to go out on a high, but in the league United slipped to 11th place, were knocked out of the FA Cup in the quarter-finals and missed out on another European Cup final when they were beaten 2–1 on aggregate in the semi-finals by AC Milan. In truth, the team was in need of an overhaul, and Busby perhaps no longer had the energy to build a fourth great side.

That season's European Cup run had ensured United further cemented their popularity in Ireland, when for only the second time in the club's history they had an official fixture against an Irish side, taking on Waterford on 18 September 1968 in a first round first leg encounter. When club chairman Don Kennedy heard who his club's opponents would be, he immediately realised that Waterford's home ground, Kilcohan Park Greyhound Stadium, was too small to host the tie. So he made the brave decision to approach the IRFU to see if the game could be moved to the capital and played at Lansdowne Road, the first football match ever to be played on the famous rugby ground.

In the weeks leading up to the game, the town of Waterford was buzzing with excitement that their local team was taking on the best team in Europe and most, if not all shops, were a sea of blue and white bunting and flags. The venue switch allowed everyone who wanted to go to the game to obtain a ticket (prices started at 4s, or 20p) and book their place on the many coaches that left Waterford for Dublin on the morning of the tie.

Paddy Lowe was one of those who travelled to the game, heading off with his brother-in-law, but nearly didn't get in when there was some confusion after they both thought the other one had the tickets. Fortunately, a swift phone call resolved the problem and they were able to take their positions. Lowe recalls one incident when Waterford's small outside-right, Al Casey, was on the receiving end of a full-blooded Nobby Stiles tackle. As the Irishman 'was lying on the ground, Nobby shouted down to him: "Get up! You're OK." However Casey got up on one elbow and said: "It's OK for you, Nobby, but I'm on the early shift in the paper mills in the morning."'

A crowd of 48,000 turned up to see Dunne and Best, as well as the rest of the United team, record a 3–1 victory, with Law scoring a hat-trick. That game also nearly produced a remarkable coincidence, for the manager who had led Waterford to European qualification the season before was Martin Ferguson, brother of the then Glasgow Rangers striker Alex, but sadly he had left the club by the time the two sides met. In the second leg at Old Trafford, United won 7–1, with Law scoring four of the goals. At the end of the game, the United players formed a guard of honour to applaud off their opponents – and the man who scored their consolation goal? Al Casey, the paper mill worker, who hit home in the 70th minute and received the biggest cheer of the night from the sporting Old Trafford crowd.

Matt Keane, from the *Munster Express*, was at both games and recalls: 'The vast majority at Lansdowne Road came to see the visitors. Six special trains left Waterford that day, in addition to dozens of buses and hundreds of cars. Johnny Matthews, the little Coventry-born winger, scored Waterford's only goal of the game and amazingly he also scored against Glasgow Celtic in 1971 and found the net against Real Madrid in 1981 when he was playing for Limerick, only for the goal to be disallowed. It would have been some treble! For the journey to Manchester, the team flew over there, and during the flight much-loved Johnny "Nish" Barns, the team kit manager and sponge man, walked the aisle of the plane with a cap in his hands and asked all on board to put a few bob into it. "What are you doing?" asked one of the players. "Making a collection for the pilot," replied Johnny. Whether that story is true or not doesn't really matter. It is now part of football folklore in this county.'

Ted Healy from Waterford recalls the first leg: 'I was twelve years old when in early July 1968 came the news of the European Cup draw: Manchester United v Waterford. United had agreed to play the first leg away, but the game was to be held at Lansdowne Road, Dublin. Soon after, my dad came in from work and said: "What do you think?" In his hand were five tickets for the game. To this day, I still can feel the sense of sheer delight of that moment and the dreams of what lay ahead.

'Wednesday 18 September finally came and the excitement in the town was at fever pitch. A day off school was the first bonus, and we set off in our car at lunchtime for the 5.45pm kick-off. We were seated in the front row of the old East Stand. It was all a magical whirlwind for me. The green baize, the teams coming out together, and there they were in the flesh just yards from us: Denis Law, who scored a hat-trick and missed a penalty, and George Best, who scored a goal of sheer genius that under today's rules would have stood, but was chalked off by a linesman's flag as Bobby Charlton was offside. Jimmy Rimmer came on for Alex Stepney and when he parried Seamie Coad's shot, Johnny Matthews flashed it to the net and the place erupted.'

The club needed to start looking towards its youth again, which gave Givens hope, especially after he scored in Ireland's next World Cup qualifier, against Hungary on 8 June 1969. He had already played for United's first team, but only in a friendly in Dublin against Shamrock Rovers on 5 May, scoring in their 4–0 victory. And during United's summer tour of Switzerland in 1969, McGuinness played Givens in both of United's games. On the opening day of the new season, United took on Crystal Palace at Selhurst Park on 9 August and Givens found himself on the bench. He came on for Dunne to make his first-team debut on his 20th birthday. After nine appearances, four of them as substitute, in which he scored just one goal, Givens was transferred to Luton Town in April 1970 for £15,000. Admittedly, competition for places up front was tough at the time, but he went on to have a long and distinguished career. At club level, after leaving Luton Town in the summer of 1972, he went on to Queens Park Rangers, then joined Birmingham City in 1978 before finishing his domestic career at Sheffield United in 1980–81.

But it was at Dalymount Park that he had some of his greatest goalscoring moments. On 30 October 1974, he scored a hat-trick in Ireland's 3–0 win over the Soviet Union in a European Championship qualifier. A year later, on 29 October 1975, he grabbed those four goals for the Irish against Turkey, the first and only time an Irish player has done this. He won his 56th and final cap for his country on 14 October 1981 in a 3–2 win over France in Dublin in a World Cup qualifier. His 19 goals for his country remained a record until it was overhauled by another United star, Frank Stapleton.

With Busby now having taken a back seat, Best's spectacular rise to superstardom was bringing with it some difficulties, as he could not go anywhere without being mobbed by adoring fans, male and female. His fan mail at the club topped 10,000 letters every week, but rather than ignore them he employed three people full-time to look after the George Best Fan Club to make sure his fans received a reply. Slogans started to appear on gable walls in Belfast and Manchester, such as 'Jesus Saves, But Best Scores The Rebound'. In so many ways, this was a pinnacle, which inevitably meant that the only way was down, for both Best and United.

After 18 months in charge, McGuinness was demoted back to reserve team coach during the 1970–71 season, and Busby took charge until the end of the campaign. The young manager had been unfortunate having to follow such a pre-eminent figure as Busby. His performance in 1969–70 – an eighth place finish and the semi-finals in both the League Cup and the FA Cup – was not bad, but the expectation was that United should be competing in the European Cup, and they were a long way behind champions Everton. There was one spectacular highlight in that campaign, and inevitably it was Best who provided it when United took on Northampton Town at the County Ground in the fifth round of the FA Cup. All possibility of an upset was extinguished by Best, who scored a club record-equalling six goals for the Reds in an 8–2 victory. Busby stabilised things in 1970–71, and Best finished the campaign with 20-plus goals for the fourth successive season, as United again ended up in eighth position and again reached the League Cup semi-final.

But for me, none of it compares to the day I got to see Best in action in the flesh. I will never forget coming home from school on Wednesday 21 April 1971 and my dad telling me that he was taking me to see Northern Ireland play that evening. I had no idea who they were playing, all I wanted to know was if George would be playing. In those days of the Troubles, this was not as straightforward as it would be now. I was an eight-year-old Roman Catholic kid going to Windsor Park in Protestant South Belfast with my Protestant father to see a game that could conceivably have been targeted by the IRA. However, all I wanted to do was get inside the ground and see George Best. He did not disappoint in that game, a European Championship qualifier against Cyprus, and scored a hat-trick which included a goal directly from a corner kick. Was there anything George Best could not do?

A few weeks later, on a sunny Saturday afternoon on 15 May, I found out that there was, when I went with my dad to see Northern Ireland take on England. The history books show Northern Ireland lost 1–0. However, it should have been 1–1, because Best scored one of the most audacious goals ever seen that day, but it was not allowed to count. Gordon Banks, the England goalkeeper, caught a pass into the area and, as he tossed the ball into the air to kick it upfield, Best, who was loitering with intent close by, toe-poked the ball upwards and headed it into the net. He started to wheel away in delight, before Banks and several other England players complained to the referee, who then disallowed the goal for dangerous play.

Another abiding memory of my childhood in supporting Manchester United is watching a goal scored by Best for United. The date was 2 October 1971, and *Match of the Day* showed brief highlights of United's home game against Sheffield United. Best collected a flick-on from Brian Kidd just in front of the centre circle inside the opposition's half. Looking around he could not see any team-mates in support and so off he set, with defenders merging on him from all directions, but none was able to dispossess him or knock him off the ball. He just seemed to be gaining momentum and speed with every stride, and when he was driven wide to the right-hand side of the Sheffield United penalty box it looked impossible for him to shoot. But Best drilled a low shot past the diving goalkeeper and into the far corner of the net, with a defender sliding in vain to catch up with the ball before it crossed the goal line. Best tilted his head back, closed his eyes and smiled as he threw both arms out in front of him as if to say 'Mission Complete'.

What happened to United in that season, and the few that followed, is outlined in the next chapter. But astonishingly and tragically, Best's career at United was nearing its end. Frank O'Farrell was the new manager, and in 1971–72 the Reds again finished in eighth place, with Best scoring 26 goals, the third consecutive time he had been the leading scorer. But years of being targeted by opposition defenders were taking their toll. Colm Devine recalls the rough-house treatment George had to put up with on the pitch: 'I remember George taking a lot of stick from Ron Yeats of Liverpool at Old Trafford. George had had enough and he swung round and decked him like a heavyweight boxer and down went Yeats. The funny side was that nobody saw it, and George was gone in a flash and was forty yards away when Yeats got up. To be fair, Yeats did not complain to the referee and just got on with the game. I met Ron Yeats many years later at a sportsman's dinner and I had a chat with him and reminded him of the incident. He just smiled and said "George Best was impossible to mark out of the game. He was the genius of our time and he was tougher than a lot of people gave him credit for."'

By now also, the distractions were beginning to take over from the football, and he began to miss training sessions. The club did not know how to handle him – there had been no one like him before – and in 1972–73 both he and O'Farrell went head-to-head on more than one occasion, and soon both men would leave the club. Tommy Docherty took over from O'Farrell mid-season and Best was briefly welcomed back during the next campaign, but on New Year's Day 1974, he pulled on the famous red jersey of United for the 470th and last time in their 3–0 loss to Queens Park Rangers at Loftus Road. In total, he scored 179 goals for United, many of them exquisite solo efforts. He was only 27 years old when he walked out on United and over the next decade he became a journeyman footballer as he drifted from club to club in England, the USA, Australia, Scotland, South Africa and back home in Ireland.

What happened next has been written about and agonised over many times, but I would prefer to remember Best the way he asked his fans to remember him: for what he did on the pitch. At his peak, Best was without question the most naturally gifted and greatest talent the British game has ever produced. An iconic figure on and off the pitch, he had perfect balance, exquisite close ball control on either foot, electrifying pace, superb vision, magnificent timing and possessed the ability to create chances from nothing and could score spectacular goals that other footballers could score only in their dreams. Pelé once remarked that George Best was 'the best player in the world'. No one argued the point.

He died on 25 November 2005, aged 59. When I heard the

news, I was devastated and admit I was in tears – the whole city seemed quiet. I took my family to visit the Best family home that evening and we laid flowers and one of my own pieces of George Best memorabilia in the garden at the house where he grew up. Just standing in Burren Way that evening, a modest little street in East Belfast, made me realise that I did not have to grieve alone. For all around me the love and admiration the people of Northern Ireland had for the Belfast Boy poured out, helping to ease the pain we were all experiencing.

Five days later, United took on West Bromwich Albion, coincidentally the club against whom he had made his debut back in September 1963, and the entire crowd of 48,924 at Old Trafford held up pictures of Best and mourned their loss. West Brom manager and former United legend Bryan Robson joined Sir Alex Ferguson in laying a wreath in the centre circle, and the fans held a minute's silence before a minute's celebration. For Best not only united Ireland, he also united football fans everywhere. John O'Shea, an Irish star from a later generation, was playing that day and commented: 'It was definitely lump-in-the-throat time, and the hairs on the back of your neck were standing up.'

How best to remember him? Perhaps the following two quotes from Best himself do the job as well as anything:

'All the bad times cannot wipe away the good memories, and despite all the ups and downs, when I look at my life as a whole, it is impossible for me not to feel blessed.

'They'll forget all the rubbish when I've gone and they'll remember the football. If only one person thinks I'm the best player in the world, that's good enough for me.'

Chapter 8

Troubled Times

By the time Frank O'Farrell took over as manager of Manchester United at the start of the 1971–72 season, there were difficulties everywhere as far as Irish Reds were concerned. In Northern Ireland, sectarian violence was on the increase and would remain a feature of life in Ulster for many years. On terraces all over England, there were growing problems of football hooliganism, making many people feel concerned about going to games, let alone make a ten-hour journey across the Irish Sea to attend one. And on the pitch at Old Trafford, the team seemed to be declining, with George Best unable to turn back the tide single-handedly. Occasionally, some of these problems would combine.

Adrian Dearnaley recalls how some fans in the Stretford End would also have allegiances to Rangers or Celtic, and that this led to trouble at Bobby Charlton's testimonial game in September 1972, when Celtic provided the opposition. 'I can recall a mass of green and white all around Piccadilly on the day of the game, and the bars and clubs were jam-packed with United and Celtic fans hanging out of every door. It looked like the city centre of Manchester had been invaded by a huge green and white army, and everywhere I went I could hear different Irish accents among the Celtic fans.'

When some United fans began chanting for Rangers before the match, the Celtic fans responded and surged towards the Stretford End. 'Had there not been a huge fence separating the warring factions, things would have turned out really nasty. Both sets of fans were pushing the fence from opposite sides, but thankfully it stood firm.' Fortunately, Celtic manager Jock Stein saw what was happening and urged his supporters back to their places, and further trouble was averted.

Iain McCartney also recalls that era, when Old Firm rivalries appeared at Old Trafford: 'Obviously, there may well have been the odd display of "dislike" between the two factions, but in the end, they were all first and foremost United supporters. If I remember correctly, it was simply something of a pre-match ritual, which did not extend to during the game.'

It was not, therefore, the easiest time for United's first (and only) Irish manager to take over the reins at the club. Francis 'Frank' O'Farrell was born on 9 October 1927 in Cork. He began his playing career with Cork United, before signing for Second Division West Ham United in January 1948. O'Farrell was extremely shy, and so it took a while for him to adapt to his new surroundings in London and establish himself at the club. However, he was a very talented wing-half and in November 1950 he was finally handed his debut. He quickly became a regular feature in the team for the following six seasons, and manager Ted Fenton appointed him the club captain. On 7 May 1952, he won his first international cap when he played for the Republic of Ireland against Austria, but they lost 6–0.

In December 1956, after 107 league games, he left the Hammers and joined Preston North End. He then helped Preston to the runners-up spot in Division One in season 1957–58. In early 1961, an injury forced his retirement from the game, and by then he had won nine caps and scored two international goals.

In May 1961, the 33-year-old was back in the game after being appointed player-manager at non-league side Weymouth. In his first managerial role, he guided the Dorset seaside club to two Southern League Cup finals and the Southern League Championship in 1964–65. Soon after, the directors of Torquay United came calling and he joined the Division Four side. He took the club to promotion in his first year in charge, after Torquay ended the 1965–66 season in third place in Division Four. In the following two seasons, the Gulls finished sixth and seventh in the table. For a club that has never reached the second tier in English football, this was a fine achievement.

In November 1968, Ipswich Town tried to lure him away, but this advance was rejected. However, the following month, when relegation-threatened First Division Leicester City approached him, the Gulls could not hold on to him any longer. O'Farrell couldn't save the Foxes from the drop to the Second Division, but there was almost a fairytale end to the season when he guided them to the FA Cup final, where they lost 1–0 to Manchester City. Having just missed out on an immediate return to the First Division, when they finished third in 1969–70, there was no mistake the following season when they won the Division Two title.

The United directors believed he was the man to follow Sir Matt Busby, with the legendary manager particularly keen to appoint him as his successor. When O'Farrell joined on 8 June 1971, Busby said he was: 'Probably the best signing I ever made.' The deal to bring him to Old Trafford was done at a deserted lay-by off a minor road halfway between Leicester and Manchester.

O'Farrell had taken over an ageing side, with the best days of Charlton, Law and Best arguably behind them. Despite this, by the end of October 1971, United were riding high at the top of Division One having lost just two of their opening 15 league games. Indeed, at one point United led the title race by five points, thanks to the brilliant form of Best, who had scored 11 times in the 15 games, including the only goal in three 1–0 victories. Then, inexplicably, United went on a run of poor form and ended the season in eighth place.

Stories began to emerge that the players were unhappy with his management style, claiming that they had to make an appointment with his secretary just to speak to him. The 1972–73 season started badly, as United failed to record a single victory in their opening eight league fixtures. O'Farrell also found it difficult to handle Best, particularly when the player had been out partying and not turned up at the Cliff for training the following morning. When Crystal Palace hammered United 5–0 at Selhurst Park on 16 December 1972, it was the final nail in the coffin of O'Farrell's reign as boss. Just three days later, O'Farrell was sacked and replaced by Tommy Docherty, who was in the stands watching the defeat to Palace. It was an unhappy time, and the only lasting recruit from his spell in charge was central defender Martin Buchan, who would go on to give the club excellent service for many years.

O'Farrell had various other management roles, finishing up back at Torquay United in the early 1980s, after which he retired from football and continued living in the town. In an interview with the *Lancashire Evening Post* on 23 October 2009, O'Farrell spoke about the difficulty he had had with his most famous Irish player: 'The first thing I did when I went to Manchester United was make George Best the best-paid player. I thought that was only right because he was the most skilful footballer. He could win games on his own and he did – George was that good. But on the flip-side I inherited the problems of George's hectic lifestyle. Some days he'd never show up for training – nobody knew where he was . . . Every week you were protecting him, explaining why he wasn't there or whatever. You tried to keep it quiet, but when it did get out, George would be on the front and back pages.'

O'Farrell did make one Irish signing in his time at United: Trevor Anderson. Anderson was born on 3 March 1951 in Belfast, and grew up in the shadow of Windsor Park in South Belfast where he supported Linfield. David Edwards, who grew up on the same Cregagh Estate where George Best was born, remembers him: 'I saw Trevor play for Cregagh Boys Club when he was probably in his teens and, if I am correct, it was on the same pitch in Cregagh Estate where George played. He was what was then called a "Hanky Ball Player".'

Jim Morgan from Belfast recalls that he used to play football with Anderson in the park on the Lisburn Road after school: 'I didn't know Trevor that well. In those days lots of kids played in the park in different groups, so you just turned up and you got picked for a game. It helped if you owned the ball, of course! We were probably only about twelve years old at the time and probably too young to recognise talent.'

He began his playing career as a striker at Portadown and scored 18 goals for Portadown in season 1971–72. The young Anderson's superb performances in the Irish League soon attracted the interest of several top English clubs, including Arsenal, Manchester City, Newcastle United, West Bromwich Albion and Manchester United. Indeed, much to his delight, Linfield were also very keen to sign him. In October 1972, after receiving glowing reports about him from scout Bob Bishop, O'Farrell paid Portadown £20,000 to take Anderson to Old Trafford. Many believed that O'Farrell saw him as a future replacement for Best, who seemed to be slowly falling out of love with football.

However, within weeks of Anderson signing for United, O'Farrell was sacked and it was Tommy Docherty who handed the slender young Irishman his Manchester United debut on 31 March 1973, when he came on as a substitute for Brian Kidd at the Dell in a 2–0 First Division victory. John Dempsey was from West Belfast, but his family sent him over to school in Southampton, and he was there for his debut: 'He was supposed to be the new George Best. Same style, long hair and pretty fast, but who could live up to those expectations?' In his first season at United, he played seven league games, and scored his first goal for the club in a crucial 1–0 win over Leeds United at Elland Road on 18 April 1973. Speaking in 2009, Anderson recalled those days: 'I had no hesitation in signing for Frank O'Farrell. It's the biggest club in the world and it was a big culture shock for me at the time. I was twenty-one when I signed and it was amazing to be training with the likes of Denis Law, Bobby Charlton and the late George Best. I recall one game away to Leeds where I scored the winner in a 1–0 win and that was probably the highlight for me.'

The following campaign, he played in 12 league games and scored once, but after just 19 appearances for United he signed for Swindon Town on 2 November 1974 in a £25,000 transfer, almost a year after his final first-team game. After 131 league appearances at Swindon, he moved to Peterborough United on 23 December 1977 (49 league appearances, six goals), before returning to Belfast in 1979 to play for Linfield where he had a hugely successful career, winning numerous trophies and making more than 300 appearances, and in 1985–86 won the Northern Ireland Football Writers' Player of the Year Award. After retiring from playing in 1987, Anderson went on to manage the youth team at Linfield before getting the post as first-team manager in October 1992. He enjoyed considerable success in this role, leading them to seven trophies, including two Irish League titles and two Irish Cup triumphs.

During his short period with United, Anderson was capped six times by Northern Ireland. He made his international debut against Cyprus on 8 May 1973 in a World Cup qualifier, scoring twice in a 3–0 win at Fulham's Craven Cottage. The game was switched to London because of the political unrest in Northern Ireland at the time. He went on to win 22 caps for Northern Ireland and scored a total of four international goals, including the winner in his last international match, against Denmark on 25 October 1978. It was his last touch of a ball in his international career.

Pat Morrison was born and bred in the 'Bone' area of North Belfast (around Oldpark Road), but now lives in Newry, County

Down. He recalls the lengths he went to in order to see O'Farrell's United in action: 'My first trip to see United was a home game against Arsenal on 20 August 1971, but the game wasn't played at Old Trafford; it was played at Anfield. United were banned from playing their first two 'home' matches of the 1971–72 season in Manchester, after some trouble at Old Trafford the previous season. Because of the Troubles, my parents had gone to England to stay with my dad's sister, who lived in a little village called Earby, which is about ten miles north of Burnley, and I joined them there after I'd been living in France.

'I went with my cousin Charlie McCann on the bus to Liverpool. It is a distance of only fifty miles, but with no direct bus service it was a marathon trek. At some point in the journey, I asked my cousin what time the bus home was, only to be told that there was no return bus that Friday night.

'There are not many United fans who can lay claim to cheering United on while standing on the Kop! However, Arsenal took a first-half lead. This, though, was the United team of Law, Best and Charlton, and they stormed back with three second-half goals by Alan Gowling, Charlton and Brian Kidd to win the game 3–1. A lot of very happy United supporters left Anfield that night, including the two of us. Only we now had to find a way to get home. We eventually managed to thumb a lift from other United supporters who took us in generally the right direction. By the early hours of Saturday morning, we found ourselves just outside Halifax and, realising that we were not going to get another lift at that time, we settled down for the night in a bus shelter. It might have been August, but boy was it cold that night. The next morning we continued our journey home very tired but very happy. I have been to many United games in the years since but few of my trips have been as eventful as that first one.

'I was also a spectator at Selhurst Park in December 1972, when United infamously lost 5–0 to Crystal Palace, a defeat which saw the end of Frank O'Farrell's reign as manager. I must admit that I didn't stay to see the end of the game.'

Belfast-born Tommy Breen in action during his last game for United, 1 April 1939. He is one of eight Irish keepers to have played for the club, making 71 appearances. (Mirrorpix)

Johnny Carey leads his team off the pitch after United had beaten Arsenal 6-1 to secure the 1952 league title. He became the first Irishman to captain a side to league and FA Cup success. (Mirrorpix)

Early days for the Busby Babes at Mrs Watson's in Manchester, September 1953. The two Irish Babes, Liam Whelan and Jackie Blanchflower, are on the left of the picture. Mark Jones, Gordon Clayton, Alan Rhodes and Duncan Edwards are also settling down for dinner. (Mirrorpix)

Jackie Blanchflower in goal during the 1957 FA Cup final – the only outfield player ever to wear a cap during a United game. (Mirrorpix)

Harry Gregg (right) watches on during training in Blackpool, February 1960. Joe Carolan, Shay Brennan and Maurice Setters (later Jack Charlton's assistant manager for the Republic of Ireland) pile on top of each other. To the left is Albert Scanlon. (Mirrorpix)

29 August 1963. Johnny Giles gets ready to leave Old Trafford to join Don Revie's (centre) Leeds United. Matt Busby (right) later admitted it was one of his biggest mistakes to let the 22-year-old Irishman go. (Mirrorpix)

Maurice Setters, Noel Cantwell and Pat Crerand parade the FA Cup round Wembley after United's 3-1 victory over Leicester City. Cantwell had just become the Reds' second Irish captain to lift the cup. (Mirrorpix)

An Everton fan sarcastically applauds Nobby Stiles and Harry Gregg as they leave the pitch after losing the 1966 FA Cup semi-final. Gregg, the hero of Munich, was one of the game's most uncompromising players. (Mirrorpix)

George Best at home with his parents in October 1966 holds on to his twin sisters Julie and Grace. Father Dickie gave him the advice to 'keep your feet on the ground'. He always did. (Mirrorpix)

Best backheels the ball to evade the Spurs defence during their First Division game in February 1968 – now you see it, now you don't. (Mirrorpix)

Best ignores Matt Busby's instructions to take things carefully against Benfica, scoring his second goal of the game after just 13 minutes as United crushed the Portuguese side 5-1 in the European Cup quarter-final. *El Beatle* was born that night. (Mirrorpix)

Tony Dunne trains at Old Trafford in 1965, while Matt Busby and Jack Crompton look on. Dunne is the Irishman to have made the most appearances for United: an astonishing 535 in total. (Mirrorpix)

Frank O'Farrell (left), United's only ever Irish manager, watches on during his side's 2-0 defeat to Liverpool at Anfield in August 1972. Within four months, the two men to his left, Sir Matt Busby and chairman Louis Edwards, would sack him. (Mirrorpix)

Top scout. Bob Bishop (second left), United's legendary talent spotter joins manager Tommy Docherty (third left) and Tommy Cavanagh (right) with a few of his discoveries: (L-R) Sammy McIlroy, Tommy Jackson, David McCreery and Jimmy Nicholl. (Getty Images)

Kevin Moran is lifted onto a stretcher during United's FA Cup semi-final against Arsenal in 1983. His thumbs-up as he was carried off was typical of the man. (Getty Images)

Frank Stapleton scores in United's 2-2 draw with Brighton & Hove Albion in the 1983 FA Cup final. He made history by becoming the first man to score in the final for two different teams. (Getty Images)

Norman Whiteside celebrates his stunning goal to win the 1985 FA Cup final against Everton. Gordon Strachan and Paul McGrath join in. (Getty Images)

Roy Keane is booked in the 1999 Champions League semi-final. Despite the fact he knew he would now miss the final, he gave an inspirational performance leading United to a sensational win over Juventus. (Getty Images)

Denis Irwin stops Mehmet Scholl's progress at the Camp Nou in the Champions League final of 1999. (Getty Images)

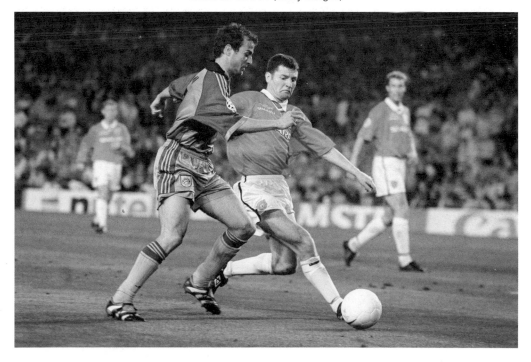

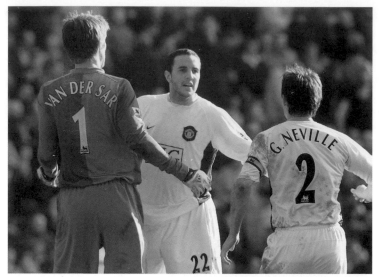

John O'Shea celebrates with Gary Neville and Edwin van der Sar after scoring the late winner for ten-man United against Liverpool in March 2007.
(Manchester United)

Darron Gibson gets a shot away in United's most recent trip to Ireland, taking on an Irish League XI in front of a packed house at the Aviva Stadium in Dublin, August 2010.
(Manchester United)

Jonny Evans in action for United against Tottenham Hotspur in the Premier League on 22 August 2011. The young Irish defender had a great start to the new campaign.
(Manchester United)

If the O'Farrell era can largely be remembered for one significant signing in Buchan, it also featured one notable debut: Sammy McIlroy's. However, Samuel Baxter 'Sammy' McIlroy, who was born in East Belfast on 2 August 1954, was in fact the last youth player signed by Sir Matt Busby, making him the last 'Busby Babe'.

He recalls his childhood: 'I grew up in Severn Street in East Belfast with our family home no more than a few hundred yards away from The Oval, home to Glentoran. My dad Samuel played for Linfield Swifts, so you can imagine the stick I took from my mates, who were all Glens fans. As very young kids we never really had any football heroes across the Irish Sea, while our heroes were local players such as Sammy Pavis of Linfield, and Walter Bruce and Eric Ross who both played for Glentoran. Of course, everything changed when I was nine years old and George Best made his debut for Manchester United. The moment he pulled on the Manchester United jersey for the first time, I decided I wanted to be just like George Best. From then on, Manchester United was my team and George Best was my idol. I went to school every day and practised as hard as I could and went to bed every night dreaming that one day I would play alongside George for United and Northern Ireland.'

He had already appeared four times for the Northern Ireland Schoolboys and was playing for Ashfield Secondary School in East Belfast when Bob Bishop, United's legendary scout, spotted him. In fact, it was Bishop who bought the young Belfast kid his first modern pair of football boots, the ones without the toecaps in them.

Sammy fondly remembers Bishop: 'Not long after George burst on to the English football scene, the word spread around my school and area that Bob Bishop, the legendary Manchester United scout who spotted George and recommended him to Matt Busby, was on the lookout for the next George Best. I first met Bob when I was nine and we got on really well together. Bob was a really lovely man and very generous, almost like a grandfather figure to us. Obviously, I was still at Mersey Street Primary School at the time and far too young to become a footballer, so Bob told my parents that he would keep an eye on me and that if I developed then there was the possibility that I could follow George across the Irish Sea to get a trial with Manchester United. And Bob was true to his word, despite the fact that he had literally hundreds of young hopeful footballers to keep track of.'

Bishop knew the 14-year-old McIlroy was a prodigious young talent after he became a regular attendee at Bishop's weekend football camps at his cottage in Helen's Bay, County Down. Eventually he was sent over to Manchester, as he recalls: 'During the Easter holidays in 1969 I travelled to Manchester for a trial. I must have done all right because I was invited back over to Old Trafford in July 1969 and a few weeks later on 2 August, the day of my fifteenth birthday, I got the birthday present every boy dreamed of: an amateur contract with Manchester United. Matt Busby sent Joe Armstrong over to Belfast to sign me and I was the happiest kid in the world.'

He signed professional forms with the Reds on his 17th birthday. Eventually, O'Farrell handed the youngster his full debut after Denis Law picked up an injury. But the game on 6 November 1971 was no ordinary debut; such was the confidence the manager had in McIlroy that he had no hesitation in throwing him into the white-hot atmosphere of a Manchester Derby at Maine Road. He revelled in the Derby atmosphere, playing alongside Best and Tony Dunne. The match was a thriller and ended 3–3, with McIlroy scoring United's opening goal (in a move started by Best) and setting up the other two for Alan Gowling and Brian Kidd. Unsurprisingly, the United fans took an instant shine to the young Irishman, who would go on to play for the Reds for another decade.

McIlroy remembers that special day: 'That Saturday, I did what I always did when Manchester United had a home game and took the bus to Old Trafford. I had my boots with me, as I always carried them around everywhere I went, and I was looking forward to enjoying the Manchester Derby because we were away at neighbours City. Strangely, one man on the bus recognised me and when I was just about to get off at the ground he looked at me and said: "All the best today, kid." I had no idea why he took the time to speak to me until I walked into Old Trafford around 11.00am and was told that Frank O'Farrell, the United manager, wanted to see me. As I walked to his office, I was wracking my brain thinking what I could have done, but before I could find an answer the manager told me that Denis Law had failed a fitness test and he was giving me my debut.

'I think I must have been as close to fainting as someone could be without collapsing. I thanked Mr O'Farrell and walked towards the changing-room areas with butterflies doing Riverdance in my stomach. For a brief moment I thought I must be dreaming, but no it was true because the team sheet was up on the wall outside the changing-rooms and there was my name, No. 10 McIlroy, sandwiched between Charlton No. 9 and Best No. 11. Now I was dreaming! The game went by in an instant and ended 3–3 and I scored one of our goals. Could things get any better I thought to myself?'

William Morrow from Belfast was one of the United fans who saw that debut: 'I remember Sammy – all skin and bones, teeth and hair – making his debut in the early seventies and scoring in a Manchester Derby. I was early in my teens and I think the game finished 3–3. He was the new Belfast Boy after Best, and he was a good servant to United, but was not playing in one of our greatest eras.'

However, McIlroy almost never made it as a United player. When he first arrived in Manchester he was deeply homesick, and in his autobiography, *Manchester United My Team*, he reveals that he went home to Belfast at every opportunity and would have gladly settled for a career in Irish football. He missed his family and his friends, but thankfully he persevered. A week after the Derby draw, he scored on his home debut in United's 3–1 win over Tottenham Hotspur, with Law grabbing the other two goals. The *Manchester Evening News* headline read: 'Sorcerer Law and his Apprentice bewitch Spurs'.

McIlroy remembers how tough those early days were: 'I found the start of a new life in Manchester was not all it was cracked up to be. I mean I was a 15-year-old kid from Belfast and several hundred miles away from my family and friends. I could not help but wonder how George coped with this transformation in his life, and he helped me get over my homesickness. The first three months were the worst and I ended up in three different lodging houses. I just could not settle in a leafy suburb of Manchester and missed the noisy bustling streets of East Belfast. Our family home was located off the Newtownards Road and thousands of men had to walk up and down my street every day on their way to work in the famous Harland & Wolff shipyard. And of course Saturdays were particularly busy when Glentoran had a home game. But, in the end, I settled in Manchester thanks to two wonderful ladies, Mrs Thomas and Mrs Barrett.

'The good thing about playing for United was that they often played friendlies back home and it was lovely to return and play before your own people. I can recall playing for United in a friendly in Ireland some ten months before I made my competitive debut for the club. On 21 January 1971, we travelled to Dublin and played Bohemians in a friendly at Dalymount Park. I was just 16 and named as one of the substitutes and I remember sitting in the dugout and looking around the ground and thinking this is just like a home game. There were 30,000 people inside the ground that day and everywhere I looked I could see red and white scarves and fans wearing Manchester United rosettes. Brian Kidd had put us 1–0 up and I was sent on to replace John Aston and scored our second goal in a 2–0 win. Not a bad start to my United career I thought.'

Within three months of his United debut, his country called upon his services and awarded him his first full international cap against Spain on 16 February 1972 at Boothferry Park, Hull.

Looking back, McIlroy says: 'It was a home game for us, but UEFA moved the game away from Belfast because of the Troubles back home. I managed to get my mum and dad to the game, but it was a long haul for them because let's not forget that the motorway system in England was not as developed back then as it is today. We drew 1–1 with Spain and I can remember someone pointing out to me that at the time I became the third youngest player to represent Northern Ireland. I was 17 years and 198 days old and I must admit that was a proud night for me. Indeed, I am extremely proud to say that I played 88 times for my country.'

He played a total of 21 games in season 1971–72, ten of them as a substitute, and scored four goals in his 16 First Division outings. In season 1972–73, McIlroy had made just ten First Division appearances for United before O'Farrell, and his coach Malcolm Musgrove, were sacked in December 1972. In came Tommy Docherty to take charge of a relegation-threatened United team. McIlroy had not played since United's 2–0 win over Liverpool at Old Trafford on 11 November, but was hopeful that he would feature in Docherty's plans. However, a car accident in January 1973 ruled him out of action for the rest of the season.

Meanwhile, Docherty quickly brought in several new players as he sought to find the right mixture to turn around the team's fortunes: George Graham, Alex Forsyth, Jim Holton, Mick Martin and Lou Macari were all signed in his first month in charge. Docherty's new signings, mainly Scots like himself, helped United to avoid relegation by finishing in 18th place in Division One. Where once Irish voices were the most common ones to be heard in the United dressing room, now it was Scottish accents: on 20 January 1973, Docherty fielded eight Scottish players. With new players coming in, it was the end of the road for many others that season: Bobby Charlton, Tony Dunne and Denis Law all made their farewell appearances for United, while George Best would play just 12 times more. Between them they had played more than 2100 times for United and scored more than 650 goals.

The one exception to Docherty's list of Scottish recruits was Mick Martin. Michael Paul 'Mick' Martin was born on 9 July 1951 in Dublin. His father, Con, played for Drumcondra, Glentoran, Leeds United and Aston Villa, and won 30 caps for the Republic of Ireland, mostly at centre-half, though astonishingly his first two came as a goalkeeper. Martin began his football career with his local side, Home Farm, and in 1968 he signed for another Dublin-based club, Bohemians. Like his dad, Martin was also quite versatile, although his strengths lay in defensive roles and in midfield. On 10 October 1971, the new Republic of Ireland manager, Liam Tuohy, awarded him his first cap for his country, against Austria in Linz in a European Championship qualifier that they lost 6–0.

Soon after Tommy Docherty took over as United manager, he travelled to Dublin to see Martin in action on the advice of scout Billy Behan. The Scot liked what he saw and immediately persuaded the 21-year-old Dubliner to cross the Irish Sea and join his new United revolution. United paid the Gypsies £25,000 for Martin, which was a record transfer fee for a League of Ireland club at the time.

Within a few days, Martin made his United debut (on 24 January 1973 in a 0–0 draw with Everton at Old Trafford) and played 16 league games that season, scoring two goals, the first of which was United's winning goal in a 2–1 victory over Newcastle United at Old Trafford on St Patrick's Day. The following season he managed just 18 games as United were relegated to Division Two. A fall-out with Docherty in September 1973 didn't help his chances. United's stint in Division Two lasted only a single season, as Docherty's young and exciting team stormed back to the top flight, but Martin made only nine appearances in the 1974–75 season.

With first-team football eluding him, in October 1975, Martin went out on loan to Second Division West Bromwich Albion, which soon resulted in a permanent move there for a £25,000 fee, the same amount United had paid for him. In December 1978, he left the Baggies, now managed by Ron Atkinson, after playing 89 league games and scoring 11 goals. He joined Newcastle United in a £100,000 transfer and stayed there until May 1983. He then crossed the Atlantic to play for Vancouver Whitecaps, before returning to the UK to play for Cardiff City, Peterborough United, Rotherham United and Preston North End. He retired at the end of the 1985–86 season, and then went into coaching and scouting with various clubs.

Martin won 52 caps for the Republic of Ireland (14 of them as a United player) and scored four goals. On 27 April 1983, he played in his last international for the Irish, a 2–0 loss to Spain in Zaragoza in a 1984 European Championship qualifier.

While Anderson and Martin were coming and going, McIlroy was settling in at Old Trafford. After making a full recovery from his injuries in the car crash, he established himself in the United midfield in season 1973–74, playing 29 league games and top-scoring with six league goals. But, as we have seen, United slipped into Division Two at the end of the season having finished 21st.

With so many experienced players gone, just as Alex Ferguson did in the mid-1990s, Docherty placed his faith in United's younger players. This would be the way he would get the team back into the top tier of English football. Docherty's trust in the abilities of his youthful side reaped the dividends he had hoped for and United won the 1974–75 Second Division title. McIlroy came on as a substitute in the opening fixture of the season, a 2–0 win away to Leyton Orient, but started every other game that season, scoring ten goals in all competitions. The race for the 1974–75 Division Two crown proved to be a three-way battle, but United's all-out attacking style won through in the end, with Aston Villa runners-up three points behind and Norwich City finishing in third spot. (Coincidentally, 18 years later, United won the inaugural Premier League title in 1992–93, with Villa runners-up and Norwich third.)

Docherty's United, captained by the immaculate Martin

Buchan, were a breath of fresh air to the First Division in season 1975–76 and finished third in the table in their first season back among the big boys. Surprisingly, though, they lost the 1976 FA Cup final 1–0 to Southampton, an unfashionable Second Division outfit who had never won a trophy before in their history. McIlroy played in that game alongside the Republic of Ireland's Gerry Daly, while another Belfast-born player, David McCreery, came on for Gordon Hill as a substitute.

One Irishman who did not make the final line-up was Thomas 'Tommy' Jackson, who was born in Belfast on 3 November 1946. A talented midfielder, he began his professional career with Glentoran in 1963, and after they won the title in 1966–67 he found himself up against Benfica in the European Cup at The Oval, Belfast, on 20 September 1967. He had a superb game and man-marked Eusébio out of the game in a 1–1 draw, impressing numerous scouts from English clubs who were there.

In February 1968, Glentoran found it impossible to hold on to their prized asset any longer and he joined Everton for a £10,000 transfer fee, helping them to the FA Cup final, even though he didn't play in the final itself. With competition fierce for places in the Toffees' midfield, up against Alan Ball, Colin Harvey and Howard Kendall, he managed just 15 league appearances in their 1969–70 title-winning season. In October 1970, he moved to Nottingham Forest, but they were relegated to the Second Division at the end of 1971–72.

The arrival of Brian Clough as the new Nottingham Forest manager on 6 January 1975 effectively signalled the end of his career at the City Ground, as he fell down Clough's pecking order of midfielders. In July 1975, he was told by Clough that he was free to leave the club if another team wanted to sign him, and in stepped Tommy Docherty, who brought Jackson to Old Trafford.

Initially, Docherty wanted the Irishman to captain United's Central League side and pass on his experience to United's new band of up-and-coming players. But after a string of impressive displays in pre-season friendlies, Docherty changed his mind and handed him his United debut on the opening day of the 1975–76 season, when United beat Wolves 2–0 on 16 August. He then played in United's next six league games before losing his place in the side to a fellow Belfast man, David McCreery. Although he did win his place back in Docherty's starting line-up and played 20 games that season as a holding midfielder, he always struggled to secure a regular position in the United team.

The following season saw him in the United Reserve team, making just three first team appearances, before he decided it was time to leave Old Trafford. In June 1978, he signed for Waterford as their player-manager in the League of Ireland, despite advances from some English clubs, most notably Fulham, to become their manager.

He led Waterford to successive FAI Cup finals in 1979 and 1980, winning the latter – their first success in the competition since 1936–37. He subsequently took charge of Crusaders in Belfast and then Glentoran, where he had a hugely successful spell in charge, before having a brief time at Ballymena United to October 1994. On 11 August 1990, he was the obvious choice to manage the Irish League team in a match celebrating their 100th anniversary. And the opposition were none other than Manchester United, with the visitors ruining the centenary celebrations by winning 3–1 with goals from Brian McClair, Mark Hughes and Danny Wallace. The Republic of Ireland's Denis Irwin and Northern Ireland's Mal Donaghy played for United. It was a unique double for Jackson, coming a decade after he managed the League of Ireland.

Jackson won the first of his 35 caps for Northern Ireland in a 3–2 win against Israel in Jaffa on 10 September 1968. His international career spanned nine years (1968–77), with the highlight unquestionably being a 1–0 win over England at Wembley on 23 May 1972 in a European Championship qualifier.

During this period, the Troubles continued in Northern Ireland, but players such as Jackson and McIlroy helped draw people together in some ways. A former soldier, 'Big Mike', who grew up in Manchester as a Reds fan, but served in the province during the early 1970s shows how this could happen in the unlikeliest of places: 'I can remember working in Long Kesh Prison at The Maze, Lisburn, in 1974. I was a tower guard overlooking what was the hospital building and at one stage this arm popped out of the window clad in red. Then it all started, with the prisoners bating the squaddies and us responding in kind. I asked this particular guy with the red sleeve what he was in for and I got the usual reply. He then asked me if I liked football and what team I supported. "I support Manchester United," I said. That was it, as we got chatting about United and I told him that I saw the great George Best play football and about the time when my dad came home from work with tears in his eyes after the Munich Air Disaster. He told me he was hoping to go to Old Trafford one day to see United play.

'The two of us talked a lot about football, but mostly we simply exchanged stories about Manchester United. Over the three days I was posted to that tower, I spoke to him quite a lot. We always talked like friends. I never did see his face, but I like to think that in the midst of all that hatred, we forgot what was going on all around us for a few hours and Manchester United was the only thing that was important.

'I often think now what ever happened to him. But two words, "Manchester United", brought two men of roughly the same age together to talk rather than fight and abuse each other. I hope that he is in full and good health and that his family is well, and perhaps if we ever met in the future we could have a drink, forget the past and watch United play. I might even pay for his match ticket! Because once a red always a red.'

Even though this wasn't the most successful period in United's history, the club still managed to attract new fans, either individually or through new supporters' clubs. Jim Wallace is the president of the City of Derry Manchester United Supporters' Club and he told me how his club started: 'All my life I have supported United – Harry Gregg was my first hero – but when I grew up and got married my dream of going to Old Trafford had to be delayed, as my family came first. Then, in 1975, I went into a barber's shop where the walls were covered in Manchester United and Glasgow Celtic posters. The owner was Jim Bradley and we discussed starting a supporters' club in Derry. We got the go-ahead from Old Trafford and a few days later we set up the City of Derry Manchester United Supporters' Club.

'As I remember, our first trip to Old Trafford was to see West Ham United and we travelled on the Belfast to Liverpool overnight ferry. We left on the Friday night and made the ten-hour return ferry crossing on the Saturday night, arriving home absolutely exhausted. To make matters worse, we lost. The next branch trip was for a game against Arsenal, and once again we were beaten, so it was not the best of starts for the branch. I don't think too many supporters would like to travel that way now, with so many flights available from Belfast to Manchester and Liverpool.

'At our first members' dinner dance, Lou Macari was our guest speaker. The next morning when I returned to his hotel to take Lou back to the airport, the Scottish chef asked me if the man at the table in front of us was Lou Macari. When I confirmed it was, he beamed with delight, and he then said: "I cooked his breakfast."

'On another occasion, we arranged for Paddy Crerand to do a coaching session with children from some local schools so the council would help sponsor some of the costs of the function. However, as soon as he set foot on to the pitch, the heavens opened. But Paddy, being the utmost professional, carried on and did the full session as the rest of us sat in the comfort of cars watching him and the kids get a good soaking. What can I say about the man other than you will struggle to find a better person to be in the company of, a true football legend and one of the most down-to-earth people you could possibly meet.'

The club also continued to build its fanbase in Ireland by making regular trips to play friendlies. In the long, hot summer of 1976, United rounded off their pre-season friendlies in

Dublin on 11 August. A good crowd of 15,000 turned out at Lansdowne Road to watch Home Farm, bolstered by some guest players, take on the FA Cup runners-up. The admission price was £2.50. United opened the scoring in the 11th minute when two Irishmen, Daly and McCreery, combined neatly to set up Gordon Hill. Seven minutes later Lou Macari made it 2–0, and the game was all over for the home side just five minutes into the second half when a McIlroy corner found Steve Coppell unmarked in the area and he wasted no time in firing the ball into the net.

Belfast-born Jim Hetherington recalls the very day his own love affair with United started, when he was just nine years old, and the horrific background to it. 'My brother Vincent was watching the final when I walked into our house in Andersonstown in West Belfast. "Who do you want to win?" I asked him. "Shush," he said, glued to the TV. "But who do you want to win?" I called out. Vincent turned around and stared at me and said, "Man United, now shush." To be honest, I hadn't a clue about football at the time and so I asked him: "Which ones are Man United?" United were trailing 1–0 and he shouted out to me: "The Red Devils."

'When the final whistle went, my brother put an arm round my neck. I don't know what made me say it, but I said: "They're not very good are they?" He just looked right at me and said: "You just watch, kid. We will win it next year." And of course we did. But our Vincent did not see it, because he was murdered in the Troubles on 6 July 1976. Ever since that losing FA Cup final in 1976, the passion for Manchester United has stayed with me and now my own kids are also United mad. When I go over to see United now, those I go with represent both sides of the religious divide here in Northern Ireland. When we travel from Carryduff to Manchester our only religion is the "Church of United".'

Sadly for many fans, there were to be more changes among the Irish contingent at United, and for one significant star of the 1976 FA Cup side, there would be no happy return the following season. Gerry Daly had seemed destined for a longer Old Trafford career, but he made just one substitute appearance in the third round in United's FA Cup run of 1977.

Gerard Anthony 'Gerry' Daly was born on 30 April 1954 in Cabra, Dublin and began his playing career with that great schoolboy academy of football, Stella Maris. He then moved to Bohemians where, despite his small physique (he was 5ft 9in tall and weighed under 10st), he was a dynamic midfielder who could ride a challenge and still retain the coolness to thread a ball through a defence to a colleague. In March 1973, he moved to Old Trafford and signed for Docherty's struggling United side in a transfer deal worth £20,000, though he did not make his debut that season. That summer, however, he made his international debut for the Republic of Ireland in a 1–1 draw against Norway in Oslo on 6 June 1973 in a friendly.

Daly made his United debut on 25 August 1973 in a 3–0 defeat away to Arsenal in Division One. He wore the No. 4 shirt in the game and was substituted for the more experienced McIlroy, but the result was a sign of what was to come that season. For some, Daly was still too lightweight to cope with the demands and the rigours of First Division football and so his appearances were somewhat intermittent that campaign, and it was only towards the end of the season, as relegation loomed, that he became a more regular starter, eventually making 17 appearances, and scoring just one goal.

With United now in the Second Division for 1974–75, Daly was almost an ever-present in the team and he scored five goals in the first four matches of the season, including a hat-trick against Millwall on 24 August 1974. Already, United were top of Division Two with a 100 per cent record and the side were playing a swashbuckling style of football, seemingly freed from the tensions of recent campaigns. Daly made 46 appearances that season and scored 13 goals as he helped the Reds go straight back to the First Division.

On their return to the top flight, United and Daly continued their good form. He missed just one game all season, making 51 appearances and scoring 11 goals. Four of his goals in 1975–76 came in the FA Cup, as United made it to the final for the first time since Daly's fellow countryman, Noel Cantwell, captained the team to FA Cup glory in 1963. He scored United's winning goals in the third and fifth rounds of the FA Cup. Docherty's young attack-minded side were red-hot favourites to win the FA Cup, but as we have seen they succumbed to Lawrie McMenemy's Southampton by 1–0.

Daly began the 1976–77 season as he finished the last – in the first team and scoring the occasional goal, and didn't miss a game until early December. However, the arrival of Jimmy Greenhoff in November meant that McIlroy was moved back to more of a mid-field role, and this cost Daly his regular place. Soon after, in March 1977, Docherty sold him to Derby County for £175,000, making him the most expensive Irish player at the time. His last match for United was a 3–1 league win over Derby County on 5 February 1977 at Old Trafford. A popular figure with the fans, who had developed a good understanding with winger Gordon Hill, Daly was also a superb penalty taker, scoring 16 times from the spot out of 17 during his time at Old Trafford. Coincidentally, within a few months, Docherty took charge of Derby, after he left United.

In the summer of 1978, Daly went out on loan to the New England Tea Men of the North American Soccer League (NASL). He stayed in Boston for two years before Derby County sold him to Coventry City in 1980 for £310,000. He spent four years with Coventry City (including a loan spell to Leicester City in 1983), before being sold to Birmingham City, then Shrewsbury Town, Stoke City, Doncaster Rovers and finally Telford United where he was player/assistant manager. In a career spanning eight different English league clubs, Daly played 472 games and scored 88 goals.

Daly went on to win a total of 48 caps for his country and scored 13 international goals. His last match for Ireland was against Uruguay on 23 April 1986 at Lansdowne Road in a friendly international. He marked the occasion by scoring a penalty in a 1–1 draw with the South Americans.

However, for United fans, the loss of Daly was compensated for by the success of new recruit Jimmy Greenhoff and the new facets to his game that came to McIlroy when he moved into midfield. United's start to the season meant they were never going to challenge for the title, eventually finishing in sixth place, but they did have a chance to fulfil Docherty's promise after the Wembley defeat in 1976 to return the following year. McIlroy played in every round on the road to Wembley, where United were faced by the daunting challenge of taking on Liverpool in the final. The Merseysiders had already retained their league title, and would go on to win the European Cup for the first time a few days later. This was United's chance not only to win some silverware, but also to prevent the Anfield outfit from having any chance of completing a Treble.

Tim Robson grew up in Rathcoole on the outskirts of Belfast and was a huge admirer of McIlroy: 'I saw Sammy play on my first visit to Old Trafford in November 1976. It was a school trip organised by our PE teacher at Rathcoole Secondary School. United's Jimmy Nicholl was a former pupil there and he kindly got us tickets for the game. After sailing on the Belfast to Liverpool boat, we arrived at the ground to meet Jimmy's parents who informed us that Jimmy had been dropped and replaced by Alex Forsyth. As we entered the ground at the old Scoreboard End, one of the older boys in the group stopped me as I was about to climb the steps and told me to take it all in and that I would remember this moment all my life. I am glad he did because he was right.'

In the 1977 FA Cup final, United lined up with McIlroy in midfield and fellow Belfast Boy Jimmy Nicholl in the starting XI. Right-back Nicholl had the inexperienced Arthur Albiston alongside him that day, as regular left-back Stewart Houston was injured. A third player from Northern Ireland, David McCreery, joined in the action, coming on as a substitute for Gordon Hill. United won the game 2–1, with all the goals scored in a swift flurry early in the second half. It was surely the first and only time that three players from Northern Ireland had played in an FA

Cup-winning side. It was also United's first major trophy in nine years and it seemed that the Docherty era was set for even greater things in the future, but a different sort of trouble came along, and within a few weeks the manager was sacked after the details of his affair with the wife of United's physiotherapist became public.

Chapter 9

On the Up

The sacking of Tommy Docherty in the summer of 1977 shocked many people, but the club moved swiftly to recruit his replacement, bringing in respected coach Dave Sexton, who, it was hoped, would ally his tactical acumen and know-how to the exhilarating skills of Docherty's side. On their day, the Reds could beat anyone, but they were occasionally prone to slip-ups and inconsistency. When he arrived at Old Trafford, Sexton had a considerable Irish contingent at his disposal. As well as first-team regulars Sammy McIlroy and Jimmy Nicholl, there was also David McCreery, Tommy Jackson, Paddy Roche and Chris McGrath, as well as Docherty's last signing, Ashley Grimes, who was yet to appear for the Reds.

The Irish element in United's squad would increase even further under Sexton, and by 1978–79 there were nine Irish-born players at Old Trafford. When combined with the increasing amount of English football shown on television in Ireland, no wonder the late 1970s witnessed a marked increase in the number of Irish people crossing the water to make the journey to Old Trafford. It was also a period when a large number of Manchester United Supporters' Clubs emerged in Ireland. From a personal perspective, it was a strange and worrying time in Belfast, and Ireland as a whole, so my love for United provided something of an escape route from the day-to-day problems surrounding me, and this seems to have been true for many others. And in the summer of 1978 a former United legend, Harry Gregg, was invited by manger Dave Sexton to become the new goalkeeping coach at United, but the big Irishman was released three years later when Ron Atkinson became manager.

Under Sexton, McIlroy and Nicholl continued to be among the first names on the teamsheet each week, with McIlroy missing just four games out of the 52 played by United in 1977–78. But while they were consistent performers, the team was less so, slipping back to tenth place in the league and not having a decent cup run in any of the knockout competitions, which included four games in the European Cup-Winners' Cup.

For Nicholl, whose second season this was as United's first-choice right-back, it was the latest episode in a long journey for him. He had been born James Michael 'Jimmy' Nicholl in Hamilton, Ontario, Canada, on 28 February 1956 to Irish parents, but moved to Belfast with his family when he was very young. The teenage Nicholl was playing for the Belfast Central School sides when United came for him. In November 1971, he signed for the club as an amateur, progressing to apprentice terms in October 1972 and then signed professional forms in March 1974. He was rewarded with his first team debut on 5 April 1975 when he came on as a substitute for United's captain Martin Buchan in a 1–0 win over Southampton at the Dell in the Second Division.

Back in the First Division for the 1975–76 season, Nicholl and Alex Forsyth battled each other to hold down the No. 2 shirt, with the Irishman playing in 20 league games for United, but he was disappointed not to make Docherty's squad of 12 for the 1976 FA Cup final. During 1976–77, Nicholl became Docherty's first choice at right-back as he was considered to be much quicker and more agile than Forsyth. He did not disappoint his manager's faith in him and played in 39 of United's league games as well as appearing in every game in the Reds' FA Cup run, including that victorious final over Liverpool.

Nicholl was unflappable on the ball and delivered a consistently high standard of performances. In 1977–78, he played 37 times for United in Division One and scored his first goal for the club in a 3–1 away loss to Manchester City on 10 September – and what a strike it was. He hit a 35-yard screamer past Joe Corrigan on a rain-soaked pitch but, because of the scoreline, barely celebrated. The first player to congratulate him was fellow Northern Ireland international David McCreery. It was a toss-up which of the Belfast boys had the longer sideburns at the time, although Nicholl's definitely stood out more with his ginger hair. Coincidentally, both McIlroy and McCreery had also scored their first United goals against City. Nicholl then missed much of the following campaign due to injury, but recovered in time to take his position for the 1979 FA Cup final against Arsenal.

While Nicholl was a regular starter, his fellow Belfast man McCreery must have hoped for a change in fortune when Sexton arrived, as he had begun to develop a reputation as United's 'super-sub'. He had been born on 16 September 1957 in the heartland of Protestant East Belfast. Like so many United stars, he had been discovered by Bob Bishop while playing for the Northern Ireland Schoolboys team. He then joined Frank O'Farrell's struggling Reds as an amateur on his 15th birthday, signing professional terms two years later. Only a few weeks later, he made his debut on 15 October 1974, coming on as a substitute for Willie Morgan in a 0–0 draw with Portsmouth at Fratton Park. He had already gained a reputation for himself as a versatile player in United's junior teams, and in the following game came on as a replacement for Gerry Daly. These two substitute appearances were the only outings McCreery got that season, but they had set a pattern for his career.

In the 1975–76 season, McCreery's flexibility meant that he lined up in five different positions during his 13 starts (wearing the No. 4, 7, 8, 9 and 10 shirts), while he also made 19 substitute appearances in all competitions, including the FA Cup final when he fulfilled his dream of playing at Wembley and came on for Gordon Hill in the 66th minute. Although still only 18 years old, Docherty knew that he had a player who would play anywhere he was asked to and give 100 per cent on every occasion.

The following season, McCreery played in 25 league games for United, 16 of them as substitute, but the focus was on the FA Cup, a challenge set by Docherty after the defeat to Southampton in the previous final. He came off the bench in the fifth round, the quarter-final and, almost inevitably, in the final against Liverpool. Once again he replaced Hill, this time coming on with just nine minutes remaining, so as to help preserve United's 2–1 lead.

Under the new manager, McCreery got his wish no longer to be the first-choice substitute, but unfortunately this did not translate into many more starting appearances. His energy and enthusiasm in training earned him the nickname of 'Roadrunner', and every time he pulled on a United jersey he ran his socks off for the team. If he wasn't hassling defenders in their own penalty area, then he would be scurrying around midfield with biting tackles or he would track back to help out the United defence. The fans loved his commitment and the fact that he never publicly complained about being on the bench. But when the same pattern repeated itself during 1978–79, when he made just 16 appearances in total, he decided that at nearly 22 years old, it was time for a move.

In August 1979, after making 110 appearances for United (53 as substitute) and scoring eight goals (three of them from the bench), he teamed up with his former manager, Tommy Docherty, at Queens Park Rangers, who signed him for £200,000. After spending almost two years at QPR, McCreery made his way across the Atlantic to join the Tulsa Roughnecks in the NASL in March 1981. Having enjoyed 19 months in Oklahoma, he returned to the UK to join Newcastle United in October 1982 in a £75,000 transfer deal, and remained there for seven years. He helped the Magpies win promotion to the First Division at the end of the 1983–84 season, playing alongside former United star Peter Beardsley as well as Kevin Keegan, Terry McDermott and Chris Waddle.

After Newcastle United were relegated back to Division Two at the end of the 1988–89 season, McCreery was given a free transfer and played briefly in Sweden before signing for Heart of Midlothian in September 1989, where he was soon managed by former United team-mate Joe Jordan. His two years at Tynecastle were followed by a stint at Hartlepool United (in 1991–92), before he moved to Carlisle United as their player-coach in October 1992. He stayed with Carlisle United for two years and then returned to Hartlepool to spend one season as their player-manager before deciding to retire. However, he was not quite finished with the game just yet, and returned to the USA to help with the setting-up of Major League Soccer (MLS) and subsequently took up an offer to become a scout for Barnet, which was followed by a period as a football consultant for Blyth Spartans. In February 2011, he was appointed technical director at Magway in Burma.

McCreery had a long and successful international career, making his debut for Northern Ireland on 8 May 1976 in the Home International against Scotland. Almost inevitably, he came on as a substitute at Windsor Park, but could do nothing to prevent a 3–0 loss to the Scots. He went on to make 67 appearances (22 as a United player) for his country, but never scored. He was part of the squad that appeared in both the 1982 and 1986 World Cup finals, and played in every match in both tournaments. The highlight was when he helped Northern Ireland beat the host nation, Spain, 1–0 in the 1982 finals. He won his last cap as a substitute on 18 May 1990 in a 1–0 friendly win against Uruguay at Windsor Park.

If the arrival of Sexton did not bring about a transformation in his fortunes for McCreery, it did at least open the door for another of United's Irish contingent, goalkeeper Paddy Roche, who had long been in the shadow of Alex Stepney, the last member of the European Cup-winning side of 1968 still to be playing for United.

Patrick 'Paddy' Roche was born on 4 January 1951 in Dublin and began his playing career with his local club, Shelbourne. Paddy played 100 times for Shelbourne in the League of Ireland and even managed to score a goal for them. At the start of the 1973–74 season, Docherty was on the lookout for a new goalkeeper as cover for Stepney, so in October 1973, he signed Roche in a £15,000 transfer deal. Roche knew he would have to bide his time, as Stepney was one of the best and most consistent keepers in the business, who rarely missed a game.

Because of this, Roche's first four appearances for United were all in friendlies; the first came just a few days after he joined United when he came on as a substitute for Stepney against Shamrock Rovers on 15 October 1973. United won 2–1 at Dalymount Park in front of 20,000 fans. However, on 8 February 1975, Docherty finally gave Roche his debut in the first team in a league game away to Oxford United, and United lost 1–0. He retained the No. 1 shirt for the following Saturday's 2–0 home win over Hull City, but that was his lot for the rest of the season.

In 1975–76 he was given a run of five consecutive matches in November. Although he kept clean sheets in two of the games, he conceded ten goals in the other three and was widely criticised in the media for his 'nervy' performance against Liverpool. He played only twice in 1976–77, conceding seven goals. So after three and a half seasons at United, he had still made just nine appearances for the Reds.

However, after six losses in the opening 13 league games of the 1977–78 season, new manager Sexton dropped Stepney and gave Roche the No. 1 jersey, and he had a run of 18 consecutive First Division starts. Sadly for him, results did not improve as the Reds won six and lost seven during that period, so Stepney was reinstated for the rest of the campaign. Then, in January 1978, Sexton signed 19-year-old goalkeeper Gary Bailey from South Africa, which had veteran Stepney and Roche looking over their shoulders at the tall, blond-haired new arrival.

After making a total of 23 appearances the previous season, Roche started the 1978–79 campaign as United's keeper for the first 14 league games. But in the last of them he conceded five goals against Birmingham City, who would later be relegated, and it was clear that changes were needed. Sexton made a £440,000 bid for Coventry City's Scottish international goalkeeper Jim Blyth, but he failed a medical, so on 18 November, Bailey was given his United debut and played well in a 2–0 home win over Ipswich Town. That was effectively the end of Roche's United career and over the course of the next three seasons he played only a further five times for the Reds, making his 53rd and final appearance for United on 5 December 1981 at Southampton in a 3–2 defeat.

In August 1982, he moved to Brentford and played 71 times for them, before joining Halifax Town in July 1984. He spent five seasons there and was a hugely popular player with the fans. After playing 184 times for Halifax Town, he moved on to Chester City, where he spent just over a year, before ending his career at Northwich Victoria.

Roche won eight caps for the Republic of Ireland and was awarded his first cap while he was with Shelbourne. It wasn't a great start to an international career as the Irish were hammered 6–0 in Vienna by Austria on 10 October 1971 in a European Championship qualifier. A future United team-mate, Mick Martin, also made his international bow that day. However, his international fortunes took a turn for the better in his next outing when he was part of the team that famously trounced the USSR 3–0 at Dalymount Park on 30 October 1974.

The other Irishman that Sexton inherited when he took over at United was Chris McGrath. He had been born on 29 November 1954 in Belfast and, after starring for the Belfast and the Northern Ireland Schoolboys side, he was signed by Tottenham Hotspur as an apprentice in July 1970. On 13 October 1973, he made his

Spurs debut in the North London Derby, a tough baptism. But he did well on the wing and helped his team to a 2–0 win over Arsenal. He played regularly that season and appeared in both legs of the 1973–74 UEFA Cup final for Spurs, collecting a runners-up medal after Feyenoord won 4–2 on aggregate.

At the end of that season, McGrath was called-up by manager Terry Neill into the Northern Ireland side for the Home Internationals. He made his debut on 11 May 1974 against Scotland at Windsor Park, helping the Irish to a 1–0 win. His teasing runs caused the Scottish defence many problems, and the future seemed bright after he won two more caps that summer, especially when Neill took over as manager of Spurs for the new campaign.

Sadly, his form dipped in season 1974–75 and he played in only nine league games for Tottenham, though he did win his fourth Irish cap early on. The momentum of his career seemed to quickly fade away and he managed just four league games in 1975–76 before Neill allowed him to go out on loan to Millwall in February 1976. He did well at the club, who were keen to retain his services, but McGrath wanted to play First Division football, so returned to Spurs, but still could not find his way into the side.

Then, in October 1976, Tommy Docherty signed him for £30,000. He made his United debut soon after, on 23 October, in a 2–2 draw with Norwich City at Old Trafford, coming on as a substitute for McIlroy. He made a total of seven appearances for United that season, all but two coming from the bench. In truth, with Steve Coppell and Gordon Hill practically ever-presents on the wings, he was always going to struggle to get a regular game. However, under Sexton, McGrath made 18 league appearances in 1977–78 (nine as a substitute) and scored his only goal for United in a 2–1 loss away to West Ham United on 10 December. Sexton preferred to use him as an impact substitute, who could run at tired defenders late in the game. As such, he took over from McCreery as the most frequently used substitute in the United squad.

But over the next two seasons he played only three times for United, though he was not helped by the fact that he broke his leg in a Central League game in 1979–80. He played his last game for United on 23 August 1980, a 0–0 league draw at Birmingham City. When his Old Trafford contract was cancelled in February 1981, he signed for Tulsa Roughnecks in the NASL, where he teamed up with McCreery. After spending two seasons in the USA, he ended his playing career at South China in Hong Kong.

Although his club progress had faltered, his international career continued and he won a total of 21 caps, scoring four goals for his country. His first international goal came against the Netherlands in a World Cup qualifier on 13 October 1976, a match that saw the return of George Best after an absence of three years. He made his final international appearance on 19 May 1979, losing 2–0 to England.

Sexton had spent heavily in his first season, bringing in Joe Jordan and Gordon McQueen from Leeds United, while in 1978–79 his most expensive new recruit was winger Mickey Thomas, though Gary Bailey was also a significant new face in the side. Sadly for Sexton, the changes to the line-up resulted in only a small improvement in United's final league position, as they ended up in ninth place. But at least there was the compensation of another good run in the FA Cup that took United back to Wembley for the third time in four years. To get there, United had to go through three replays and overcame the runaway league leaders Liverpool in the semi-final.

Arsenal were United's opponents in the final, and as they had finished just two places above United in the league, it was very hard to call who would win, though the Gunners were seeking revenge for losing the previous year's final to Ipswich Town. Just two of United's nine Irishmen lined up that day – Nicholl and McIlroy – but the final seemed to be one of the more dull affairs. With only five minutes of the game remaining, United trailed 2–0 and hadn't looked like staging a fightback. Then they were offered a glimmer of hope when Gordon McQueen rampaged up the pitch from his centre-half position to pull a goal back. Three minutes later, amazingly United were level after McIlroy scored: he raced into the area, squeezed past one defender, then nutmegged another before sliding the ball past his Northern Ireland international colleague, Pat Jennings, for the equaliser. He became the first Irishman to score an FA Cup final goal for United, and seemed to have earned his side a replay. But no; Alan Sunderland almost immediately put the Gunners back into the lead to secure a 3–2 victory.

Frankie 'Dodger' Dodds from the Falls Road in Belfast remembers the game well: 'I first fell in love with United during the 1979 FA Cup final when they somehow came from two goals down in the last four minutes, only to throw it away in the last minute of the game. It helped that a fellow Irishman, Sammy McIlroy, had slalomed through the Arsenal defence to score a glorious equaliser, after what looked like a consolation goal from big Gordon McQueen. I was eight years old at the time and dreamed of being the next great Irishman to play for United. I still have the same slightly unrealistic dream and I am forty now!'

That 1978–79 season saw three more Irishmen make their United debuts: we will cover Kevin Moran's career in more detail in the next chapter, but he joined Tom Sloan and Tom Connell in putting on the famous red jersey for the first time during this campaign.

Thomas 'Tom' Sloan was the first of the three to appear for United. He was born on 10 July 1959 in Ballymena, County Antrim, and began his football career with his local side, Ballymena United, where the midfielder played alongside his elder brother John. He helped them to the Irish Cup final in 1977–78, where they lost to Linfield. That summer, a number of English clubs were anxious to secure his services, with United and Tottenham Hotspur heading the queue. And, as was the norm with most young Irish footballers offered the chance to join United, he opted for Old Trafford.

In August 1978, United paid the Irish League side £20,000 for

Sloan. A few weeks later, on 18 November, Sexton gave him his United debut, wearing the No. 10 shirt in place of Lou Macari. United beat Ipswich Town 2–0 in the league at Old Trafford that day. He went on to make three further first-team appearances in his first season at United, one as a substitute. At the end of the 1978–79 campaign, he was called into the Northern Ireland squad by manager Danny Blanchflower and won his first cap on 22 May 1979 in a 1–0 defeat to Scotland at Hampden Park. He then made two appearances as a substitute in the next two internationals, but by 6 June his Northern Ireland career was over.

Over the course of the next three seasons he found himself on the periphery of the first team and managed only eight appearances in 1979–80 and 1980–81. Not having featured at all in season 1981–82, Sloan was given a free transfer to Chester City in July 1982, where he played 44 league games. However, after just one season at the club, he moved back to Northern Ireland and signed for Linfield, and also recommenced his original trade as a plasterer. After a three-year term with Linfield, winning the Irish League title in 1983–84 and 1985–86, he was transferred to Coleraine. He spent three seasons there before finishing up where it had all started for him, Ballymena United. His second stint with the Sky Blues was from 1989–91 and after he decided to retire in 1991, he turned out regularly for Raglan Homers in the Ballymena Sunday Morning League.

If Sloan's career at United was brief, then unfortunately that of Thomas Connell was even briefer. He was born in Newry, County Down, on 25 November 1957 and began his football career at Newry Town, before moving on to Coleraine in the Irish League. He was confident in either full-back role or at centre-half and won a full international cap while he was on the books of Coleraine, making his one and only appearance for Northern Ireland as a substitute on 19 May 1978 against Wales in a 1–0 defeat at the Racecourse Ground, Wrexham.

In August 1978, Sexton paid £30,000 to bring the young Irishman to Manchester. After a number of excellent displays for

United's Central League side, Sexton handed the 21-year-old his United debut on 22 December 1978 at Bolton Wanderers when left-back Stewart Houston was injured. United lost the league encounter 3–0, but Connell retained his place in the United team for the visit of Liverpool four days later. Once again United lost 3–0. Although he remained at Old Trafford until the end of the 1981–82 season, he never saw first team action again. That summer Glentoran paid £37,000 to bring Connell to Belfast, and he later played for Portadown.

In the 1979–80 season, Sexton continued to remodel the United side, with Ray Wilkins joining the club from Chelsea for a record fee of £777,777. Mid-season Yugoslavian international Nikola Jovanović joined the club – the days of United looking throughout just the British Isles for the best players were coming to an end. Soon the club's scouts would be searching across the globe for the best talent. And that meant that the nine Irishmen used in 1978–79 set a club record that is unlikely ever to be matched again.

Sexton had a much more settled line-up this season, with several players lining up in every game of the campaign. Jimmy Nicholl was one of them, while Sammy McIlroy missed only one league game and a League Cup tie. The result was United's best finish in the league since 1967–68, as they ended up in second place, two points behind champions Liverpool.

Robert Dallas from Jordanstown, County Antrim, remembers this season as the time he became a Red: 'It was on 8 December 1979 when a friend of mine asked if I wanted to go to Old Trafford to see United play Leeds United. I took him up on his offer and was blown away by the whole thing: the massive 58,000 crowd, when most fans were standing, especially in the Stretford End. It was quite breathtaking, but devastating when Terry Connor scored for Leeds and Ashley Grimes missed a penalty. Thankfully, Mickey Thomas equalised and the day was saved. Through that whole experience there seemed to be an aura about George Best, even though he had left the club years ago. Hearing my accent, everyone I spoke to asked me if I lived near George Best or did I remember him playing in Belfast.'

Indeed, in the late 1970s it seemed an Irish accent acted almost like a passport in some parts of Old Trafford, as John Conran from Clonmel MUSC recalls: 'More than thirty years ago, I went to Old Trafford with my friend Sam Gill to see United play City. As we walked around the front of the ground, we noticed the BBC trucks and vans together. We then saw some crew members entering a lift for the executive suite, manned by a gentleman dressed like the head doorman at the Savoy. Sam said we should try to get up in the lift and see where it takes us. We put our United hats and scarves in our pockets and rang the bell. When the lift door opened, the operator looked at us and said: "BBC?" We answered "Yes" and up we went.

'We arrived in this suite and went straight to the bar. The barman was Irish and asked if we were from the press. I told him we were with the *Clonmel Express* [a small free paper from home]. We ordered two pints of Harp and wondered how much longer we were going to get away with this. Then, one of the two men sitting in the corner of the room drinking coffee called over to us and asked us if we were Irish and what part of Ireland we came from. It was Sir Matt Busby and Louis Edwards, and I thought, this is it, game up, call security.

'Believe it or not, they could not have been nicer. Mr Edwards took a special interest when he realised we came from Tipperary, and went on to describe the woodland from Tipperary Town to Clonmel and from Clonmel to Waterford. Sir Matt was a gentleman to speak to and we left after a short time, as they appeared to be having a private conversion. So that gamble paid off.'

For Grimes, penalty miss or not, the 1979–80 season was his busiest at United. Augustine Ashley Grimes was born in Dublin on 2 August 1957 and grew up a United fan. With his long curly ginger hair, he began his football career at Stella Maris, like so many other former United stars. In August 1972, he was invited over to Old Trafford for a pre-season trial, but it was an unsuccessful visit for the 15-year-old schoolboy, and so he concentrated on carving out a career for himself in the League of Ireland. His performances in midfield and at left-back soon attracted Bohemians to sign him up, but United did not forget about him.

Almost five years after being rejected, Docherty signed Grimes in March 1977 for a fee of £20,000, though they could have had him for free originally. But it was Sexton who gave Grimes his United debut on the opening day of the 1977–78 league season. He came on as a substitute for Stuart Pearson in United's 4–1 win over Birmingham City at St Andrew's on 20 August. In a creditable first full season, he played a total of 17 games, eight of them from the bench, and scored two goals, both in April.

After making 21 appearances in 1978–79, 11 as substitute (he thus followed Belfast-born McCreery and McGrath as the most frequently used player from the bench), he had his best season in 1979–80, starting in 20 of United's league games and making a total of 27 appearances in the campaign. His adaptability meant that he wore the No. 3, 7, 10 and 11 shirts, though he was always happiest playing on the left side of the team. In Sexton's final season, 1980–81, he made just ten appearances in all, but the arrival of Ron Atkinson as manager brought little change in his fortunes, as he was a peripheral figure in 1981–82.

Now aged 25 at the start of the 1982–83 season, Grimes was approaching the peak of his career, and indeed he did play more often for the Reds. But he achieved some notoriety on 30 October, when United played West Ham away in the First Division. It was a bit of a niggly game, and shortly after United were refused a penalty by referee Dennis Hughes. The official then proceeded to give the home side a spot kick after Grimes had handled the ball in his own area.

Grimes, who had been involved in United's claim for a penalty at the other end, was enraged and grabbed the referee's sleeve to attract his attention. However, when Hughes attempted to pull his arm away, the hand of Grimes smacked the referee on the head. Hughes accused the Irishman of striking him and sent him off.

The following month Grimes found himself appearing before an FA disciplinary committee and he was handed a £750 fine and banned for two games. It was the highest financial punishment ever given to a player at the time.

At the end of the season, he won an FA Cup winners' medal as a non-playing substitute against Brighton & Hove Albion in the FA Cup final replay (he was also a unused substitute in the first game). After that, he left United and joined Coventry City in a £200,000 transfer deal. He had played 107 times for United, scoring 11 goals. However, he stayed at Highfield Road for only a single season before signing for Luton Town in August 1984. Grimes played 117 times for the Hatters, and in 1988 he collected a League Cup winners' medal with them, coming on as a substitute to set up Luton Town's winning goal in a shock 3–2 win over Arsenal. The following year he was back at Wembley with Luton to try to retain the League Cup, but this time Brian Clough's Nottingham Forest claimed the trophy. In August 1990, Grimes headed for a warmer climate and joined Osasuna. His stay in Spain lasted only a matter of months before he returned to England to take up an offer from Lou Macari, his former United team-mate and now the manager of Stoke City, to assist him in a coaching role at the Victoria Ground. He later worked as a player-coach at Glasgow Celtic in season 1993–94 before returning to Stoke.

Having made his United debut in 1977–78, he also made his first appearance for the Republic of Ireland that season. On 5 April 1978 he won his first cap in a 4–2 friendly victory over Turkey at Lansdowne Road. Grimes won 18 caps (15 while with United) for his country and scored his only goal for the Republic against Spain on 17 November 1982 in a European Championship qualifier. He played his last game for Ireland against Romania on 23 March 1988.

However, leaving United in 1983 was not the last connection Grimes had with the club, as not that many years ago he was somewhat surprisingly to be found working in the Legends Chip

Shop on the corner of Sir Matt Busby Way serving fans fish and chips on their way to and from the game. Despite his ginger hair and pale complexion, not that many United fans were aware that the man behind the counter getting their order sorted out was a former United footballer. All of which may provide the answer as to why the mural on the shop wall features not only the likes of Denis Law, Cristiano Ronaldo and Eric Cantona, but also Ashley Grimes.

The 1980–81 season not only proved to be Sexton's last in charge of United, it marked the end of the Reds' two longest-serving Irishmen as regulars in the side. Having pushed Liverpool so hard the previous campaign, United had hoped that Sexton could lead them to the title, especially after he bought the club's first million-pound player, Garry Birtles, in October. But the ex-Nottingham Forest man struggled to settle down, and United finished a disappointing eighth. Even seven successive wins at the end of the season were not enough to save the manager.

That season also saw one of the briefest United careers ever by an Irishman, but even so Anthony Gerard 'Anto' Whelan did get to run out at Old Trafford wearing the famous red shirt. He was born in Dublin on 23 November 1959 and began his football career with the Bohemians, making his debut on 9 September 1979. The central defender played 25 league games that season, scoring four goals, and appeared in the UEFA Cup. He also helped his side win the 1979–80 Leinster Cup, all of which had several English clubs taking note of him. That August, Sexton signed him up for a fee of £30,000.

On 29 November 1980, just six days after celebrating his 21st birthday, he made his debut for United, coming on as a substitute for fellow Dubliner Kevin Moran, in a 1–1 draw with Southampton at the Dell. However, his first taste of life in the United team was his last, and he spent the rest of his time at Old Trafford in the Central League side.

Two days later, United visited Whelan's place of birth to play in an exhibition match against a Home Farm side that featured a number of guest players to mark the inaugural use of their new floodlights. An expectant crowd of 20,000 saw two Irishmen in United's starting line-up, Sammy McIlroy and Ashley Grimes, while three more came off the bench, Whelan, Tom Sloan and Chris McGrath, the latter netting United's third of the game as the Reds ended up comfortable 3–0 winners. But this was a rare career highlight for Whelan during his time at United.

Loan spells at Rochdale and in the USA preceded a return to Ireland in June 1983, when he signed for Shamrock Rovers. In his first season with Rovers he won an FAI League title medal. After a short spell with Cork City in season 1985–86, he very briefly rejoined Rovers in the summer of 1986 before moving on to Bray Wanderers. In 1988, he signed for Shelbourne, where he played the best football of his career, winning more honours. A third FAI League winners' medal came his way in 1994–95, this time with Dundalk. He then took up a role as assistant coach with Drogheda United and helped them win promotion to the Irish Premier in 1996–97. He ended his career back with Bray Wanderers for one season in 1997–98.

A few weeks after United's previous trip, on 10 February 1981, the Reds crossed the Irish Sea again, but this time they took on Linfield in Belfast, although several players were more than a little apprehensive about visiting the city because of the sectarian violence at that time. However, Sexton insisted his players 'had an obligation not only to meet this fixture, but with the football lovers over there who have shown us such loyalty.' The Northern Ireland public turned up at Windsor Park in their hordes to watch their United heroes take on the local side – 35,000 in total, which was a higher attendance than any Northern Ireland side had attracted for a World Cup qualifier over the previous decade. Indeed, the game had to be delayed by 15 minutes to allow the fans to make their way into the ground such was the pull of United.

I was there and must admit to sharing the same apprehension as some of the United players about the fixture, and remember my father saying to me: 'Remember, son, if you go looking for trouble, you will find it.' United won 1–0 in a drab game, thanks to a goal from Garry Birtles in the 22nd minute, his first ever goal for United. Former United player Trevor Anderson was probably the best player on view that night as he did his best to help Linfield attempt to cause a major upset, while Nicholl and McIlroy played for United.

In Sexton's place came a much more extrovert figure, Ron Atkinson, who had done well at West Bromwich Albion and who was not at all fazed by the fact that he had not been the board's first choice to take charge. He quickly moved to put his stamp on the club, and that meant that one or two familiar faces were soon on their way. McIlroy and Nicholl were both victims of this, and it was the midfielder who was the first to go.

McIlroy played in United's opening five league games of the 1981–82 season (all at No. 11), but then lost his place to Remi Moses, who Atkinson had signed from his old club. But on 3 October, he realised his time at United was almost at an end when Atkinson went back to West Brom to sign Bryan Robson for a British record transfer fee of £1.5 million. That day a table was brought out on to the Old Trafford pitch and out of the tunnel walked Atkinson and Robson, who took their seats at the table. The stadium announcer introduced the man who would go on to become a United legend to the 46,837 fans inside the ground who watched as Robson signed his contract.

McIlroy's response was typical: he went out and scored a hat-trick in United's 5–0 thumping of Wolverhampton Wanderers. They were the last goals of his United career, and it was his only hat-trick for the club. After that, he played just seven more times for the Reds, and after 419 appearances and 71 goals his United career was over when he played in a 1–1 league draw against Everton at Old Trafford on 6 January. In February 1982, aged only 27 and still at his peak, he signed for Stoke City in a £350,000 transfer. And so departed the last playing link with the Busby era.

When McIlroy left Stoke City in August 1985, after making 133 league appearances for the club, he briefly joined Manchester City (spending some time on loan at Örgryte IS in Sweden in 1986), before moving to Bury in March 1987, for whom he made 100 league appearances. He also had a spell in 1988 playing for the Austrian club VfB Mödling. But in February 1990, he was appointed player-coach under John McGrath at Preston North End, which proved to be a stepping stone to his new career as a football manager.

For Northern Ireland, McIlroy won a total of 88 caps, scoring five goals. He played in all of Northern Ireland's matches during both the 1982 and 1986 World Cup finals, captaining the side in the latter tournament. He was also a member of the Northern Ireland team that won the last Home International tournament in 1984. He played his final game for his country, coming on as a substitute, on 15 October 1986 in a 3–0 defeat against England in a European Championship qualifier. During his United career, 1971–82, he won the most caps for Northern Ireland of any player while playing for the same club, 52.

McIlroy has had numerous managerial posts, starting with non-league Northwich Victoria in July 1991, before joining Ashton United for a brief spell in December 1992. He then took charge at Macclesfield Town in 1993, eventually guiding them into the Football League in 1997 (they would have been promoted in 1995 but their ground did not meet Football League requirements) and to promotion the following campaign, though they came straight back down the following year. In January 2000, he became manager of Northern Ireland, remaining in charge for 29 games until 2003. Thereafter, he had just over a season at Stockport County (October 2003 to December 2004) and finally a long spell at Morecambe from 2006 before leaving the club at the end of the 2010–11 season.

For Nicholl, the end was even more abrupt. Atkinson's first move in the transfer market on joining United was to swap left-sided midfielder Mickey Thomas for right-back John Gidman from Everton in August 1981. The United stalwart made only one substitute appearance in the league for United in season 1981–82, as Gidman made the position his own. When Gidman was missing, Mick Duxbury was usually selected ahead of Nicholl. In December the Irishman went on loan to Sunderland and this preceded a £250,000 transfer in April 1982 to Toronto Blizzard in the NASL. He had made 248 appearances for United, and scored six goals.

In his international career, Nicholl made his debut for Northern Ireland on 3 March 1976 against Israel in an away friendly that finished 1–1. He went on to make 73 appearances for his country and scored one goal (in a 3–0 home win over Sweden on 15 October 1980). Like his long-time United team-mate McIlroy, Nicholl played in every match for the Irish at the 1982 and 1986 World Cup finals, after which his international career was over. How good was he? Well, Sir Matt Busby was so impressed with Nicholl's ability to play practically anywhere on the pitch he said: 'Jimmy reminds me of Johnny Carey.' High praise indeed.

Nicholl returned to Sunderland in September 1982 before going back to Toronto Blizzard. Between October 1983 and April 1984 he played on loan for Glasgow Rangers before teaming up with the Blizzard for a third time in May 1984. In November 1984 he completed a £65,000 move to West Bromwich Albion, then went back to Rangers in July 1986, where he helped Graeme Souness's side to the SPL title and Scottish League Cup; he was also the Reserve Team coach.

After three seasons at Ibrox, in July 1989 he joined Dunfermline Athletic before becoming Raith Rovers' player-manager on 27 November 1990. Exactly four years to the day after taking charge, he helped them to Scottish League Cup glory when they won a dramatic penalty shootout 6–5 to beat Celtic, after the game ended 2–2 after extra-time. For this achievement, and gaining promotion to the SPL, he won the Scottish Football Writers' Association Manager of the Year Award. He left Raith Rovers in February 1996 and later that month was appointed manager of

Millwall, but was unable to stop them from being relegated to Division Two that season.

He stayed with Millwall until February 1997 and then in August 1997 returned to Raith Rovers for two seasons. When Jimmy Calderwood was appointed manager of Dunfermline Athletic in December 1999, Nicholl became his assistant and stayed for five years. Nicholl followed Calderwood to Aberdeen in May 2004, and they stayed there for five years. In January 2010, he teamed up with Calderwood for a third time, this time at Kilmarnock, before he accepted an invitation from Cowdenbeath to be their new manager on 25 June 2010. After they were relegated at the end of 2010–11, he returned to Kilmarnock as assistant manager in June 2011.

Although the Atkinson era had brought a close to these long-standing servants of the club, it was also the beginning of a new era of Irish talent. Rugged defender Kevin Moran was already established at the heart of United's back line, alongside Martin Buchan and Gordon McQueen, and before Atkinson's first season was over he would have discovered another great Irish defender. The manager also moved quickly to sign an established Irish international striker, and he would soon find out that his junior ranks possessed one of the finest talents to cross the Irish Sea since George Best. As so often, before and since, the Irish would be crucial to United's fortunes in the years ahead.

Chapter 10

The Four Irishmen of the Eighties

Ron Atkinson joined United as manager in the summer of 1981, and immediately looked to change things around after the disappointments of the Sexton era. More of a showman than his predecessor, he perhaps reflected his era – a time when the New Romantics were putting the emphasis on style and glamour. Before his first season was over, he would have a trio of players from the Republic of Ireland on his books who would not only make an enormous impact for the Reds, but also for their country. And they were accompanied by another Belfast Boy to ensure that the new era was going to have a very heavy Irish element to it.

While Atkinson altered many things, he knew the importance of catering to the club's Irish fanbase. So, three weeks before the opening game of the 1981–82 season, United visited Dublin to face Bohemians in a friendly at Dalymount Park. The home side, with several guest players boosting their ranks including former United star Gerry Daly, took the lead. But United eventually won through 3–1, with Jimmy Nicholl (getting an early sign of what was to come when he was substituted for John Gidman) being one of three Irishmen to line up for the Reds, alongside Sammy McIlroy and Kevin Moran.

If Frank Stapleton's career as a United player is viewed in a slightly lesser light by some fans to that of his two fellow countrymen who shared the Old Trafford spotlight with him throughout much of the 1980s, Kevin Moran and Paul McGrath, it is only because he arrived at the club having already had plenty of success at Arsenal, and he was 25 when he joined. However, had United not rejected Stapleton as a schoolboy, then his story, and that of United, may well have been very different. On the other hand, Moran and McGrath got their first breaks at United, which always gave them a special place in the hearts of fans. The gifted Irish triumvirate were unfortunate to be at United at a time when the team, although capable of romancing the fans by turning on the style, were always just a step away from true greatness. But they made a major contribution to the cup success the team enjoyed during the mid-eighties.

Arguably, Kevin Moran spilt more blood in United's cause than any other player in the club's long history and it could be claimed that if the fans did not see the Irishman leave the pitch swathed in bandages or with blood streaming from a head wound, then Moran must have had a poor game. Moran put his body where others would never consider, a defender in the true sense of the word and a United player through and through. Paul McGrath was a footballer similar in style to Rio Ferdinand today, playing the game with his brain, compared with Moran's brawn, and had he been a few years younger when Alex Ferguson arrived at Old Trafford in November 1986, then his career might have taken a different path. Injuries also played a major part in McGrath's career, but it is to his immense credit that after leaving United he continued to play to such a high standard with Aston Villa.

Kevin Bernard Moran was born on 29 April 1956 in Dublin. He grew up in Rialto, Dublin, until his early teens when his family moved to the Long Mile Road in Walkinstown. He was educated at the James's Street Catholic Boys School and Drimnagh Catholic Boys School, where Gaelic football was the main sport, and soccer was not permitted on the school grounds, though pupils would often play it on the streets near their homes.

Moran recalls those days: 'When I was a young boy growing up in Dublin the big English football clubs at the time were Arsenal, Liverpool and of course Manchester United. Glasgow Celtic was also hugely popular among Irish boys. I actually supported Liverpool when I was a young boy, because one of my older brothers had already chosen United. We adopted this policy in our house that each one of us would support a different team, and I chose Liverpool as United was not available. One of my brothers supported Queens Park Rangers and another followed the exploits of Nottingham Forest. However, by the time my two younger brothers were born, we relaxed the one-team-per-household rule and they grew up United fans.

'In contrast, my father never supported any soccer team as he was an out-and-out Gaelic football man and Leitrim was his team. From an early age, and thanks to my father's influence, I too was a GAA fan and played both football and hurling at school. However, GAA football was my first love and I played for Good Counsel in Dublin. When I was around fourteen years old I began to take an interest in soccer and played for a local team at Bushy Park in Terenure, the Parish of Rathfarnham, County Dublin. Interestingly the team was called Rangers and they are still active today.

'Being a Liverpool fan, my boyhood hero was the legendary Roger Hunt. "Sir Roger", as he was affectionately nicknamed by the Liverpool fans, was a magnificent player who possessed tremendous skill and was a prolific goalscorer. However, my principal sporting heroes were the members of Dublin's famous GAA All-Ireland Senior Football Championship winning side in 1974.'

As well as Gaelic football, where he was an inter-county player for Dublin and won two All-Ireland Football Championship medals in 1976 and 1977, Moran played soccer as a full-back for Bohemians in his home city and also for his college team, Pegasus.

However, as both sports were played on a Saturday afternoon, he often found himself torn between the two.

In January 1978, Billy Behan was one of a crowd of just 150 when he spotted Moran playing for Pegasus against Dundalk in the first round of the FAI Cup, and recommended the 21-year-old to Dave Sexton. Later that month, Moran signed for United and it caused shockwaves in Ireland among the Gaelic football fraternity as he was on course to become one of the sport's great stars.

He recalls leaving home for Manchester: 'When I moved to Manchester on 1 February 1978 I did not know anyone personally. I found it difficult to settle in Manchester at first, and really missed my family and mates back home in Dublin. I had also just left behind my Dublin GAA football team-mates, all close personal friends, and really did miss the camaraderie we enjoyed together. To their credit, my Dublin team-mates all wished me well when I decided to join United, and that meant a lot to me at the time. However, I wasn't a kid and just buckled down to the job in hand and that was to become a professional footballer with Manchester United.

'The club was also great to me and allowed me to return home to play for Dublin in the 1978 GAA All-Ireland Senior Football Championship final. The game was played at Croke Park on 16 September 1978 and we went into the match against Kerry seeking to claim our third consecutive Sam Maguire. However, we were well beaten on the day.

'What I recall most about my early months at United was the boredom. Back home in Dublin I had a busy daily schedule, learning to be an accountant from nine-to-five, and then heading off to training with the Dublin team. But in Manchester there was very little for me to do once training ended for the day. When I moved to Manchester, I was placed in digs in the Chorlton-cum-Hardy area of the city by the club with a lovely lady named Elizabeth "Beth" Fannon. Fellow Dubliner Ashley Grimes was already in digs there and we became good friends instantly, and Beth was like a second mum to us and two other young lads who never made it at United. No one from the club ever really checked up on us, but then again I was twenty-one years old at the time and I suppose the club just trusted us to do the right thing.

'Ashley and I had a car, so the four of us would travel together to the Cliff for training every morning. Not too long after my arrival, I became very close to another fellow Dubliner, Paddy Roche, and very good pals with Jimmy Nicholl. A lot of the Irish lads in the United set-up hung around together, while two of the Scottish lads, Arthur Albiston and Alex Forsyth, were regular members of our company when we went out for the evening. We used to go to a nearby club called Woodheys which was in Sale.'

Moran began life at Old Trafford in United's Central League side and his full-blooded commitment in games convinced Sexton that he was ready for bigger things. 'I made my debut for Manchester United on 30 April 1979 in a First Division away game against Southampton. The game was played at Southampton's old ground, the Dell, and we drew 1–1 thanks to a goal from Andy Ritchie. Dave Sexton handed me my debut as he was resting a number of the players ahead of our FA Cup final versus Arsenal less than two weeks later. However, the game against the Saints wasn't actually my first game for United, as I played in a testimonial match for Peter Bonetti at Stamford Bridge the previous month. At the end of the game, Harry Gregg, who was on the coaching staff then, came up to me and said: "You did well out there today, son." Harry's words of encouragement meant a lot to me, and from that moment on I was determined to succeed in establishing myself in the Manchester United team.'

Gregg was impressed with what he saw of Moran from the touchline, and recalls: 'Kevin was an outstanding player and without question one of the bravest footballers I have ever seen. I had the privilege of working with the young Moran when I was in charge of United's Reserve team for a period under Dave Sexton. I jumped at the chance. Kevin gave it everything whether it was a training match or a Reserve fixture. His enthusiasm and commitment knew no bounds and along with the imposing figure of the young Yugoslavian international, Nikola Jovanovic , they scared the living daylights out of opposing players.

'Kevin was a big lad and could handle himself. I mean you don't win two GAA All-Ireland Senior Championship Football winners' medals with Dublin if you are not prepared to mix it up with some of the hardest men in the sport. Kevin took to soccer from Gaelic football like a duck takes to water and wasn't afraid to get hurt. And Big Kevin's partner in the centre of defence was a giant of a man. Nikola was bought from Red Star Belgrade and stood 6ft 3in tall and weighed about 15st. Honestly, he was built like Charles Atlas, and if he or Kevin tackled you, or fought with you for the ball in an aerial challenge, you had no hope of coming out of it the winner, or without feeling a great deal of pain. There are physical footballers and then there is Kevin Moran, one of United's greatest ever defenders.'

The Southampton game was Moran's only appearance in his first season at Old Trafford. In 1979–80, he made nine appearances in total and scored his first goal for the club in a 5–0 hammering of Norwich City at Old Trafford on 24 November 1979. As injuries began to take their toll on first-choice central defenders Martin Buchan and Gordon McQueen, Moran (now usually deployed in the centre of defence, rather than at full-back as earlier) began to establish himself in the first team in 1980–81, playing in 32 league games. When Atkinson arrived at United, Moran was already very much a part of the team, and made another 30 league appearances in 1981–82, scoring an impressive seven goals, as his fearless approach to the game proved highly effective in the opposition box as well as in defending his own goal.

But the man who was paid to be a threat in the opposition box was Francis Anthony 'Frank' Stapleton. Born on 10 July

1956 in Dublin, he began his career with local side St Martins before moving on to another Dublin side, Bolton Athletic. As a junior he travelled to England and had trials with United and Wolves, but both clubs passed up on the chance to sign him. In June 1972, Arsenal snapped him up as an apprentice and in September 1973 he signed professional terms. He played for the Arsenal junior sides, but for a while couldn't get into the first team. However, his combative style and his domination over opponents in the air did not go unnoticed. On 29 March 1975, he made his First Division debut. By season 1976–77, he was a regular in the Arsenal team and his strike partnership with Malcolm Macdonald was prolific, the pair scoring 46 goals between them.

Over the following three seasons, he was Arsenal's leading goalscorer and was on target against United in the 1979 FA Cup final. After making some 300 appearances for the Gunners, scoring 108 goals, Atkinson signed him for United in August 1981 for a fee of £900,000, describing him as 'the best centre-forward in Europe'. He was seen as a direct replacement for Joe Jordan, who had left the Reds for AC Milan the previous month.

Stapleton made his United debut on the opening day of the 1981–82 season at Coventry City, partnering Garry Birtles in attack, but the Reds lost 2–1 in a disappointing start to the new era. In his first season, Stapleton missed just one game in all competitions, and was the top scorer with 13 goals, as United finished in third place, a big improvement on the previous campaign. The only fixture he missed was the last game of the season, a 2–0 home win over Stoke City on 15 May 1982, when a certain Norman Whiteside took his place and scored his first goal for United.

Atkinson's side earned themselves a new fan that year as well – but in the most bizarre of circumstances. Noel Flannery from Belfast tells the story: 'I was born in January 1974 and grew up in Moyard, West Belfast. At that time, Liverpool and Celtic were the teams many in our street supported. I would love to say that I became a United fanatic because of Sammy McIlroy or David McCreery or Jimmy Nicholl, but to be honest I started supporting Manchester United because Andy Gray couldn't score for Wolverhampton Wanderers! The date was 3 October 1981 and United were playing Wolves at Old Trafford. It was the day Robbo signed his contract. I watched the game on TV and I decided there and then that I would support the winner of this game. I was watching it with my dad and, although he is a United fan, he also had a soft spot for Wolves and he was a big fan of Andy Gray, who he felt sure would score that day. Happily, the game finished 5–0 in United's favour and so I ended up a United fan.'

Noel Johnston from Ballynahinch, County Down, was already a United supporter when he made his first trip to see United in action that season: 'During the eighties I followed United through thick and thin (mostly thin) as they struggled to win any major trophies. My first live match at Old Trafford was on 6 January 1982, when our youth group took the Belfast to Liverpool ferry so we could watch United v Everton. I remember feeling ill the whole time before the match, after a ten-hour ferry crossing in the middle of winter. Two of our leaders thought this was funny and kept telling me I'd be fine when the game started. After the game I had fully recovered, but one of the leaders had eaten a half-cooked burger at one of the chip vans near the ground and was sick as a dog for the rest of the trip. Revenge was sweet and the game was good value for the 1–1 draw, with Frank Stapleton scoring our goal.'

For Robin Wallace from Temple, County Down, his first trip to United (also that 1981–82 season) had a more wholesome ending: 'It wasn't until 28 November 1981 that I managed to see my first game at Old Trafford. That day United played Brighton & Hove Albion and the trip was run by the *Belfast Telegraph*. United won 2–0 thanks to goals from Garry Birtles and Frank Stapleton. That evening in the hotel where we were staying, I could not believe my eyes when in walked Garry Birtles. I have still got the United Review match programme which he signed for me.'

Still waiting in the wings at that stage of the season was Norman Whiteside. He was born in the Shankill Road area of North Belfast on 7 May 1965. When he was only eight years old his PE teacher at Edenderry Primary School informed his parents that Norman would be a professional footballer before his 15th birthday, but even he couldn't have imagined just how quickly Whiteside's career would eventually take off. He then attended Cairnmartin Secondary School on the Ballygomartin Road, Belfast, where his giant physique made him stand out above all the other pupils on the football pitch.

Tim Robson remembers a very young Whiteside playing in a Belfast Schools Cup final in the late 1970s: 'As a fifth-year pupil at Rathcoole Secondary School, I went along to see our fourth-year students play Cairnmartin Secondary School at Solitude, home to Cliftonville in North Belfast. All the talk at the time was about this big fella – at that time Norman was known as 'Smilie' – and how we could possibly contain him. As it happened we couldn't, and Cairnmartin ran out 5–2 winners, with Big Norm scoring at least two goals against a team including Jackie Evans – Corry and Jonny's dad. I happened to meet Norman outside Old Trafford before a game a few years ago and mentioned the first time I had saw him play. He just smiled and said: "Aye I stuck a few in that day."'

Whiteside was the third player of the famous triumvirate discovered by the legendary United scout Bob Bishop, after George Best and Sammy McIlroy. Even at 13, Bishop knew Whiteside was destined to be a United great and wasted no time in contacting the club, and in September 1978 he signed for United as a schoolboy apprentice – news that spread around the schools of Belfast, excited that the city had clearly produced someone truly special. United flew Whiteside over to Manchester on a Friday evening so he could play for the Juniors on the Saturday morning.

William Morrow from Belfast remembers Whiteside joining United and the buzz around his area at the time: 'I was just leaving school when Norman signed as a thirteen-year-old for United. There was some footage of him in action shown on the news at the time, and he was twice the size of his team-mates and opponents! At that stage it was hard to tell if he was a phenomenon or not, but he was fearless (easy to say I suppose when you are twice the size of the opposition). However, he was also very tactically aware for his age and simply had a natural instinct for scoring goals.'

In May 1979 Whiteside played for the Under-16 Northern Ireland Schoolboys team against Wales. Despite being up against much older boys, he was the Man of the Match, scoring the first goal and setting up their second in a 2–1 win. The next day a Manchester newspaper carried the back-page headline: 'Have United found the new George Best at last?' It would not be the last time the comparison was made.

Whiteside's outstanding ability shone like a beacon in the United Reserves side and during training sessions with the first team. So, on 24 April 1982, Atkinson unleashed him on the First Division, giving him his United debut just a fortnight before his 17th birthday, when he came on as a substitute for Mike Duxbury at Brighton & Hove Albion in a 1–0 win. He became United's youngest-ever Irish debutant. Eight days after his 17th birthday, he became United's youngest goalscorer when he found the net in their 2–0 Division One win over Stoke City at Old Trafford on 15 May 1982. It was only his second game for United, but it was enough to convince the Northern Ireland manager, Billy Bingham, to include him in his 22-man squad for the World Cup finals in Spain that summer.

At Espana '82, Whiteside broke Pelé's record as the youngest player ever to appear at the World Cup finals when he made his international debut in Northern Ireland's opening game against Yugoslavia on 17 June 1982. He was just 17 years and 41 days old, and was booked in the game that ended 0–0. He started in all five of Northern Ireland's games at the tournament, including the historic 1–0 win over hosts Spain. Hot on the success of his performances for Northern Ireland in Spain, he was an obvious choice for inclusion in the United squad that toured Ireland later that summer as United prepared for the 1982–83 season.

First up was a testimonial for the former United and Republic of Ireland international Don Givens on 10 August at Dalymount Park. United won 4–2, in front of a crowd of about 20,000, with Whiteside scoring twice and recent recruit Paul McGrath getting another of United's goals. The Reds faced not only Givens, but also two other former Reds in Gerry Daly and Mick Martin. Two days later, United beat Limerick United 3–1 in another testimonial game, with Moran among United's goalscorers. The last game of the tour, on 14 August, saw United travel north, and even the presence of local hero Whiteside did not get the most attention when the Reds took on Glentoran to mark the club's centenary. Instead, the focus was on a player the Belfast outfit had rejected some 20 years previously as being too slight to cope with football at that level, but who had gone on to play for United: a certain George Best.

As soon as he took to the pitch, Best received a standing ovation from the crowd of 19,000 and his every touch that day was cheered. He nutmegged Garry Birtles, much to the crowd's delight, and then when Scott McGarvey fouled him, Best just got up, smiled and handed the ball to the star-struck United player. But despite his best efforts, United still won 2–0 to complete a highly successful tour that won yet more Irish hearts and minds for the club.

After signing up John Gidman, Stapleton, Remi Moses and Bryan Robson in the previous campaign, Atkinson made only one major signing in the summer of 1982, bringing in the skilful midfielder Arnold Mühren from Ipswich Town, and the Dutch midfielder would have an immediate impact on the side. But it was a recruit from Irish football at the end of the previous campaign who would go on to have an arguably greater impact.

Paul McGrath was born on 4 December 1959 in Ealing, London, to an Irish mother and a Nigerian father. Perhaps as a result of feeling guilty about being unmarried, McGrath's mother made her way to London, where she knew no one, to give birth to Paul. After she returned to Ireland, the baby was passed from orphanage to orphanage in Dublin for the first 16 years of his life.

He began his football career with his school side, Pearse Rovers, before joining the junior side Dalkey United, where scout Billy Behan saw him in action. However, in 1981, the 21-year-old signed as a full-time professional with St Patrick's Athletic, after working as an apprentice sheet-metal worker and a security guard in Dublin. Although he spent only one season at St Patrick's, the fans took to him instantly and nicknamed him 'The Black Pearl of Inchicore', and he won the PFAI Player of the Year Award in his only season in League of Ireland football.

In April 1982, Atkinson signed McGrath in a bargain £30,000 transfer deal. However, a niggling injury prevented his senior debut until 10 November 1982 when he played in United's League Cup third round 0–0 draw away to Bradford City. Three days later, he made his First Division debut in place of Moran in a 1–0 win over Tottenham Hotspur at Old Trafford. His assured performance in the heart of the defence won over the United faithful instantly. However, when Moran was available again, McGrath returned to the reserves and did not reappear again in the first team until 2 March.

A few days later, on 15 March, United took on St Patrick's in a friendly, as part of the deal that saw McGrath leave the Dublin club. A crowd of 16,000 turned out at Dalymount Park to see United record a rather tepid 2–0 win in which McGrath, Ashley Grimes, Whiteside and Stapleton all took part.

McGrath played in 16 games for United in his first full season at the club, scoring three times, with his first two goals for the Reds coming in a 3–0 home win over Luton Town on 9 May 1983. This game was the first in which the famous Irish quartet of McGrath, Moran, Stapleton (who scored the other goal) and Whiteside all played together.

Although United again finished in third place in the league, the main story of the season concerned runs to the final in both domestic knockout cups, where McGrath was very much a bit-part player. The same could not be said of Stapleton, who missed just one of United's 60 games in 1982–83, an extraordinary effort that saw him finish the campaign once more as top scorer, with 19 goals. Whiteside was not far behind, missing just three games, though he turned 18 only at the end of the season, and he scored 14 goals playing up front alongside Stapleton.

First of all, United reached the League Cup final for the first time in the club's history, meeting Liverpool on 26 March. Stapleton and Whiteside both scored at Highbury in the semi-final when United stunned the Gunners, beating them 4–2. Moran then scored in the second leg, as United won through to the final 6–3 on aggregate.

In the final itself, when Moran went off injured in the 69th minute, Stapleton slotted into the centre-half position alongside Gordon McQueen, while United's substitute, Lou Macari, partnered Whiteside up front. The teenaged Whiteside made more history in that final, when he scored United's only goal in a 2–1 defeat to their fiercest rivals, thus becoming the youngest player ever to score in a Wembley final. He had not done with setting records that season, either.

After that disappointment, the Reds were more determined than ever to get back to Wembley. Stapleton had scored the only goal in the quarter-final against Everton, to ensure they were just one match away from that target. Once again, Arsenal awaited them in the semi-final, and Whiteside was again on the scoresheet against the Londoners, striking a magnificent half-volley. But for many at Villa Park that day, it was Moran who took most of the plaudits.

He was as hard as they come, but fair with it. Opposing players knew that if they attempted to rough him up there would only be one winner and that would be United's amiable Irish centre-half. He was as brave as they come and carried on playing through pain barriers some of today's footballers would faint from. Is it any wonder, after all the blood he spilled, that the United fans nick-named him 'Captain Blood'. That semi-final summed up why. You knew Moran was badly injured when the St John Ambulancemen had to come on to the pitch and stretcher him off. And who can forget him lying on the stretcher and sticking his thumb up in the air to tell everyone he was OK, even though he clearly wasn't.

Happily, Moran recovered in time for the final, when United took on relegated Brighton & Hove Albion, and two of United's Irish contingent made FA Cup history. First of all, Stapleton scored for United in the 2–2 draw against the Seagulls, becom-ing the first player to score for two different clubs in an FA Cup final. In the replay, United ensured things stayed true to the formbook, and crushed Brighton 4–0, with Whiteside scoring one of the goals, thus becoming not only the youngest player to score in an FA Cup final, but the first to score in both domestic finals.

Not surprisingly, Whiteside was gathering his own fanclub, as Marshall Angus from Bangor, County Down, recalls. 'My youngest memory of being a Manchester United fan was getting a cracking white kit for my birthday in 1983. The kit itself came from a workmate of my dad's. He was a plumber and he worked alongside many other tradesmen, among them a painter called Norman Whiteside; not the famous one but his father. My father kept well in with Norman because of his links with United through his gifted son. I was six years old at the time and, as far as I was concerned, the kit had been sent over from Old Trafford by the young Norman Whiteside just for me!'

That summer of 1983, by and large, Atkinson kept his chequebook in his pocket, believing his side could go on from their cup-winning exploits to mount a serious challenge for the title. Before the campaign got under way, United and Liverpool played an exhibition match at Windsor Park before an expectant crowd of 30,000 on 3 August, just a few days before the two sides would meet again in the Charity Shield. The two most popular English sides in Ireland put on a great show, and the atmosphere was superb. United won 4–3, with goals from Lou Macari (2), Moran and Whiteside. Five Irish players played in the game for United: Whiteside, Moran, Stapleton, McGrath and Grimes.

Sadly, although the team garnered more points (74 compared to the previous season's 70), United slipped back to fourth place as Liverpool completed a hat-trick of league titles. In 1983–84, Stapleton did not miss one of United's 58 games, and for a third season in a row was the top scorer, with 19 goals. Moran and Whiteside also both played more than 50 times for the Reds, scoring seven and 12 times respectively. For McGrath, however, there was disappointment as he made just 12 appearances, with Graeme Hogg emerging to challenge for a place in the side.

There was no significant domestic cup run, but in Europe United did well as they faced up to some of the continental giants. Few who were there will ever forget the European Cup-Winners' Cup quarter-final against Barcelona. In the first leg, United had lost 2–0 and so had a massive task against Barça. Moran recalls that game: 'The atmosphere that night was amazing, something I will never forget. The crowd knew that they had to get behind us and the buzz about the place was just incredible.' Against Diego Maradona and Bernd Schuster, it was Bryan Robson who bossed the game, scoring two goals before Stapleton scored the vital third goal that secured the Reds' progress to the semi-finals, in front of 58,547 fans in full cry. Sadly, despite a Whiteside goal in the second leg of the semis against Juventus, United could not make it through to the final.

During the summer of 1984, Atkinson invested heavily in his squad, bringing in Gordon Strachan and Jesper Olsen to reinforce the flanks of his midfield, while striker Alan Brazil joined for £700,000 from Tottenham Hotspur. However, it was the emergence of 20-year-old Mark Hughes from the youth ranks that would have the biggest impact on the side during 1984–85.

As usual at this time, Irish fans had a chance to see Atkinson's new-look team ahead of the season's start. On 5 August, United played a pre-season friendly against Shamrock Rovers at Glenmalure Park. Olsen gave the Irish side the run-around and was the star of the show. He capped his first performance in a United shirt with a goal to help United to a 2–0 victory (Hughes also scored). Moran was the only Irish representative in the United team.

With two new strikers in the squad, this obviously put pressure on the established men in those positions – Stapleton and Whiteside. However, Atkinson decided to move the latter into the heart of the United midfield to play beside captain Robson. Ray Wilkins, Robson's midfield partner at United and for England, had left Old Trafford to join AC Milan, so there was a vacancy in the position. Whiteside would be the first to admit that he never possessed great speed, but what he did have was a magnificent football brain and he was as hard as they come and well suited to the heated battle of midfield. He was very strong and, for a big man (6ft 2in), he had a deft touch and contributed his fair share of goals from his new combative role. United fans loved him because he was a warrior who gave his all every time he wore the shirt, never flinching from a tackle and standing toe-to-toe with some of the hardest players around at the time.

Stapleton was not so lucky. An injury at the start of the 1984–85 season ruled him out of United's opening 11 league games, although he did manage six league goals in his 24 games. By the time he returned, coming on as a substitute at Goodison Park, it was clear that Everton were the new force in the league, as they thrashed the Reds 5–0 and went on to claim the title, with United 14 points adrift in fourth place.

At the heart of United's defence, there was no settled pairing, with McGrath starting 23 league games and Moran just 19. At the beginning of the campaign, Moran and Graeme Hogg were the regular starters, with McGrath having to bide his time in the Central League team. However, his strength, speed, stamina and coolness under pressure could not be ignored any longer by

Atkinson. When Moran suffered an injury, McGrath slotted in at centre-half and his excellent form saw him play in every one of United's last 21 First Division games of the season.

Moran recalls their partnership: 'My all-time favourite Manchester United footballer has to be, without any shadow of a doubt, Paul McGrath. Paul was a magnificent player, courageous in the air and in the tackle, aggressive but not dirty, tremendous stamina, powerful, a great reader of the game and a man you could always rely on to dig you out of trouble if you happened to be having an off day against an opponent. I loved and still cherish every minute of every game I had the honour and privilege of playing alongside Paul in the red of United and the green of Ireland. Paul's dominating presence on the pitch frightened the life out of even the toughest of centre-forwards, but off the pitch he was a very quiet and shy man – and I should know because I shared a room with him.

'Paul's place in the history of United's most famous Irishmen is assured, as is another one of my good mates – Norman Whiteside. What a player Norman was and what a ferocious pair he and Paul made, but having said that, they are two of the nicest lads you will ever meet. I remember Paul, Norman and myself going to a Wolfe Tones concert at an Irish Centre located in the Levenshulme area of Manchester during the mid-1980s. To say we had a bit of *craic* that night would be a gross under-statement. I don't think Big Norman had ever heard of the Wolfe Tones prior to that memorable night out, but by the time we left the place he knew all about the history of one of Ireland's most famous bands.'

Robert Dallas was there that night, too: 'The Wolfe Tones were playing in Manchester. My mates and I were puzzled as to who owned the table at the front, as we were eyeing it up to take over. Then in trots Kevin and we soon wised up and stayed where we were, not wishing to mess about with the Big Man. What a great bloke he was, as he signed autographs and stood for photographs with us and we even had a brief chat with him. I can still remember that he had a magnificent game that day, 21 January 1984, in our 3–2 win over Southampton at Old Trafford in the old First Division. Absolutely great memories and none of could speak for a week after it!'

So, yet again, in spring 1985 United's hopes of silverware rested on the cups. Everton ensured there would be no glory in the League Cup, while a decent run in the UEFA Cup was somewhat surprisingly ended by Videoton, which just left the FA Cup. And in the oldest cup competition of them all, the Irish were in stunning form. Stapleton scored in a comfortable 3–0 win over Bournemouth in the third round, while McGrath got his first FA Cup goal to help beat Coventry City 2–1 in the next round. He was on the scoresheet again in the following round, as Blackburn Rovers were beaten 2–0.

In the quarter-finals, it was Whiteside's turn, as he scored the only hat-trick of his United career in a 4–2 victory over West Ham. That set up a semi-final tie against Liverpool. Stapleton seemed to have scored the winner, until Paul Walsh grabbed an equaliser in the last minute of extra-time for the match to finish 2–2. In the replay, McGrath scored his third goal of the campaign, but unfortunately it was past his own keeper, but United came back in the second half to win through to the final.

All four of United's Irish contingent were selected for the final, where champions Everton were looking to complete a Treble, having won the league and the European Cup-Winners' Cup – and they would have a significant role to play in the game. Moran was back at Wembley with United for a third time on 18 May 1985, and he was to make a very unwanted piece of English football history. In the 78th minute of the game, Peter Reid was chasing on to a through ball, and Moran slid in and caught him. Most expected referee Peter Willis to caution him, but instead he sent him off. He was inconsolable, despite the commiserations of even the Everton side, as the TV cameras zoomed in on him and showed him shaking his head in disbelief and close to tears. Stapleton had to urge him away from the referee, and then when the game restarted slotted in beside McGrath in central defence.

The seeming injustice fired up the Reds. Thankfully, Whiteside scored the only goal of the game in the 20th minute of extra-time, curling a stunning left-foot shot round the diving Neville Southall from the edge of the box – it was a goal that deserved to win the final. Colm Devine is one who will never forget that strike: 'The goal he scored against Everton in the 1985 FA Cup final was sheer class. It was like the kind of goals that we used to see Johan Cruyff score and everyone marvelled and sang the Dutch maestro's praises, so why did Stormin' Norman not get the same accolades?' At the time, Moran was not allowed to go up to collect his medal, but happily he was subsequently presented with it.

While Moran and Whiteside gained all the headlines, and Stapleton had to play in two positions, it was McGrath who actually ended up as Man of the Match. Atkinson had picked him ahead of Graeme Hogg, and the decision was utterly vindicated. He was a colossus and snuffed out attack after attack from the Merseysiders, with Andy Gray and Graeme Sharp barely getting a touch of the ball, despite United going down to ten men after Moran was sent off. It was to be his only honour at the club.

Once again, cup success created hopes that United's long wait for the league title would finally come to an end, and when the Reds started the 1985–86 season with ten straight wins, it seemed as though Atkinson had finally got everything in place. But sadly, the squad picked up a few injuries and lost momentum. United finished fourth in the league, and there was little excitement in the cups, either. Furthermore, following the events at Heysel in the European Cup final, English teams were banned from Europe, too. It was, however, a good season for three of the Irish contingent, as Stapleton (50 appearances, nine goals), McGrath (48 appearances, four goals) and Whiteside (46 appearances, seven goals) turned out more frequently for United than anyone else. Sadly, Moran's season was blighted by injury.

After those disappointments, everyone at United went into the 1986–87 campaign under pressure – none more so than the manager. As so often, there were a couple of early season trips to Ireland. On 14 August, United took on Shamrock Rovers in a testimonial match to honour the former United hero, Shay Brennan. A crowd of 10,200 turned out to pay tribute to the 1968 European Cup winner and former Republic of Ireland international. Brennan had recently suffered a heart attack and was scheduled to go into hospital for a by-pass operation. Clearly things weren't right for the Reds, as United lost 2–0, and one of the best players on the pitch that day was the home side's Liam O'Brien. A few weeks later, on 10 September, United went to Belfast to play Linfield in a friendly at Windsor Park, partly to help skipper Robson in his comeback to fitness, and he scored twice in the Reds' 3–0 victory.

Moran, who played in the Shamrock game, recalls how he viewed these friendlies: 'When I first returned home to Dublin after making my debut for United, my family and friends did not treat me any different to how they had done when I left for Manchester. I think it is fair to say that my family and friends kept my feet firmly on the ground and I respect them so much for this. After all, I was one of six boys in the family home and we were all loved equally by our parents. And on top of that, I was a Dublin boy first and foremost and I am extremely proud to say that I have never forgotten my roots.

'Playing for United means regular visits back home, as the club plays so many friendly games against Irish sides. Between 1981 and 1987 I played in nine such games, and no matter where we played the fans turned out in vast numbers with their United scarves, flags and shirts turning the ground into a sea of red, white and black. I played in Dublin five times, Belfast three times and Limerick once. I will never forget a game in Belfast just two days after we beat Limerick United 3–1, when we took on Glentoran at The Oval. George Best played for the Glens that day and I wasn't afraid to incur the wrath of the home support by tackling the legendary Belfast Boy. The problem was I couldn't get anywhere near him! He may have left United eight years earlier and was thirty-six years old, but believe me he still had it. For me it was just one of those special games that you can put your hand on your heart and say: "I played in that match."'

United got off to a terrible start to the 1986–87 league season, and by the beginning of November they were languishing in 19th place, one above the relegation spots. Atkinson was dismissed and in his place came Alex Ferguson, who had had such a remarkable impact on Aberdeen. His first job on arriving at Old Trafford was to keep United in the First Division, but longer term he wanted to make sure that the Reds became the best team in the country. His arrival would have a dramatic impact on all four of United's established Irish stars.

Stapleton soon realised that he would not be featuring in the long-term plans of the new manager. By the start of the 1987–88 season, he would be 31, but the summer purchase of 23-year-old Brian McClair from Celtic showed Ferguson's thinking. There was some speculation that the popular Irishman might be converted to a central defender, having filled the role on several occasions for the club, but this always seemed unlikely to happen. Instead, after 288 games and 78 goals, he was given a free transfer to Ajax by United for his loyal service to the club.

His time at Ajax was an unhappy one (he played only four games) and so he moved on loan to Derby County before joining Le Havre in France. In the summer of 1989, he signed for Blackburn Rovers. And after spending two years at Ewood Park, he played a game for Aldershot before becoming player-coach at Huddersfield in October 1991. In December 1991, he was appointed player-manager of Bradford City where he remained until he was sacked in May 1994. After Bradford City, he played two games for Brighton & Hove Albion in season 1994–95 and then coached the New England Revolution in the USA in 1996.

His tally of 78 goals in six seasons at United may be looked upon by some as a relatively low return for a player of his ability. However, it was his contribution to the team effort that secures Stapleton's lofty position as a true United legend. His workrate was second to none, as he constantly pulled defenders out of position thereby allowing his fellow strikers a clear path to goal. He led the United attack imperiously and was always acutely aware of what was happening all around him. He covered at centre-half with the utmost ease when the situation arose, and was superb in the air both when heading towards the net and when laying cushioned headers off. His timing was excellent, his touch for a big man was superb and he possessed the ability to kill a ball and delicately flick a pass on to a team-mate. He had a powerful shot and, although he wasn't the quickest of strikers, he could hold off defenders and had the skills to twist and turn them out of position.

In international terms, Stapleton made his Republic of Ireland debut on 13 October 1976 against Turkey in a friendly in Ankara, and it proved to be a dream start as he scored the first Irish goal in a 3–3 draw three minutes into the match. He played for Ireland at Euro 88, and famously captained the side when they beat England 1–0 on 12 June in Stuttgart. He scored his record-making 20th international goal for Ireland in a friendly against Malta in Valletta on 2 June 1990 before the 1990 World Cup. The game also marked his 71st and last cap for his country. In May 1988, a testimonial was played in his honour in Dublin.

Moran was the next to go, as Ferguson continued his clearout. But the new man got an early idea of what the Irishman gave for the cause. On New Year's Day 1987, he almost lost his life in a United shirt. During a goalmouth scramble against Newcastle United, he got a smack in the face and when he hit his head on the rock-hard pitch he suffered concussion. Thankfully, United's physiotherapist, Jimmy McGregor, rushed on to the field and knew right away that the big Irishman was in trouble. He lay motionless on the ground for three or four minutes as McGregor saved him from swallowing his tongue. The hush inside Old Trafford burst into a roar and a rapturous round of applause when he got to his feet and walked off the pitch, assisted by the physio. True to form, Moran wanted to return to the game, but the club doctor refused him permission to do so.

After making 289 appearances for United, scoring 24 goals, the 32-year-old Moran left Old Trafford in August 1988 and moved to Sporting Gijón in Spain. United rewarded his service to the club by arranging a testimonial match for him against neighbours Manchester City on 21 August. A bumper crowd was expected at Old Trafford after George Best announced during an interview on television that he would make a sensational return to pay tribute to the defender. Sadly, he never made it, but 25,432 did come, and saw City beaten 5–2. After one hour's play, Moran left the game to a standing ovation.

After 18 months in Spain, Moran returned to England to sign for Second Division Blackburn Rovers in January 1990, where he once again lined up with Stapleton. He helped them to promotion to the Premier League for its inaugural season in 1992–93. Rovers had a successful season, finishing fourth, and the following campaign they finished runners-up to United. At the end of 1993–94, Moran hung up his boots.

Not surprisingly, he had a long and distinguished international career. He made his debut for the Republic of Ireland in 1980 and still remembers the occasion as if it were yesterday: 'I still look back with enormous pride when recalling my debut for my country. We played Switzerland on 30 April at Lansdowne Road in a friendly, which we won 2–0. I still get a tingling sensation in my spine today when I think about pulling on that famous green jersey of Ireland for the first time. A truly magical moment for me and one I will never forget.'

He was an integral part of the Jack Charlton squad that made the historic breakthrough, when Ireland qualified for the finals of a major tournament for the first time in their history, Euro '88 in West Germany. He was at the heart of the Irish defence against

England in their opening match in Stuttgart. In a monumental rearguard action, Moran played a major part in the historic 1–0 victory. He also played in the 1990 World Cup finals in Italy and, although he didn't play, he was also in the squad for the 1994 finals. He won his 71st and final cap on 24 May 1994 in a friendly against Bolivia at Lansdowne Road, and he scored six international goals.

He was never a dirty player and would more than often put his head where others dared not even place their boot. After he left United, Jimmy McGregor paid a fitting tribute to Moran's commitment in a United jersey saying: 'There can't be a player with more stitches in his face and head, unless they have been involved in a motorway smash. I have logged more than eighty stitches in my medical records and that is only over the last seven years.'

To this day, Moran is still a huge United fan and his affection for the club and its history is evident: 'If I could be transported back in time to play in a United team from any era, then I would set the date for 29 May 1968 when three Irishmen, Shay Brennan, Tony Dunne and George Best, helped Manchester United conquer Europe by winning the European Cup. Growing up in Dublin, I had heard all about George Best, while my brothers and I played the VHS tape of his days at United that many times we wore the video recorder out.

'When I arrived at Old Trafford in February 1978, George's name was still on the lips of many United fans, who clearly missed the mercurial genius. I remember my school going on a trip to Blackpool during the late 1960s and we were taken to Old Trafford to see Manchester United play. George did things with a football that day I had never seen any other player do before and I suppose today you could say that Lionel Messi is Best-like, because he causes havoc among defences every time he steps across the white line. I would have loved the opportunity to play in the same team, any team, that George Best played in.'

He also gave his thoughts on why United are so well supported in Ireland: 'I have been asked so many times by United fans all over the world why the club is so popular in my homeland. To be honest, I don't think it is possible to answer this question, as there are a myriad of reasons why the Irish are United fanatics. However, there is no doubt that the Great Famine of 1845–52, when so many Irish families moved to Manchester from all over Ireland, was the catalyst for the Irish support the team has enjoyed throughout its history. Without question the Munich Air Disaster of 6 February 1958 plays a significant role in the Irish's association with United, with Dublin's Billy Whelan one of the eight legendary Busby Babes who lost his life in the crash and of course the heroics of United's Northern Ireland international goalkeeper, Harry Gregg, who pulled survivors from the burning plane. And finally, perhaps two words more than any others will explain just why the Irish fell in love and remain fixated with Manchester United – George Best.'

McGrath and Whiteside stayed on at Old Trafford until the end of the 1988–89 season, though both were associated with the 'drinking culture' that surrounded the club, and indeed much of football at that time. The fact that both men were often battling with injury problems did not help matters, as they had time (and money) on their hands. But Ferguson was anxious to stamp out this approach and both men were transferred.

However, there is no question that Ferguson knew what he was losing when he allowed Whiteside to leave the club. He saw an example of his commitment on 24 January 1987, when he faced Arsenal for the first time as the manager of United, in a game that set the benchmark for subsequent ill-tempered meetings between the pair. Arsenal arrived at Old Trafford on the back of a 22-game unbeaten run, while United were in 13th position. Whiteside bossed the midfield as he constantly harassed the Arsenal players, who simply could not handle his aggression. Eventually, David Rocastle tried to hit back – all too literally and was sent off. United won the game 2–0 and after the game Ferguson said, 'Norman got away with about forty-five fouls in the game without even getting booked.'

When fit, Whiteside continued to have a big impact, often in the most crucial games. On 4 April 1988, United went to Anfield and fell 3–1 behind in their league encounter. Whiteside came on as a substitute to put a bit of grit and muscle into the United attack in what was already a very feisty game. The manager's plan worked wonders, as the Irishman caused fear and havoc among the Liverpool players, many of whom had the bruises to show for it, as he galvanised United's comeback to 3–3. One tackle on Steve McMahon nearly took his head off. Looking back on it, Whiteside smiled and said: 'I kicked lumps out of them.' Some of his tackles would warrant an instant red card today, but that day he got away with it.

Cathal Mullan from Derry remembers Whiteside's all-action style: 'I can recall seeing Norman playing in the third First Division game of the 1985–86 season. It was 24 August 1985, an away game versus Arsenal, which I attended with some mates while I was on student placement in London. The game had just literally kicked off when Norman threw himself into a tackle on Steve Williams, Arsenal's talented midfielder, which resulted in Williams being stretchered off with a broken toe. This was ten seconds into the game! The Arsenal players were not too happy and, as they considered themselves tough at the time, the incident set the scene for a pretty rough game. However, United had Paul McGrath, Mark Hughes, Frank Stapleton and Bryan Robson in their team, as well as young Norman, and so they knew how to handle themselves. But I do him a disservice by singling out this foul, because he was a great player, incredibly strong and brave, a great header of the ball, a great tackler and what he lacked in speed he most certainly made up for in skill and artistry. Norman also possessed great passing ability and a tremendous shot, scoring many fantastic goals over the years.'

A knee injury in 1987–88 saw him miss 15 league games, as United recovered their league form to finish second behind

Liverpool, and towards the end of the season Whiteside handed in a transfer request, but he stayed at the club for another year. His knee problem returned in 1988–89 and, coupled with an Achilles injury and a hamstring injury, he was restricted to just six games, the last of which came at the Dell on 6 May in a 2–1 defeat. When Ferguson bought midfielders Neil Webb and Mike Phelan in the summer of 1989, Whiteside joined Everton in a £650,000 transfer. He had played 274 times for United, scoring 67 goals, and was undoubtedly one of the most popular Irish stars ever to play for the Reds.

In his first season with Everton, 1989–90, he played in 35 games and scored 13 goals, but his knee injury returned the following season limiting him to just two outings. After 13 knee operations during his eventful career, Whiteside was forced to retire at just 26. Unsurprisingly, having to quit so young hit him hard. He recalled in an interview with *Players' Club* magazine how he tried to reinvent himself: 'You mope around for a couple of weeks, there are tears, and you try to consider what you're going to do. But I knew that I couldn't carry on. I just thought I've got to do something about this. Through school and university I made a second career for myself at the age of thirty-two. I wouldn't say it was more pleasing than scoring the winning goal in a cup final, or captaining your club and country, but I took a huge amount of satisfaction from doing something I never thought I was capable of.'

In October 1991, Whiteside was appointed assistant manager to Sammy McIlroy at Northwich Victoria, but left the club before the season had ended to concentrate solely on his new career as a physiotherapist, after graduating as a podiatrist from Salford University.

He explained to *Players' Club*: 'I had that many injuries during my career that I got very friendly with Jim McGregor. I was in the medical room so often that I started to ask him about his job, and he would give me the names of muscles to go home and learn. I'd come in the next day and say "the rectus femoris", that's the big muscle in your thigh. From that stage I started to get interested in the anatomy, and Jim began explaining about physio techniques, such as dealing with ankle injuries. After I retired, I wanted to be a physio from the beginning, but I didn't have the qualifications. However, I went on day release to Salford University and had a look at their podiatry course. I was really taken by it and decided to apply.'

As we have seen, Whiteside's international career got off to the most spectacular start in the 1982 World Cup finals. He went on to score his first goal for his country on 21 September 1983 against Austria in a 3–1 win at Windsor Park in a European Championship qualifier. He won 38 caps in all, the last of which was in a 3–0 defeat to the Republic of Ireland at Lansdowne Road on 11 October 1989 in an Italia 90 qualifying game, and he scored nine goals for his country.

Today, Whiteside is a popular after-dinner speaker and can very often be seen on a match day at Old Trafford giving guided tours of the stadium and entertaining fans in the executive suites.

Having been a regular in season 1986–87, McGrath's career at Old Trafford also went on a downward spiral. Drinking sprees, coupled with chronic knee injuries, took their toll on his body and severely restricted his ability to train and therefore he played fewer games. During his last two seasons at United he played in 42 league games and scored three goals. In August 1989, Ferguson allowed him to leave United after making 199 appearances for the club, scoring 16 goals. He joined Aston Villa in a £425,000 transfer. Many sports writers at the time wondered why the Villa manager, Graham Taylor, would pay so much money for a player who was just weeks away from his 30th birthday, had dodgy knees, was injury prone, could hardly train and, according to reports, brought some social baggage with him. But he went on to play some of the best football of his career in his seven years in Birmingham.

In his award-winning book, *Back From the Brink*, McGrath said that he found the move to Aston Villa a very traumatic one and he even attempted suicide. Taylor gave him all the support he needed and, after he recovered, he was determined to repay the faith Taylor had shown in him, helping them to the runners-up spot. Three years later, and now managed by his former boss at United, Ron Atkinson, Villa were again runners-up in 1992–93, and McGrath was voted the PFA Player of the Year. A year later, he helped Villa defeat United in the League Cup final. In the summer of 1996 he left the club, where he remains a hero to the fans. He played 252 times for Aston Villa, scoring nine goals. Following brief spells with Derby County (24 games in 1996–97) and Sheffield United (11 games in 1997–98), he retired from the game aged 38, with eight knee operations behind him.

Colm Devine gives a fan's assessment of the man: 'Paul McGrath was an excellent player and was naturally gifted. He was a fantastic reader of the game. His knees were giving him so much trouble that he did not train during the week after Tuesday. He was still an automatic choice on Saturday, because of the way he could read the game. He didn't have to chase around, because he could position himself where he was most effective and command all around him. A truly great player, he was loved by all United fans.'

But while his exploits for United and Villa won him high praise, it was perhaps in the green shirt of Ireland that he earned the biggest plaudits. He won his first cap for the Republic on 5 February 1985, coming on as a substitute for Mark Lawrenson in a friendly against Italy in Dublin. At that stage, he was in competition with Lawrenson, Mick McCarthy, David O'Leary and his United team-mate Kevin Moran for one of the two centre-half spots in the team. However, he became an established figure in the Irish side after Jack Charlton took charge of the national team in March 1986, as he recognised that he could be as valuable in the Irish midfield as he was in their back four.

The vast majority of Irish fans cite McGrath's two magnificent performances against Italy as his best. In the first of these, Ireland faced the host nation in Rome in the quarter-finals of the 1990

World Cup finals. The Italians were short-priced favourites to beat Ireland, but McGrath was the star in Ireland's narrow 1–0 loss. Four years later in the USA, McGrath helped his country to an unlikely 1–0 revenge win over Italy in New York when he formed an impenetrable barrier in front of the goal. He played his last game for his country in a 0–0 draw against Wales on 11 February 1997 in Cardiff. In total, he won 83 caps and scored eight international goals.

With the departure of four such influential Irishmen in quick succession, the United line-up was suddenly no longer so reliant on those who had come across the Irish Sea to play at Old Trafford, but all that would change again, and within a short period of time would arrive a man who grew up in the northern suburbs of Cork who would stand comparison with just about any other who had made that journey from Ireland to play for United.

Chapter 11

In Pursuit of the Title

When Alex Ferguson arrived at Old Trafford in November 1986, he soon realised that United was a club that needed to be changed from top to bottom. As we have seen, many of the squad – including all four established Irish stars – were moved on over the first few seasons he was in charge.

However, he also inherited two recent recruits, bought in Ron Atkinson's final year at United. William Francis 'Liam' O'Brien was one of them. Born in Dublin on 5 September 1964, like so many before him he began his football career with Stella Maris in Drumcondra. In 1982 he signed for Bohemians and, having made just five league appearances, he then moved to Shamrock Rovers in September 1983.

In his first season with the Hoops, he won the League of Ireland Championship and then clinched the Irish league and cup Double in 1984–85, followed by another Double the next year. After so much success, it was no surprise that he attracted the attention of some English clubs, and eventually Atkinson signed him in a £50,000 transfer in October 1986 – it was to be his last transfer deal at the club. United also agreed to play two friendlies against the Hoops as part of the deal, the first of which took place on 18 March 1987.

Within weeks of Ferguson taking charge, O'Brien was given his United debut. He played against Leicester City on 20 December 1986 in a 2–0 home league win. In his fourth game, on 3 January 1987, he was in action against Southampton at the Dell, but it all went horribly wrong for him. After just 85 seconds, he went into a tackle with Mark Dennis which left the home full-back lying in agony on the pitch, and was immediately shown the red card. When interviewed after the game, O'Brien was almost in tears when he told reporters: 'I have never deliberately kicked anyone in my life.' His red card remains the fastest-ever sending-off of a United player, and some while after it he remarked: 'I still think it was harsh. It was the first tackle of the game. I was devastated, as it was the first live game shown in Ireland and all my family and friends were watching it.' Despite that, he made a total of 11 appearances in his first campaign at United.

One thing that hadn't changed under Ferguson was the regular trips to Ireland for pre-season friendlies. A visit to Belfast on 10 August 1987 to take on an Irish League XI drew a crowd of 10,000, but they saw a rather dull 0–0 draw. O'Brien was a part of that match, and during the 1987–88 campaign that followed, the elegant midfielder made a respectable 21 appearances, but 15 of them were from the bench, though he did score two goals in that time.

Frustrated at not being able to command a regular place in the side, O'Brien joined Newcastle United for £275,000 in November 1988. He had played just 36 games for United, 19 of them coming off the bench, scoring twice. The Magpies were relegated at the end of that season, but he then helped them back into the top flight at the end of the 1992–93 season. However, in January 1994 he signed for Tranmere Rovers after enjoying a successful loan period with them. In the summer of 1999, he moved back to Ireland and played for Cork City for one season before returning to play for Bohemians. He helped guide them to the Double in 2000–01. After he retired at the end of the 2001–02 season, he then went on to serve as the assistant manager at Bohemians and Shamrock Rovers.

O'Brien won 16 caps for the Republic of Ireland (six of them while at United), his first coming on 23 April 1986 in a friendly against Uruguay at Lansdowne Road. The game ended in a 1–1 draw, and also marked the end of Gerry Daly's international career. Only two of his games for his country were in a competitive fixture. He played his last international on 9 October 1996 in a home tie against Macedonia in a World Cup qualifier. He never scored for Ireland.

Derek Michael Brazil was another Irish recruit who struggled to make an impact at United. Born on 14 December 1968 in the Finglas area of Dublin, he played his early football at St Kevin's Boys National School and then at Finglas Patrician College. Although keen on Gaelic football, he followed in the steps of his father, also named Derek, who played for Shamrock Rovers. Initially a striker, he was converted to a centre-half, and by the age of 17 he had trials with various clubs, including United.

In March 1986, Atkinson beat several other clubs to Brazil's signature and brought him to Old Trafford. He arrived at Old Trafford when McGrath and Moran had United's centre-half partnership sewn up. When Ferguson bought Steve Bruce from Norwich City in December 1987, Brazil's chances of a first-team place looked even slimmer. However, at the end of the 1988–89 season, on 10 May, he made his debut in a 2–1 First Division loss to Everton at Old Trafford, coming on as a substitute for Clayton Blackmore. When Gary Pallister joined United during the summer, his chances of making the side became even more remote. He did, however, play his second and last game for United on 10 February 1990 in a 2–1 Division One away win over Millwall. While at United, he had loan periods at Oldham Athletic and Swansea City.

In August 1992 Cardiff City made a bid of £85,000 for the young Irishman after he impressed there during a two-week trial. He spent four years at Ninian Park and later played for Newport County before moving on to Welsh Premier League sides Inter

Cardiff and the New Bridge Meadow Bluebirds, ending his playing career with the latter. In October 2006, he was appointed team manager of Haverfordwest County but was dismissed in November 2010, only to be re-appointed three months later. He also runs his own business teaching physical education and coaching football in and around the Cardiff area. He was never capped at full international level by his country.

Unlike O'Brien and Brazil, Ferguson's first Irish signing did become a regular starter for United, but his route to Old Trafford was a very long one. Malachy Martin 'Mal' Donaghy was born in Belfast on 13 September 1957 and was a United fan from an early age. He began his football career with his local team, St Agnes in the Down and Connor League in the city, and with the Post Office Social Club's works team (he worked there as a clerk), before joining amateur side Cromac Albion in 1976–77. He also represented County Antrim in Gaelic football. He then joined Larne and spent just one season with the club, before Luton Town manager David Pleat snapped him up for a fee of £20,000 in June 1978.

Donaghy spent ten happy years with the Hatters, which coincided with the most successful period in the club's history. In season 1981–82, he helped them clinch the Second Division title and with it promotion to the top flight of the English game. Luton finished in a record high seventh place in Division One in 1986–87, and the following season Pleat's team caused a huge upset by defeating Arsenal 3–2 in the League Cup final to claim the club's first and only major success. In six of the ten seasons he was with Luton, he did not miss a game, and averaged 41 league games per season in his time there, a truly remarkable level of consistency.

In October 1988, Donaghy left Kenilworth Road having made a staggering 415 league appearances for the club, scoring 16 goals, and moved to Old Trafford in a £650,000 deal, with other clubs eyeing up the reliable defender. He later said that: 'I would have only left Luton for one other team, and that team was Manchester

United.' He was 31 at the time, but Ferguson had the utmost confidence in his ability to do a good job in the United back four. The manager liked the fact that Donaghy could play at centre-half or at full-back with equal ease, and saw him as the ideal replacement for the recently departed Kevin Moran.

On 30 October, Donaghy made his United debut alongside Steve Bruce at centre-half in a 1–1 away draw with Everton in the First Division. The match was the first to be shown live by ITV, following one of the biggest changes in the history of English football on television when the broadcaster gained exclusive rights to show Football League matches, both in live and highlights form. After making his debut, he never missed a single league game for the rest of the season, when United ended up in a modest 11th place.

By now Ferguson was making radical changes to his team, and the summer of 1989 saw him spend millions to bring in Mike Phelan, Neil Webb, Gary Pallister, Paul Ince and Danny Wallace. It remains arguably the biggest overhaul he has made in his time at United, but the results of the changes were not immediately apparent. In fact, in the league United slipped back to 13th, leaving many fans disappointed at the rate of progress and there was a great deal of media pressure on the manager's position. But in the Old Trafford boardroom, there was confidence in the Scot and an appreciation of the work he was doing to bring the club up to the best standards.

With Pallister and Bruce in tandem in the centre, Donaghy was moved to left-back for 1989–90, and he made only 16 appearances in all competitions, partly due to injury, but he also had a brief spell back at Luton, on loan. But there was some compensation, in terms of another FA Cup run. Donaghy played only in the fourth round FA Cup tie at Hereford United, which the Reds won 1–0, as young Lee Martin was the regular pick in the left-back position. After a hard-fought semi-final against Oldham Athletic, when the Latics' adventurous Irish full-back Denis Irwin caught the eye, United took on Crystal Palace in the final. For the first time since 1909, United took to the field for a final without an Irishman in their side. After a 3–3 draw, United won the replay 1–0, with Martin scoring the winner.

The next season things improved for United, as they finished sixth in the table, and for Donaghy, who made 38 appearances in all competitions, albeit often coming from the bench. He also picked up his first winners' medal with United as an unused substitute in the European Cup-Winners' Cup final in Rotterdam on 15 May 1991, when United beat Barcelona 2–1 with two goals from Mark Hughes.

On 19 November 1991, he was once more a non-playing substitute in United's 1–0 European Super Cup win over Red Star Belgrade at Old Trafford, but made just 26 appearances during the 1991–92 season, the last of which was a 3–1 win over Tottenham Hotspur on 2 May. That was not only his final appearance in United's colours, but also the last league game before the famous Stretford End was knocked down and subsequently converted into a new all-seater West Stand. Not content with the odd game here and there, in August 1992 Donaghy left Old Trafford to join Chelsea in a £100,000 transfer deal. He never managed to score a goal for United in 119 games.

With Donaghy's departure, it meant that for the first time in more than four decades, since Jackie Blanchflower's arrival in 1951, United did not have a single professional footballer from Northern Ireland on their books until Keith Gillespie signed professional terms with the club in January 1993.

The 35-year-old Irish international helped Ian Porterfield's Chelsea side finish in 11th place in the inaugural Premier League season in 1992–93. The following campaign Donaghy missed out on a place in Glenn Hoddle's Chelsea squad that faced United in the 1994 FA Cup final. In the summer of 1994, after making 68 league appearances for the club, he decided to retire and returned to Northern Ireland where he accepted the position of manager of Newry Town. Donaghy later worked as the assistant manager of Cliftonville in Belfast. In 2000, he was appointed to his present position as the coach of the Northern Ireland Under-19 side.

Donaghy won the first of his 91 caps for Northern Ireland on 16 May 1980 in a 1–0 Home International win over Scotland at Windsor Park. He played for the Irish at the 1982 and 1986 World Cup finals, and made his final appearance for his country in a 3–0 friendly defeat to Mexico in Miami, USA, on 11 June 1994. He is Northern Ireland's most-capped outfield player, but as with United, he never scored for his country.

Jim Hetherington has fond memories of Donaghy: 'Mal grew up just two streets away from me in Andersonstown, West Belfast. He went to La Salle Secondary School and all of the kids in our area always had a great sense of pride in the fact he lived so close. And when he joined United, well that was him raised up to automatic superhero status. I remember on one occasion he came back to our school to present trophies to our football team, and afterwards we all went to the gymnasium for a cup of tea and a chat. Today, Mal spends a lot of time back in the area coaching kids and you can still find him playing snooker with his brother Joe, who was an excellent Gaelic footballer. Mal was a fairly tough player who always gave one hundred per cent when he played for United and Northern Ireland, and he represented our wee country with immense pride.'

John Dempsey grew up in West Belfast and began to follow United closely after the 1968 European Cup final, a decision that was reinforced soon after when he was working at a petrol station and 'a very large limousine pulled in and who was sitting in the back but George Best himself, along with some other Northern Ireland players. I couldn't sleep for a week afterwards.' Despite seeing United play at the Dell on several occasions when he was living in Southampton, he had never been to Old Trafford to watch the Reds in action until 1991, soon after the foundation of the Carryduff MUSC: 'I had the chance to go along to Old Trafford for my first ever United home game against Norwich City on 7 September 1991. There were twenty-three of us on a small coach travelling overnight for a two-night stay, all travel and match ticket for £67. Our seats were in the North Stand Lower. It was fantastic and we won 3–0, with goals from Denis Irwin, Brian McClair and a young kid the media were describing as the new George Best, Ryan Giggs. I couldn't wait to get back there again.'

Dempsey recalls the impact that the arrival of satellite TV had on the ability of people in Northern Ireland to have a much closer link to the games United played, when he was unable to get to the matches himself. He would often join other members of the Carryduff MUSC to watch games in their living rooms and to share in the drama of it all. But it was better to be watching in person: 'Usually four of us, sometimes five, would jump in the car on a Saturday morning and get the 8.00am sailing from Larne to Cairnryan and race down the A75, M6, M61 and M62 and arrive in Manchester just before the kick-off. Those were the days when most games kicked off at three o'clock on a Saturday. It was in our blood to be there. I can remember us deciding late on the Friday night before our home First Division game against Nottingham Forest that we would catch the early ferry on the morning of Saturday 20 April 1992 and go to the game. And we didn't even have tickets for the match!

'Fortunately, we were able to get some tickets. The Forest match was a vital game for us, as we were neck and neck with Leeds United in the race to win the First Division title. We longed for United to bring an end to our twenty-five-year wait for the title and unbelievably it was an Irishman who spoiled our day. His name was Roy Maurice Keane and he ran the show that day as the visitors won 2–1 with him scoring. I am also convinced that it was the day that Fergie decided he had to buy Keano, which thankfully he did just over a year later.'

Ed O'Riordan from Tipperary is clear about just how big an impact United has in Ireland, partly because of his young son, Vincent: 'It's interesting that Vincent became a fan without ever hearing anything about football in his home. He must have developed the interest in school with his young schoolmates. He would kick a ball around the garden with me as he grew up, and he was always Beckham or Giggs or Cantona. I once heard it recounted that when a student of sociology conducted a survey among primary school children in County Kerry some twenty years ago, he discovered that in a year when Kerry won the All Ireland Gaelic Football final, the children were better able to name the players on the Manchester United team than they were the Kerry team. Kerry is the stronghold of Gaelic football and that survey result was astounding. Manchester United must be doing something right.'

Vicky Fisher from the Castlereagh area of East Belfast explains one reason why the pupils at schools in Ireland grew so close to United: 'My earliest childhood memory of Manchester United was a trip I took to Old Trafford back in 1990 when I was in primary school. We took a tour around the ground and visited the museum. I remember the buzz I felt once I entered the Theatre of Dreams, walking up the steps and seeing the pitch for the first time just took my breath away. Another amazing memory I have was when George Best came to my high school [Lisnasharragh] and he talked about the goals he scored for Manchester United and how he started off playing football in my school when he was just a boy himself. I was thirteen years old at the time. What made this visit even more special for me was that I was picked to make him tea and give him a guided tour around the school.'

With interest in United rising rapidly in Ireland at this time, the club recruited another hero from that country during the summer of 1990. Denis Joseph Irwin was born in Cork on 31 October 1965 and played a lot of Gaelic football and hurling during his schooldays at Coláiste Chríost Rí (CCRí), on Capwell Road on the south side of Cork. However, Irwin was also an excellent footballer and was capped at schoolboy level by his country. It came as no surprise to his family and friends when he left Turners Cross College football team and crossed the Irish Sea to join Leeds United as an apprentice in March

1982. But it wasn't until January 1984 that he made his debut for the Elland Road club. He went on to make 72 league appearances for Leeds, scoring one goal, but in May 1986, he was placed on the transfer list and was on the verge of moving to Chesterfield. However, the Oldham Athletic manager, ex-Everton striker Joe Royle, moved in for him immediately, picking him up on a free transfer – a superb deal. Irwin later commented: 'When Leeds let me go, I was devastated. I was only a youngster and I felt like I'd run into a dead end. I'm sure that if I'd not been picked up by Oldham I'd have been tempted to go home to Ireland.'

Irwin spent four highly enjoyable and successful seasons with the Boundary Park club and quickly established himself as the best full-back outside the First Division. He was a vital member of Royle's team, who lost the 1990 League Cup final to Nottingham Forest and gave United a scare in the semi-final of the 1990 FA Cup, which they took to a replay. Irwin's performances in both semi-finals were firmly embedded in Ferguson's mind. He was calmness personified when placed under pressure and rarely made a mistake in the Latics' defence. A solid performer who was hard but fair in the tackle, he was a player of immaculate timing, excellent distribution and he posed an attacking threat from his full-back berth.

After the season was over, on 8 June 1990, Ferguson persuaded Royle to sell Irwin in a £625,000 transfer deal. 'When I heard United were interested in me, I didn't even want to talk to anyone else,' said Irwin at the time of his move. However, as Ferguson explained to Royle, it wasn't just those performances in the semi-final that had swayed him: he had had Irwin watched more than 20 times by his team of scouts and advisers, and he never once received a negative report.

Sir Alex recalls that time when he was checking up on the full-back: 'I liked the fact that he was versatile. Denis was a two-footed player and I had tinkered with a few players at left-back, including Lee Martin, Clayton Blackmore and I even played

Lee Sharpe in the left-back position. We did not sign Denis on the back of his two fine performances against us for Oldham Athletic in the 1990 FA Cup semi-final, we had him watched all that 1989–90 season. I can remember going to see Denis play in all of Oldham's games that took them to the 1990 League Cup final. Denis had been on our radar for a long time. In fact, I can recall one Saturday afternoon, St Patrick's Day 1990, going to Barnsley to watch Denis as we had Liverpool at home the following day.'

It was appropriate that Irwin's first appearance in a United shirt should take place at Musgrave Park, as the Reds took on Cork City in a pre-season friendly on 3 August. A crowd of 10,000 saw a rather dull 0–0 draw. United continued their tour of Ireland by playing against Waterford United, Derry City, an Irish League XI and Bohemians. Such was the draw of United at the latter game, that kick-off at Dalymount Park had to be delayed by 15 minutes to allow the huge crowd of 20,000 to get inside the ground. While United's team no longer had such a large Irish component, the club's support continued to be strong. What was about to happen over the next few years would only reinforce that. And the new full-back would play a vital role in it all.

Irwin made his United debut at right-back on 18 August 1990 in the Charity Shield against Liverpool, which ended 1–1. He played in 34 of United's 42 league games in his first season at Old Trafford and, unlike fellow Irish full-back Donaghy, was selected for the League Cup final on 21 April, which United lost 1–0 to Sheffield Wednesday. A few weeks later, on 15 May, he won the first of many medals with United when they beat Barcelona 2–1 to claim the European Cup-Winners' Cup.

If anyone still doubted the closeness of the ties between United and Ireland, the testimonial game for Sir Matt Busby played on 11 August 1991 in front of a crowd of 33,410 surely proved the point. For the opponents chosen to take on United by Busby were not a Scottish side, or one of United's major domestic or European rivals, but the Republic of Ireland. The game ended in a 1–1 draw.

Donaghy played for United, while Irwin and Moran played for the Irish. It was confirmation, if any was needed, that the links were unbreakable.

With the improvement in United's league position, and the cup success of the previous two campaigns, the feeling was that the Reds were in a strong position to make a challenge for the title in 1991–92. The defence was further reinforced in August 1991, when Ferguson paid £1.7 million for the Queens Park Rangers and England right-back Paul Parker, which meant that Irwin switched to left-back, and proved to be an inspired move for both manager and player. There was a new goalkeeper as well, with Peter Schmeichel joining the club.

In season 1991–92, Irwin made 38 league appearances for United and scored four goals; his first for the club coming in the home game against Norwich City on 7 September in a 3–0 win. That game was the first trip to Old Trafford that I organised for the Carryduff MUSC, following our affiliation to United that July, and since then I have organised more than 350 trips to Old Trafford for our members.

The hopes that United would be contenders for the big prize of the league title proved to be justified, as they led the title race for large parts of the season. On 19 November 1991, Irwin was in the side that won the European Super Cup, beating Red Star Belgrade 1–0 at Old Trafford. On 12 April, United finally won the League Cup for the first time in their history when they beat Nottingham Forest 1–0 in the final at Wembley. Lining up against Irwin that day was a fellow Cork man, Roy Keane.

That season at left-back, Irwin would regularly feed Ryan Giggs or Lee Sharpe on the wing, as they formed a formidable left flank for the Reds. The fans loved his swashbuckling style as he was capable of turning defence into attack, robbing an opposing winger of the ball and then racing off up the line to start an attack at the opposite end of the pitch. Sadly, however, his efforts weren't quite enough, as the league title eluded United again, and they finished second, four points adrift of champions Leeds United – it was the fourth time since their last league title back in 1967 that they had just missed out on the prize by one place.

I was one of the 30,069 fans inside Lansdowne Road on 9 August 1992 when I travelled down to Dublin to see the pre-season game against a Republic of Ireland XI. A couple of us had made a banner out of one of my wife's bed sheets to welcome the arrival of our new striker, who we hoped would give United the extra impetus up-front finally to bring home that league title. It read: 'Welcome To Dublin Dion'.

But it wasn't to be Dublin who made the difference, as he picked up a serious injury early in the campaign, and so encouraged Ferguson to go back into the transfer market where he signed up Eric Cantona. He was the final piece in the jigsaw of a side that was bursting with talent and brimming in confidence, helped by a very settled defence. Between them Irwin, Bruce, Pallister and Schmeichel missed just two league games all campaign, though Parker was out for a few more matches. Irwin was a key player in the United team that clinched the inaugural Premier League title in season 1992–93 to end the club's 26-year wait to be crowned champions of England. He even weighed in with five goals, becoming the second man to score a Premier League goal for United when he hit home in their 1–1 draw against Ipswich on 22 August.

A few days after winning the title, United were in Belfast to give the club's Irish supporters a chance to share in the celebrations. A crowd of 20,000 poured into Windsor Park that lovely sunny May evening to see United take on Aston Villa. It didn't matter that the only Irish player on display for United was Cork-born Brian Carey. He had been signed from Cork City on 24 August 1989, but he never made a competitive appearance for United and six months after his Belfast outing he was sold to Leicester City.

At the beginning of that 1992–93 season, United had been in Northern Ireland for a very different reason: to sign up Patrick

Colm 'Pat' McGibbon. He was born in Lurgan, County Armagh, on 6 September 1973 and won schoolboy honours with Northern Ireland. He began his senior career at Portadown in 1991, but had hardly had a chance to make an impact at the club when he left Shamrock Park and signed for United for a fee of £100,000.

Following a number of impressive games at centre-half in United's Central League side, Ferguson decided to try out McGibbon in a League Cup second round tie on 20 September 1995 against York City. It was an inauspicious start, as he rushed into a late challenge in his own box, culminating not only in the referee awarding the visitors a penalty, but also showing the debutant the red card. United went on to lose the game 3–0. It proved to be McGibbon's first and last game for United.

In September 1996, McGibbon went to Swansea City on loan, as Bruce and Pallister occupied the centre-half positions in the team, with David May in reserve. An injury and then a double hernia operation sidelined the young Irishman for a lengthy spell, so he played only one game for the Welsh side. In March 1997, he joined Wigan Athletic on loan and played ten times for the Latics, helping them to promotion to Division Two.

Wigan Athletic then signed him for £250,000 during the summer, with the fee later rising to £380,000 as he made over 150 appearances for the club and scored 11 goals. In 2002, he had brief loan spells with Scunthorpe United and Tranmere Rovers, but soon moved back to his first club, Portadown. After two seasons there, he moved to Glentoran in the summer of 2004 and ended his career there in March 2006. Although qualified as a physiotherapist, he got his UEFA coaching badges and became player-manager at Lurgan Celtic from 2006 until January 2009. He was then appointed assistant-manager at Monaghan United and in February 2011 he took charge of Newry City.

McGibbon made his debut as a substitute for Northern Ireland on 22 May 1995 in a 2–0 away defeat to Canada. It was the first of seven caps for his country, the last of which came on 23 February 2000, again as a substitute, in a friendly 3–1 win away to Luxembourg.

It is fair to say that the next Irish recruit signed by United made a far greater impact on the club than McGibbon was ever able to do. Roy Maurice Keane was born in Mayfield, Cork, on 10 August 1971. He came from a working-class background and his family were all interested in sport. As a boy, he was a fan of Celtic and Tottenham Hotspur, with Liam Brady and Glenn Hoddle as his favourite players, and then later United's Bryan Robson. Although he boxed and played Gaelic football, it was soccer that soon dominated his life, beginning when he played for Rockmount's Under-11 team. He almost gave up football completely at 14 when he was turned down following a trial with the Republic of Ireland Schoolboys in Dublin, as he was deemed to be too small. Unsurprisingly, when he recovered from the disappointment, he decided to prove them wrong. He got no further with English clubs, either, though he wrote to almost all of them asking for a trial. Keane then took up temporary jobs involving manual work while waiting for the one chance that would be his stepping stone to a career in professional football.

In 1989, he joined the semi-professional League of Ireland club Cobh Ramblers, thanks to the persistence of their youth team manager, Eddie O'Rourke. By 16 he was playing for the Ramblers' senior side, as well as their youth team, and would often play two games at the weekend. This was where Keane learned to look after himself on a football pitch, as it was an uncompromising league where no prisoners were taken and hard tackles were the norm. It was not a place for shrinking violets. But then no one ever said Roy Keane was a shrinking violet.

In February 1990, Keane was approached by Noel McCabe, Nottingham Forest's scout in Ireland, who invited him over to England for a trial with Brian Clough's side. He did well and on

12 June a deal worth £10,000 was struck with Cobh Ramblers for their 18-year-old star.

Keane found it very difficult to settle in Nottingham and was often homesick. However, just as Busby had done with Best, so too did Clough with Keane, allowing the young Irishman to make regular visits home to spend time with his family. Clough, not always renowned for his caring side, did this even though it interfered with Keane's training routine. But Clough was an astute judge of talent and he knew that in Roy Keane he had a rare football gem and he did not want to lose him. He played his first games for Forest in the Under-21s team during a 1990–91 pre-season tournament in the Netherlands, and did so well that Clough believed he was ready for first team action. Clough didn't play him in the first game of the season, a home tie against Queens Park Rangers, but waited a few days until the second fixture – at Anfield against champions Liverpool. Clough knew his man would not wilt in the toughest game of the season, and on Tuesday 28 August, he remained unflustered throughout and more than held his own, despite Forest losing 2–0.

Keane played 35 league games that first season for Forest (scoring eight goals), and even displaced the England international Steve Hodge from the side. He also scored three goals during Forest's run to the 1991 FA Cup final, but he could not prevent Tottenham Hotspur from winning 2–1. The cup run wasn't entirely smooth, however: a mistake by Keane in their third round tie resulted in a punch in the face from Clough.

A year later, Keane and Forest were back at Wembley, this time for the 1992 League Cup final, but again they lost out, this time to United. The following season, 1992–93, was not only Clough's last at the club, but also Keane's, as Forest were relegated. The battle to sign up the 21-year-old midfielder was fought out between United and Blackburn Rovers, who would contest the Premier League title between themselves for the next two years. In the end, Keane signed for Manchester United for a transfer fee of £3.75 million on 19 July 1993, a British record at the time. Keane had played 154 matches for Forest and scored 33 goals in his three years at the City Ground. Ferguson was ecstatic about capturing Keane, for he had been a huge admirer of the Irishman for a while and had been impressed by his obvious lack of respect for reputations. The first time he had played against United, he went in for a tackle with Bryan Robson and unceremoniously upended his opponent. It was the sort of spirit he needed if his side were going to become not just the best side in England, but the best in Europe.

Keane made his United debut on 7 August 1993 in the Charity Shield against Arsenal at Wembley. The game ended 1–1 after extra-time and was decided by a penalty shootout, with Keane scoring in United's 5–4 victory. In his first season with United he played in 54 games (including four as a substitute) and scored eight goals.

If the 1992–93 season had been a huge relief for United fans everywhere, then the following campaign was one of enormous enjoyment, as the Reds came very close to winning all three domestic trophies. In the League Cup, they reached the final, but lost 3–1 to Aston Villa. The Premier League was secured with an eight-point margin over Blackburn Rovers, and Irwin was the solitary ever-present player during United's league campaign. In a season when United played 63 games, Irwin missed just one of them, though one of his appearances was as a substitute. Along with Steve Bruce he set a new record for most appearances in a season for United of 62 games in 1993–94. In today's era of squad rotation, it is a record that looks likely to remain unbroken for many years. With Irwin and Keane having won their Premier League title medals, they both lined up for United against Chelsea on 14 May in the FA Cup final, where a 4–0 victory secured the club's first ever Double of league and cup titles.

As usual, United warmed up for the season ahead with a trip to Ireland, taking on Dundalk (who were beaten 4–2) and Shelbourne (beaten 3–0), but by the start of the 1994–95 campaign, Irwin's and Keane's were not the only Irish voices regularly to be heard in the dressing room. Now there was a young, skinny, dark-haired winger from Northern Ireland, who seemed ready to make a breakthrough into the team and who was attracting inevitable comparisons with a certain George Best.

Keith Robert Gillespie was born on 18 February 1975 in Larne, County Antrim. He attended Whitehead Primary School and later went to Bangor Grammar School. Spotted by United scout Eddie Coulter when he was playing for St Andrews in Belfast, he signed for United as a trainee when he left school in July 1991. In his first season at Old Trafford, Gillespie helped United win the Youth Cup, defeating Crystal Palace in the final. That side was packed with so much talent, among them Ryan Giggs, David Beckham and Gary Neville, that they attracted big crowds whenever they played. It was the first time they had won the trophy since 1964, when Best had played.

Coulter, from Lisburn, was one of United's leading scouts in Northern Ireland and was also responsible for sending David Healy, Darron Gibson and Jonny Evans to Old Trafford. Sadly, he passed away on 3 September 2011, aged 70, with Evans among the mourners who attended his funeral.

On 5 January 1993, Gillespie made his United debut in the third round of the FA Cup against Bury, and he helped United to a 2–0 win at Old Trafford. He set up United's first goal in the seventh minute, when he crossed for Mike Phelan to score his first senior goal for the club since joining them from Norwich City in July 1989. He then went on to score United's second goal himself – it was a spectacular start, and it earned him a substitute appearance in the next round.

At the start of the 1993–94 season, Premier League teams adopted the squad number system and Gillespie was allocated the No. 31 shirt. With Giggs, Lee Sharpe and Andrei Kanchelskis in scintillating form for United, it proved impossible for Gillespie to break into the first team and so he was loaned out in September 1993 to Wigan Athletic, who were playing in Division Three at the time. Gillespie played eight games for the Latics, scoring four goals. When his loan spell ended he returned to Old Trafford, and in 1994–95 made 12 appearances (half of them from the bench), but he remained on the periphery of the first team.

On 10 January 1995, he was transferred to Newcastle United as part of the transfer deal (valued at £7 million) that saw Andy Cole move to Old Trafford. The Toon Army were devastated to see Cole leave them, but Magpies manager Kevin Keegan had seen Gillespie score one of United's goals in a 2–0 win over his side at Old Trafford on 29 October 1994 and believed the young winger had enormous potential.

Indeed, when Kanchelskis was sold by United later that year, newspaper reports linked Gillespie with a return to Old Trafford to fill the void on the right wing left by the flying Ukrainian. However, Gillespie remained on Tyneside and Beckham began to occupy that flank instead. He stayed at St James' Park for three and a half years and played 143 games for the club, scoring 13 times. In the summer of 1998, he was signed by Blackburn Rovers in a £2.3 million transfer and stayed at Ewood Park for five seasons, helping them to win the League Cup in 2002. Thereafter, he played for Leicester City 2003–05, Sheffield United 2005–09, Charlton Athletic on loan in 2008, Bradford City 2009, Glentoran 2009–10, Darlington 2010 and on 24 March 2011 he joined Longford Town in the League of Ireland First Division.

Gillespie made his international debut for Northern Ireland on 7 September 1994 in a 2–1 loss to Portugal at Windsor Park in a Euro 96 qualifier. He scored his first international goal in his second appearance for the Irish a few weeks later, a 2–1 away win over Austria on 12 October. In total he won 86 caps for his country and scored just two goals. Only Pat Jennings, Mal Donaghy and Sammy McIlroy have made more appearances. But although his career was in so many ways a successful one, he has admitted to gambling too much from an early age, and how this has caused him enormous financial problems.

While 1994–95 saw the end of Gillespie's career at United, Irwin and Keane were regulars in the side. But the campaign was to end in frustration, as the Reds lost their title by one point to Blackburn Rovers, and were then beaten 1–0 by Everton in the FA Cup final. Matters had not been helped by the controversy surrounding Cantona's 'kung-fu' kick on a fan at Selhurst Park on 25 January, which resulted in a long ban.

Ferguson's response to the disappointment took many by surprise: Hughes, Ince and Kanchelskis were all sold, and he sent out a team of 'kids' at the start of the 1995–96 season, who were duly outplayed by Aston Villa and lost 3–1. But they bounced back strongly, winning the next two games, with Keane scoring three goals, and a new generation of stars was born. But the midfielder's disciplinary record began to be questioned when he was sent off for the third time in six months in October 1995. Despite that, he and Irwin helped United to a third title in four years, and then both played in the 1996 FA Cup final against Liverpool, won by Cantona's late strike, that secured a second Double for the club.

But that summer of 1996 was to provide a very different sort of association between Manchester and Ireland that had some questioning whether the relationship could survive. A few months before, on 5 December 1995, United travelled to Belfast to play in a fundraiser for Co-Operation North, an organisation that had been established to promote mutual understanding and respect in the communities in the trouble-torn province. A crowd of 20,000 watched the game, raising in excess of £160,000. Irwin, McGibbon and young Irish prospect Philip Mulryne all played for United.

Martin Roche from Derry, who was there that night, remembers how it was his father's excitement when United won the European Cup-Winners' Cup in 1991 that began his enthusiasm for the Reds, but it wasn't until that Belfast game that he saw them play live for the first time: 'It was a cold wintry night when United played an International Select side. We were standing behind the goal and unfortunately we were beaten, but at least we saw Scholesy score. The main memory I have from the game is watching Cantona warm up; I was in complete awe at the tricks he was doing with the ball. I ended up with a kidney infection a few days after it, which my mum blamed on standing in the freezing cold all night – but it was well worth it, though.'

What could have changed things was what happened on 15 June 1996: the Provisional IRA exploded a bomb in the heart of Manchester, in Corporation Street outside the Arndale Shopping Centre, where it went off at 11.20 am causing widespread damage. More than 200 innocent people were injured by the blast, but mercifully there were no fatalities. The day after the bombing, Old Trafford played host to the Euro 96 match between Germany and Russia. After the mess had been cleared up, Manchester underwent a massive programme of regeneration and rebuilding, creating a superb new city centre.

Given the previously close links between the city and the Irish, there was some concern as to what the impact would be. When I returned to Manchester for the first time a couple of months after the attack (with my wife and two young children), I was extremely apprehensive and could not help but wonder how I would be treated by my friends there, let alone those I did not know. I made sure we had as little contact as possible with people that day, fearing that our accents might spark some anger or bitterness from our fellow United fans, who might have blamed all the Irish for the actions of a few. However, my concerns were unfounded and we enjoyed a 2–2 draw against Blackburn Rovers that featured a debut goal from Ole Gunnar Solskjaer. It is at moments like this that one realises just how close the ties are. United made sure they did their bit, too, by ensuring they played their pre-season friendly in Northern Ireland against Portadown on 27 July 1996. The Reds eased to a 5–0 victory in front of a crowd of 6,100.

During the next season, Keane's campaign was interrupted by injuries, so he played only 21 league games, while Irwin was as usual a regular in the side. Once more the Premier League was to be United's, but within Old Trafford the focus was moving to Europe. Since winning the European Cup-Winners' Cup in 1991,

United had not had a decent run in Europe. This season was different, and the Reds reached the semi-finals of the Champions League, only to lose both legs of the tie 1–0 to Borussia Dortmund, with neither Irishman playing in the second leg at Old Trafford.

After United had paraded the Premier League trophy around the stadium at the end of the 1996–97 season, things were about to change for both of the Reds' Irishmen. For Keane, the news was initially good, but not long after they would both find how fragile success can be.

Chapter 12

Captain Keane

After United had completed their fourth Premier League title success, all seemed to be going well for the club, until skipper Eric Cantona stunned fans by announcing his retirement from the game with immediate effect during the summer of 1997. Club captain and team talisman, it seemed he would be impossible to replace. But fortunately, Alex Ferguson had an obvious successor in his squad: Roy Keane.

Sir Alex explains how he came to that decision: 'When Eric left I had quite a young team at the time. Old warhorses like Bryan Robson, who was my best-ever captain, and Steve Bruce had left the club, and I always look for a player who can change a game and inspire others around him to be my captain. So when Eric left, I looked around the dressing-room and saw Ryan Giggs, David Beckham, Paul Scholes, Nicky Butt and Gary Neville. However, they were all still very young, although I did consider handing the captaincy to Gary. Gary was a natural leader and more importantly, he was a winner. But in the end I chose Roy because of the dynamism of his personality.'

Keane thus became United's third Irish club captain, following Johnny Carey and Noel Cantwell. However, his first season in the role was a personal nightmare for him. In the early hours of 25 September, he was involved in a fracas at a Manchester hotel following United's 2–2 draw with Chelsea at Old Trafford the day before when a Cork–Dublin argument got out of hand and into the papers. As Keane admitted in his autobiography, he had had too much to drink at the time, a problem he would subsequently deal with. Two days later, perhaps still feeling the after-effects of the late night, he injured his knee while attempting to tackle Alf-Inge Haaland of Leeds United at Elland Road in a 1–0 Premier League defeat. A few days later the club confirmed the diagnosis: Keane would miss the rest of the season with cruciate ligament damage.

A few weeks later, on 5 November, Denis Irwin's glittering career was almost brought to an end by a bad tackle. United were playing Feyenoord in a Champions League group game in the Netherlands, and were 3–0 up after 76 minutes of play. An Andy Cole hat-trick had United in full control of the game, and then in the 82nd minute Paul Bosvelt's badly timed lunge caught Irwin in the calf, and he was stretchered off. At the time, Irwin feared his career was over and recalled the incident in an interview with Ted McCauley for the *Sunday Mirror*: 'I was furious because it was such a bad challenge – and even when I was lying on the floor, I was having a right scream at the referee because he didn't do anything about it. I was in a lot of pain, too. But players are always getting stretchered off and then sprinting straight back on again, so the fans probably don't recognise that a man can get hurt. The thought was there, that my injury was serious and I didn't really know how bad it was. It was only when the physio told me in the dressing room that it was probably the medial ligaments, that I knew I would be OK. I thought it was a terrible challenge and there's no place for that against a fellow professional.'

In fact, Irwin was back in action by the beginning of January 1998, as United started their FA Cup run; and in the fourth round, on 24 January against Walsall, he was part of the team that featured a new Irish star, though the two men would never be on the pitch at the same time that season. Philip Patrick Stephen Mulryne was born in West Belfast on 1 January 1978. He moved to Manchester in 1994 and joined United's blossoming youth set-up. In 1995, playing in the same team as Phil Neville, he collected an FA Youth Cup winners' medal, beating Tottenham Hotspur 4–2 on penalties after the game ended 1–1.

His senior debut came not for United, but on 11 February 1997, when he won his first cap for Northern Ireland. The Irish entertained Belgium in a friendly international at Windsor Park, and he was introduced as a substitute and scored in a 3–0 win. It was the first of 27 caps (scoring three goals), the last of which he would win in 2005. Eight months later, on 14 October, the midfielder made his United debut in a third round League Cup tie away to Ipswich Town, which they lost 2–0. However, competition for places in the United team was tough, with David Beckham, Paul Scholes and Nicky Butt among those keeping the talented Mulryne out of the side.

Mulryne got his Premier League debut on the final day of the 1997–98 season, against Barnsley, but by then United already knew they would finish runners-up, a point behind Arsenal. It was to be his only Premier League appearance for United. The following season he played in just two League Cup ties for United before he was sold to Norwich City on 25 March 1999 for £500,000.

Mulryne's career with the Canaries began well, but a broken leg saw him miss the vast majority of the 1999–2000 season. Then in 2001–02 he helped Norwich City reach the Division One play-offs where they lost out to Birmingham City on penalties, with Mulryne missing his spot kick. Two seasons later, 2003–04, he helped the Canaries clinch the First Division title and with it promotion to the top flight, though he was mostly used from the bench. When Norwich City came straight back down, Mulryne was released and joined Cardiff City, but struggled to be selected.

He had trials at various clubs, until on 23 January 2007 he joined Leyton Orient in a free transfer until the end of the

2006–07 campaign. Having made only a couple of appearances for them, he joined King's Lynn on 25 October 2007 before being released after two months. In March 2008, Mulryne returned to Belfast and trained with Cliftonville and then went on trial with Linfield in June 2008, but things did not work out for him at Windsor Park.

Mulryne's next move surprised everyone: he announced in July 2009 that he would be entering the priesthood. This is the first time in the history of Manchester United that a former player has set out to become a priest, opting to change his career from a football luminary to that of a clerical seminary. Frankie 'Dodger' Dodds from Belfast was astonished when he came across the former United star in his new vocation recently: 'I attended my youngest daughter Paula's "Service of Lights" mass in preparation for her confirmation on 12 March 2011 and Philip Mulryne was doing work experience in preparation for his ordination ceremony to become a priest in the Roman Catholic Church. I suppose this makes a welcome change to ex-footballers going on silly reality TV shows.'

With United having suffered early exits from both domestic cups, and a quarter-final defeat in the Champions League to Monaco, the 1997–98 season had ended without a major trophy, and left some commentators questioning if United could recover from the loss of Cantona. The 1998–99 season would give them their answer – and in the most emphatic terms. Before the campaign got under way, however, Alex Ferguson had another summer of heavy investment in the transfer market, bringing in Jesper Blomqvist, Jaap Stam and Dwight Yorke.

And there was one other important player available again: on 27 July 1998, Keane made his long-awaited United comeback in a pre-season friendly against the Norwegian side Vålerenga IF in Oslo. But the new campaign didn't immediately give any signs of what was to come; Aston Villa were the surprise league leaders until December, when Chelsea took over top spot. But when United beat Keane's old club Nottingham Forest 3–0 on Boxing

Day, it would be the start of an astonishing run of form that would see the Reds go unbeaten for the rest of the campaign.

Nothing seemed to stop the Reds: 1–0 down to Liverpool with two minutes left in the fourth round of the FA Cup? Goals from Yorke and Ole Gunnar Solskjaer sorted that out. By April, it was neck-and-neck in the title race with Arsenal, and the Reds were also in the semi-finals of the FA Cup and the Champions League. People began to talk about the possibility of an unprecedented Treble.

On 14 April, United met Arsenal in the FA Cup semi-final replay at Villa Park. First Keane was sent off and then, with the score at 1–1, Peter Schmeichel saved a penalty. As if that wasn't enough drama, Ryan Giggs's wonder goal in extra-time saw United through to the final.

A week later saw what was surely Keane's greatest-ever performance in a United shirt. It was the second leg of their crucial Champions League semi-final, against Juventus at Stadio delle Alpi. United had drawn the first leg 1–1 at Old Trafford, but conceded two goals in the first ten minutes to the Italian side. Keane remained focused and calm, and this transmitted itself to everyone in the side. He pulled a goal back in the 24th minute, and suddenly United were in contention. But before half time, he was booked and he knew that if United made it to the final he would not be part of it. He did not falter, and drove his team on to a stunning 3–2 victory – their first ever in the competition in Italy.

On 5 May, United won a precious point in a 2–2 draw with Liverpool at Anfield. Irwin scored United's second goal that day to give the Reds a two-goal cushion, but was then sent off. Ferguson described the decision as: 'An affront to common sense . . . it ruled out one of the best-behaved and most respected pros in England out of the FA Cup final.'

So the Premier League race came down to the final day, 16 May 1999, when United took on Tottenham Hotspur, knowing they had to win to regain the title from Arsenal. Irwin and Keane both played, but the goals came from David Beckham and Cole. It was a case of one down, two to go as Keane was presented with the Premier League trophy. After playing 35 league games (scoring twice), it was his fourth Premier League winners' medal with United and his first as captain, while for Irwin it was title No. 5, after making 29 appearances (two goals).

For Keane, unfortunately, the celebrations ended with him being arrested after a woman alleged he assaulted her in a bar, but he was quickly released without charge. As he commented in his memoirs: 'I went home vowing . . . I wouldn't make the same mistake again. Of course I'd made that vow before.'

Next up, 22 May, was the FA Cup final against Newcastle United. With Irwin absent because of his red card earlier in the month, Irish involvement in the game for United did not last for long, as Keane picked up an injury inside ten minutes. But the 2–0 victory gave the Reds their third Double, and both men still picked up FA Cup winners' medals.

Finally, on 26 May, came the Champions League final against Bayern Munich in Barcelona; it was the 90th anniversary of the birth of Sir Matt Busby. This time it was Keane who was suspended, but Irwin was back in the defence as United won 2–1 in one of the most astonishing comebacks of all time. With the dream of European glory seemingly all over as the game went into added time, and United trailing 1–0, up stepped Teddy Sheringham to score the equaliser in the first minute of injury time, followed by Solskjaer's winner a minute later to send the United fans inside the Camp Nou into a frenzy. United had won a historic Treble, with Keane leading from the front throughout the season. He had played 55 times all told, his busiest campaign ever for United, scoring five goals, while Irwin made 48 appearances and scored three goals.

On 3 August 1999, the Treble winners visited St Julian's Road to play Omagh Town. Sadly, this was no ordinary pre-season game in Ireland. Instead, it was a fundraiser for the victims of the horrific Omagh bombing, which occurred on Saturday 15 August 1998, killing 29 people and devastating the town. United entertained the 7,000 crowd by scoring nine goals, with Sheringham getting four of them, while Cole (2), Michael Clegg (2) and an own goal completed the scoring. Irwin, Keane and John O'Shea from the Republic, as well as Northern Ireland's David Healy, all played for United in the game as the club reinforced its links with the Irish in the most public way it could.

But before the 1999–2000 season had progressed too far, there were newspaper reports claiming that Keane would leave United if his new contract did not meet his demands. He said: 'I was a bit annoyed with the first offer put to me. Deep down they must have known it wasn't something I could sign. Our dealings have to be realistic. I am not naive enough to settle for anything less than a reasonable valuation of my worth.' It took a while, but by December agreement was reached, and the Reds' talisman had committed his future to the club for the next four years.

Not that the negotiations seemed to distract him. On 30 November, he scored the only goal of the game in United's Intercontinental Cup final win over Palmeiras of Brazil in Tokyo, to help the Reds become the first British club to lift the trophy. That season, he was in unstoppable form, scoring 12 goals (his best season tally for United), and was deservedly named both the Professional Footballers' Association and Football Writers' Association Player of the Year.

Not long after collecting his individual honours, he claimed his fifth Premier League winners' medal and his second as captain when United beat Aston Villa 1–0 on the final day of the season. But the margin of the Reds' dominance was clear: second-placed Arsenal trailed them by 18 points. Irwin missed a third of the league season, but was absent for only one Champions League game, his experience now a vital part of the European strategy, but there was no repeat glory this time, as Real Madrid knocked out United in the quarter-finals.

Keane always demanded utter commitment to the cause, not just from himself, but also from his team-mates, and even the fans. Sometimes, this could lead him into trouble: when United played

Chelsea on 13 August 2000, in the Charity Shield at Wembley, he was sent off in United's 2–0 defeat. Following a rather tepid but important 1–0 win over Dynamo Kiev in the final Champions League group game on 8 November, it was the supporters who he felt had let down the team. In one of his most famous utterances, he complained about a lack of atmosphere at Old Trafford saying: 'Sometimes you wonder, do they understand the game of football? Away from home our fans are fantastic, I'd call them the hardcore fans. But at home, they have a few drinks and probably the prawn sandwiches, and they don't realise what's going on out on the pitch. I don't think some of the people who come to Old Trafford can spell football, never mind understand it.' The 'prawn sandwich brigade' was born.

But of course not all fans are like that. And sometimes, as Martin Roche from Derry explains, you get an even more special moment than usual when you come to Old Trafford: 'The best experience I ever had with players was in October 2000 when we played Leeds United. We were at the ground hours before kick-off and I was away getting something to eat. When I came back, my dad and his mate were standing with a man and a girl talking about football. He was introduced to me as Ted Beckham – David's father. The girl was Becks's sister, Joanne. Ted stood and chatted for ages before he apologised and said that he had to go. However, before Mr Beckham went into the stadium, he asked a security guard to ensure that when David came in that he signed our shirts.

'We waited for ages and then a huge buzz went around the large crowd, which was gathered at the back of the Stretford End where the players park their cars and walk into Old Trafford. Becks had arrived, and all I was thinking about was: would he sign my shirt, but more importantly would the security guard remember to tell him about us. I could not believe it when David came over to us and signed my shirt. I also got autographs from Dwight Yorke, Andy Cole, Fabien Barthez, Ronny Johnsen, Raimond van der Gouw and Quinton Fortune. Then, after the match, we bumped into Fergie and I managed to get my ticket stub signed. What a magical day!'

Although Keane remained club captain, just occasionally others would take the role on the pitch, and on St Patrick's Day 2001, Sir Alex handed Irwin the captain's armband for the Premiership home game versus Leicester City, even though Keane was playing. It was his 500th appearance for United, who won the game 2–0 thanks to two very late goals from Yorke and Mikaël Silvestre. On the final home fixture of the 2000–01 campaign, Irwin was again given the honour of captaining United for the visit of Derby County. United had already clinched their third successive Premiership crown, their seventh overall, despite the fact that they still had three games to play, such was the team's dominance.

A much-changed United side lost 1–0 to the Rams that day, but fittingly it was Irwin who stepped on to the purpose-built platform on the pitch at Old Trafford to hold aloft the Premier League trophy before 67,526 fans. It was a very special moment for the Irishman, who had helped United win all seven Premiership crowns to that date (only Giggs had matched his achievement). He may have been a much underrated player by certain sections of the media and opposing fans, but his team-mates and his adoring United fans knew just how much of an asset he was to the club.

Marshall Angus from Bangor, County Down, was one of those fans, and he recalls visiting Old Trafford with his father at the start of the next campaign when United took on Fulham: 'It is not the 3–2 win for United that sticks out most in my mind; it was the look on my dad's face. That day was his first trip to Old Trafford since the 1960s and he looked like a child on Christmas morning when we walked out of the tunnel to take our seats in the stand. I am extremely proud to follow the team my father taught me to love. Thanks Dad!'

The 2001–02 season would be the last for the hugely popular Irwin at Old Trafford, and the first for Ruud van Nistelrooy and Juan Sebastián Verón. The Irishman had spent 12 memorable years with the club and in that time he made 529 appearances for

United (33 goals), which places him eighth in the table of all-time appearance-makers for the club. The only other Irishman to have played more for United is Tony Dunne (535 appearances), another unsung hero of a full-back who also won the European Cup with the Reds.

Irwin scored many important goals for United, he had a ferocious shot, was a cool penalty taker and was lethal from free kicks. His playing motto seemed to be: keep it simple; keep it plain. He remains United's most successful Irish player in terms of winners' medals and at a bargain £625,000 represents one of the best transfer deals Ferguson ever did. Even in his mid-30s, he was Sir Alex's first choice left-back, with Phil Neville waiting in the wings, and he was unquestionably one of the most consistent performers in the United team season after season.

On 16 August 2000, Irwin was given a thoroughly deserved testimonial in recognition of his first ten years with United, and Manchester City provided the opposition. He walked out of the tunnel at Old Trafford with his three young children, Liam, Lauren and Katy, and was welcomed by a standing ovation from the United fans and received a guard of honour from his fellow professionals. Sadly, he was forced to leave the game early after being caught by a late and clumsy challenge.

Irwin won just about everything the domestic game could offer, but was never arrogant about his success as a professional footballer. When he was at United he was perceived as being extremely shy, but he maintained that this was a false image of him, as he commented during an interview in 1999: 'I think it's a bit false. It's one that seems to have been created by the media. The supporters don't know me, so they accept that view of my personality. I'm not complaining. I know I don't get the headlines – but I'm happy to leave that to the forwards because when the stick is being dished out they're usually the first in line.'

Irwin played his last game for United on the final day of the 2001–02 season, 11 May, which ended in a 0–0 draw with Charlton Athletic. In honour of his sterling service to United, Sir

Alex made him captain for his final game, and he received a stand-ing ovation before and after the match. Irwin's longevity with United is shown by the fact that not one of his team-mates, including substitutes, from the 1990 Charity Shield game (his debut) was still with the club on the day of his last game for the Reds.

Sadly, he was not able to go out on a high, as that season was one of only two in his time at United when he did not collect a winners' medal (1994–95 was the other one), with the Reds fin-ishing in third place in the league and exiting the Champions League to Bayer Leverkusen in the semi-finals. When he was asked for his best moment at United he said: 'Winning the Champions League in 1999 was great, but my favourite memory is that first league title win in 1993.' Sir Alex Ferguson labelled Denis as 'the best two-footed player in my time here'. He also gave me this assessment of the man and the player: 'Denis was a fabulous player and so dependable. I never had to tell him what to do, because he knew instantly what was required of him every time he pulled on the jersey of Manchester United. Denis was a tremendous servant to both Manchester United and his country and one of the best full-backs the game has ever seen.'

Many United fans over the years have lamented over a post-match drink or two how impossible it has been to replace the likes of Bryan Robson, Mark Hughes, Eric Cantona or Peter Schmeichel. But Denis Irwin is surely in that category, too.

Two months after his final appearance in a United shirt, Irwin was on his way to Wolverhampton Wanderers in a free transfer and scored twice for Wolves in his first season with the Black Country club. On 26 May 2003, Wolves beat Sheffield United 3–0 in the Division One Play-Off final to win promotion to the Premier League. Three months later, he received one of the loud-est welcomes I have ever heard an opposing player receive from United fans when he played for Wolves against United in the Premiership. United won the game 1–0, with a goal from his former United and Ireland team-mate, O'Shea. Sadly, even with all his experience, he could not prevent Wolves from being relegated at the end of the 2003–04 season. The 38-year-old Irwin then announced his retirement, having made 75 league appearances for the club.

In his autobiography Bobby Charlton chose Irwin in his personal 'very best of Manchester United'. This was despite the fact that Sir Bobby played in the same team as two other legendary United full-backs, Roger Byrne and Tony Dunne. He explained why: 'You never worried about Denis Irwin. I remember him once making a mistake, an occasion so rare I found myself thinking: really, I never thought I would see that.' Meanwhile, Sir Alex Ferguson was equally full of praise for his Irish gem and stated in his autobiography: 'Nowhere in football is there a more popular player than the unassuming Irishman, who is the ultimate professional, one of those quiet, under-praised heroes who constitute the bedrock of all great teams.'

As if his club career was not impressive enough, Irwin had a long and distinguished international career. He made his debut for the Republic of Ireland on 12 September 1990 at right-back (the position he would more usually take for his country) in a 1–0 friendly win over Morocco at Dalymount Park. He represented Ireland at the 1994 World Cup finals in the USA, and played in the famous 1–0 win over Italy in Ireland's opening group match at Giants Stadium. He pulled on the Irish shirt for the 56th and final time on 17 November 1999 in the second play-off leg against Turkey for Euro 2000. The game ended 0–0, and having drawn 1–1 against the Turks in Dublin four days earlier, the Irish missed out on the finals on the away-goals rule. Jack Charlton was his manager for much of this time and commented: 'There are certain types of players who give managers headaches, and I've come across a few in my time in the Ireland job. Denis, though, is a manager's dream, a class act, a nice guy and a player you could always bank on to come up trumps.'

In 2002, it was little surprise when Irwin was named in the 'Overall Team of the Decade' for the Premier League's first ten seasons. He then made a welcome return to Old Trafford in 2004, taking up a job as a presenter for MUTV and he has also worked for RTÉ covering several football tournaments for the Irish television broadcaster. Today, he is also a football columnist with Ireland's *Sunday World* newspaper.

Supporter Dessie Roche paid his own tribute to Irwin: 'He was quite simply one of the greatest full-backs ever to play for our famous club. During my early years of supporting United, Denis was first-choice left-back and a permanent fixture in the team. He wasn't the most rampaging of full-backs, like Rafael or Evra, but he knew how and when to attack. His primary job as a defender was to make sure he patrolled his area of the pitch and he did that masterfully. Although he wasn't very tall I can hardly remember an occasion when this potential weakness was exposed, because he read the game so well.

'He was an extremely popular figure in Ireland. I remember one occasion when United had sent a team to play in my home town of Derry and rumours had spread that he was among the travelling party from Old Trafford. The stadium was a buzz of excitement about the possibility of Irwin playing in the relatively modest surroundings of the Brandywell, home to Derry City. I remember the feeling when the team was announced and his name was missing. The disappointment was tangible and this demonstrates the affection for Irwin in our small part of the world.'

Des's older brother, Marty, added: 'I've never had the fortune of meeting him, but I have met people who have, and they all say he is a gentleman. United fans love players who work hard, are modest, and can play football. Denis falls into all three of those categories with consummate ease. He was a very intelligent player also, which again is something he didn't get the credit for that he deserved. I would say that Denis is probably the most consistent player to play for us in my time following the team. I would love Denis no matter where he came from, but his being Irish makes him that wee bit more special.'

Irwin always seemed to have time for the fans and could often be found standing out in the pouring rain signing autographs and posing for photos. Sometimes today's Premier League footballers seem distant from the rest of us, driving to matches in Ferraris or Bentleys. But on a match day, Irwin pulled up in his club car or his Volkswagen Golf, which says everything about the character of the man. He was a truly down-to-earth bloke who was extremely modest and just concerned himself with putting in a good performance for the team on the pitch. A family man first and foremost, and a really nice guy with it, he was the perfect gentleman on and off the pitch.

While Irwin was leaving the club in the same understated way he had played for it for so long, his fellow Irishman Keane was still driving himself and everyone else along. It could be glorious and inspirational, but it could be something much darker, too. United's failure to regain the Champions League title frustrated him, and after United lost out to Bayern Munich in 2001 he commented: 'The great teams get back to finals and win it, and this just shows we are not a great team. We're just an average team in a lot of areas. The players gave it their all tonight, but we are just not good enough and maybe it's time to move on. Maybe it's the end of the road for this team.'

As we have seen, Sir Alex had obviously come to similar conclusions, as he brought in van Nistelrooy and Verón. Within another year, Rio Ferdinand would also join the Reds. The process of rebuilding is a constant one.

Three days after that Champions League exit, Keane saw red once again when he fouled Alf-Inge Haaland in the Manchester Derby at Old Trafford. The Norwegian had not been forgiven for his comments when Keane tore his cruciate ligaments a few seasons earlier. His description of that incident in his memoirs, published a year later, would land him in even greater trouble. Early the following season, on 16 September 2001, Keane was dismissed for the ninth time in his United career after trying to hit out at the Newcastle United captain, Alan Shearer, at the end of a 4–3 Premiership defeat at St James' Park. However, later that campaign, there was good news when he signed a new contract, agreeing a four-year deal with the club.

None of Keane's United controversies were to compare with what happened that summer, when Ireland set off for the World Cup finals in Japan and South Korea. Keane had already had his differences with both the manager, Mick McCarthy, and the FA of Ireland. On 26 May 1996, he was a no-show at Lansdowne Road for McCarthy's testimonial match and the following month he failed to turn up to train with the national side, opting instead to go away on holiday with his family to Italy. As a consequence McCarthy stripped him of the captaincy and left him out of the following six internationals.

Then, in March 2001, having scored twice in the Republic of Ireland's 4–0 away victory in Cyprus, Keane criticised the Irish FA over the facilities at the team's training base and hinted that he might quit the international scene: 'Where we trained last Monday, in Clonshaugh, was abysmal and it has been for as long as I've known it. I was fairly critical about our seating arrangements on the flight out here, when the officials were sitting in the first-class seats and the players were sitting behind.'

As preparations for the World Cup got under way, Keane was sent home from the Irish squad on 23 May after a row with McCarthy in Saipan. No controversy had ever hit Irish sport quite like the Roy Keane–Mick McCarthy disagreement. After a Keane-inspired qualifying campaign that included a fantastic victory over the very talented Dutch team, the Irish had travelled with realistic hopes of improving upon the quarter-final place achieved in the 1990 World Cup. Keane was again unhappy about the training facilities and equipment in Saipan, and this formed the background to the row. In midst of it all, he gave an interview to Tom Humphries of the *Irish Times*. The content of the interview infuriated McCarthy, who called a meeting of the entire squad to thrash out matters. The consequences of the meeting were that Keane returned to his home in Manchester and took no part in the World Cup finals, despite various attempts at reconciliation.

To this day, Irish people are divided on the issue. On one side of the argument there are those that say he was wrong to leave the team when his country needed him most. The pro-Keane camp are certain that he was right to stick by his principles and that the FAI is more professional now because he took the stand that he did. However, regardless of which side is right, it is clear that Keane paid a high price, missing out on a chance to show off his skills on the biggest stage of all.

Instead, when he returned to action on 20 July 2002, it was in a very different atmosphere to the World Cup: at Tolka Park, Dublin, in front of a crowd of 8,000. Shelbourne were beaten 5–0, with van Nistelrooy scoring a hat-trick while Diego Forlán and Yorke also found the back of the net for United. Northern Ireland's international goalkeeper Roy Carroll also played in the game for United. It was the first of eight pre-season friendlies, which also took United to Denmark and Norway. By now, such was the club's worldwide fame that the Reds had to tour much further afield for its pre-season games than it had in the past so that everyone had a chance to see them live. It would be another two years before United returned to Ireland, when they took on Keane's first club, Cobh Ramblers, in July 2004.

With Keane the biggest story in sport at the time, he released his autobiography soon after in August 2002; it proved explosive stuff. In particular, his comments about his tackle on Haaland landed him in trouble. While the controversy raged, on 1 September, Keane was sent off after lashing out at Sunderland's Jason McAteer during United's 1–1 draw at the Stadium of Light, with his Irish team-mate scribbling in an imaginary book. Two days later, Sir Alex announced that Keane would miss up to three months of the season after undergoing a hip operation. An FA disciplinary committee then banned him for five games and fined him £150,000. Brian Kerr, the new Ireland manager, unsuccessfully attempted to persuade Keane to play for his country again, but the player announced that he intended to retire from the international scene.

Keane returned to action for United just before Christmas 2002, with the Reds trailing Arsenal in the title race, but after a Boxing Day defeat the side went on an unbeaten run to the end of the campaign that resulted in him lifting the Premiership trophy for the seventh time with United, following a 2–1 win over Everton at Goodison Park on the final day of the season. He had played 21 times in the Premier League, but did not score in the league all season, a sign that he was now playing in more of a holding midfield role.

By the start of the 2003–04 season, Keane was 32 years old, but anyone who was hoping that he would mellow was soon disappointed. When United finished the campaign in third place, 15 points adrift of Arsenal, he was quoted as saying: 'We have one or two young players who have done very little in the game. They need to remember that and not slacken off. They need to remember just how lucky we all are to play for Manchester United and show that out on the pitch.'

However, the disappointment of failing to land the Premiership was compensated for when on 22 May 2004 Keane captained United to FA Cup glory at the Millennium Stadium with a 3–0 win over Millwall. He lifted the famous trophy for the fourth time, setting a record with his sixth appearance in an FA Cup final. It was also a record 11th victory for United. That day he was joined by another Irishman, John O'Shea, who was in his second full season in the team, having won a Premier League medal the previous term.

Although Chelsea, backed by Roman Abramovich's vast wealth, would go on to win the title comfortably in 2004–05, the rivalry between United and Arsenal remained intense. The two clubs had divided up the title between them since 1995, and their meeting at Highbury on 1 February was all set to be another intense clash. This was the moment Keane single-handedly won a game for Manchester United before a ball was even kicked.

Prior to the game, Keane had a row in the tunnel with the Arsenal captain, Patrick Vieira, when the United captain believed that the Frenchman was 'bullying' some of his team-mates, particularly Gary Neville. Keane invited Vieira out onto the pitch before kick-off to 'settle their differences'. As the match referee, Graham Poll, tried to calm down Keane, it was clear that the job had been done as the Irishman bossed the game. United won 4–2, with O'Shea scoring the last goal.

There was still hope that United could end the season with some silverware when Keane captained United in the FA Cup final against Arsenal on 21 May at the Millennium Stadium. After an uninspiring game, United were beaten in the penalty shootout, despite the best efforts of Northern Ireland goalkeeper Roy Carroll. Speaking of United's disappointing season Keane said: 'Our performance levels have not been good enough. Everyone at this club needs to look at themselves and ask whether they are giving one hundred per cent.'

By now, Keane was beginning to suffer from an increasing number of injuries: his all-action style and complete commitment to the cause was taking its toll on his body. On 18 September 2005 he was at Anfield for a Premier League against Liverpool. However, with just two minutes of the game remaining, Keane hurt his foot and was substituted as the game ended 0–0. Afterwards, it was announced that he would be out of action for two months after breaking a bone in his left foot. No one realised it at the time, but they had just witnessed his last game as a United player.

He might have been out of action, but when United lost 4–1 away to Middlesbrough on 29 October, slipping to sixth in the table, Keane was interviewed by MUTV. His comments were deemed too outspoken to be aired and still haven't been. Some thought he had gone too far this time, and on 18 November he left United by mutual consent. It was a sad end to a remarkable career at the club (he had made 480 appearances, scoring 51 goals), and the decision to let him go divided the fans who had so loyally supported him.

In a statement released at the time, Sir Alex said: 'Roy Keane has been a fantastic servant for Manchester United. The best midfield player in the world of his generation, he is already one of the great figures in our club's illustrious history. Roy has been central to the success of the club in the last twelve and a half years, and everyone at Old Trafford wishes him well in the rest of his career and beyond.'

In an interview for this book he added: 'Roy was a marvellous captain for the club, captaining the team to four Premier League titles, two FA Cups and the World Club Championship. He always performed for United and without question his best-ever performance for Manchester United was our 1999 semi-final win over Juventus in Turin, because it was a performance of sacrifice. When Roy got booked he knew he would miss the final if we got there, but it never changed the way he played because he was a winner first and foremost.'

Four weeks later, on 15 December, United fans discovered where the rest of that great career would be played out when Keane signed for Glasgow Celtic, one of the teams he idolised as a boy growing up in Cork. But six months after joining Celtic and helping them secure the Scottish Premier League title and Scottish League Cup, Keane announced his retirement from professional football on 12 June 2006 following medical advice.

Before then, however, on 9 May, Keane received a rapturous welcome back to Old Trafford with his new team. A record testimonial crowd of 69,591 turned out to pay tribute to him. He played for Celtic in the first half and, much to the delight of the United fans, he walked out of the tunnel for the second half wearing a United shirt. All of the proceeds from the game were donated by Keane to his favourite charity, Guide Dogs for the Blind.

Keane's international career was also a long and successful one, despite the controversy. He made his debut for the Republic of Ireland on 22 May 1991 in a 1–1 friendly against Chile at Lansdowne Road under Jack Charlton, and would pick up 15 more caps while playing for Nottingham Forest. He won his first

Irish cap as a United player on 8 September 1993, a 2–0 win over Lithuania at Lansdowne Road in a World Cup qualifier.

He first captained Ireland on 27 March 1996 in a friendly against Russia at Lansdowne Road, when he took over from Andy Townsend after he was substituted. By then, Mick McCarthy was the manager. He won his 67th and last cap for his country in a 1–0 loss to France at Lansdowne Road on 7 September 2005 in a World Cup qualifier, after making a brief comeback to international football under the management of Brian Kerr. But for injuries and a reluctance to play friendlies, he would surely have won many more caps.

The 1994 World Cup finals in the USA under Charlton was the only major international tournament in which he competed, and he performed superbly in the competition. But his efforts during the qualifying campaign for the 2002 World Cup were surely even better. In a group that included an outstanding Netherlands side and a superb Portugal, Keane produced a succession of performances that drove Ireland to Japan and South Korea. He was at his best in Ireland's 1–0 victory over the Dutch at Lansdowne Road on 1 September 2001. The win effectively guaranteed the Irish runners-up spot in the group, behind Portugal, and qualified them for a two-leg play-off game versus Iran, in which they won through by 2–1 on aggregate.

Frankie Dodds from West Belfast remembers that game against the Dutch: 'Roy Keane crunched Marc Overmars in the first minute and it seemed to really unsettle the Dutch team, particularly Patrick Kluivert, who missed a great chance shortly afterwards. Ireland's goal in a famous 1–0 win that day came as a result of a typical barnstorming run from Keano. He covered every blade of grass that day – as good an international performance against a team full of quality players as you will ever see. Sheer willpower and determination, maybe, but Keano was close to being at his peak at the time and possibly the most influential player in world football. Despite his lack of height, he struck such fear into opposing players – a true force of nature!'

But for Marty Roche, the essence of Keane came not in that game but in the previous game against them: 'I remember Ireland drawing 2–2 with the Dutch in Amsterdam, on 2 September 2000. Ireland had taken a 2–0 lead, but the Dutch fought back to equalise and Ireland held on to the draw. At the end of the match, all the players were congratulating each other, but Keane was fuming. He couldn't understand why everyone was so happy at throwing away a 2–0 lead. For me, this typifies exactly what Roy Keane was all about – WINNING!'

Unsurprisingly, after he retired from playing, it wasn't long before he was approached to become a manager. In August 2006, he took charge of Sunderland and steered the Black Cats to the Championship title and promotion to the Premier League in his first season at the Stadium of Light. But then, with Sunderland struggling during the 2008–09 campaign, he stood down on 4 December 2008. Following some time out of the game, he surprised many by taking on the role of Ipswich Town manager on 23 April 2009, signing a two-year deal with the Championship side. But sadly it never really worked out for him there, and he left the club on 7 January 2011.

So how does one assess Keane? Sammy McIlroy comments: 'If I had to pick one former Irish United player from any era that I wished I had the opportunity to play alongside, that player would be Roy Keane. Keano was my type of player with his insatiable will to win, his desire, his fitness, his aggressive style of play, his commitment, his passion and, above all else, his leadership abilities. In many ways Keano was an Irish Bryan Robson, and I think Sir Alex saw that in the young man from Cork when United signed him from Nottingham Forest in the summer of 1993.'

For me personally, when Keane left United I felt the same level of shock and pain as when Eric Cantona retired in May 1997. All I could think about was: 'How are we going to replace Keano?' Other great players have come in, but there has been no one similar to him yet.

Keane was the ultimate football warrior and a truly outstanding captain. Some players thought they were hard, some players acted hard and some players were as hard as steel, but Keane was harder still. He was a midfield destroyer who had no peer; a player with intense desire, power and technique whose commitment in a United shirt was second to none. But he was also skilful, and it was his combination of attributes that gave him the priceless ability to take control of a game, but also to win a game. His passion and full-blooded approach lifted his team-mates, as he showed so well against Juventus in 1999.

He played in one of the greatest United midfields of all time, a quartet of footballers to match anything British football has ever witnessed. While it is true to say that Keane did not possess the majestic close control ball skills of Giggs, or the pinpoint accuracy of Scholes's passing, or the flair and goalscoring exploits of Beckham from free-kicks, he could do pretty much everything else.

In his autobiography, Ireland team-mate Niall Quinn gave this assessment of Keane: 'You understand that not only is Roy very good, he's always very good. Usually, people with presence on a pitch are loud bawling centre-halves, or the centre-forwards who can score a goal out of nothing, or the midfielders whose tackling and passing dictates the rhythm of the game. Roy is all three.'

At his peak he was the most dominant midfield player in Premier League history and some would argue the greatest midfielder the game has ever seen. Sure his explosive and intensive style of play was not the flavour of many, but these dissenters were not United fans. Sir Alex Ferguson labelled him the best he's ever worked with. For me, Keane has to go down as the most dominant player United has ever had and the greatest player that has ever worn the green jersey of the Republic of Ireland.

Martin Roche remains a huge admirer of Keane, highlighting another aspect of his personality, one that is often ignored: 'What people don't realise is the amount of charity work Roy did and still does, particularly in his native Cork. The reason why this is not publicised is because Roy keeps it very private. He doesn't do this to get his name into the newspapers; he does it because he wants to help people.'

But whatever anyone thought of Keane, the fact of the matter was that he was no longer at United, and that the club would have to find a way of restoring themselves to the top of the table in England and to search out yet more European success. As so often in the past, the Irish would play a vital part in it all – both on and off the pitch.

Chapter 13

United We March On

The modern game of football in England is a far cry from its roots, or even the days before the Premier League. The players of today earn such huge amounts, compared with their predecessors, that they can sometimes seem distant from us, the fans. But now, with wall-to-wall television coverage from both Sky and MUTV, not to mention highlights packages and Champions League games on terrestrial TV, some fans in Ireland find there is no longer the same need to leave home at inconvenient hours to set off to go and watch a game. Indeed, in the current economic climate, how many can afford to do so on a regular basis, when one considers the cost involved in travel and accommodation? Because of this, many have taken the option that they believe gives them the best of both worlds: they can watch their favourite team in the comfort of their own home or in a nearby pub with like-minded devotees. In short, while the players may seem to live increasingly different lives, we are also closer to them than ever before – able even to watch them in 3D on our screens. Of course, many fans in Ireland cannot live without their regular visits to Old Trafford to see their team in action.

This doesn't make those Irish followers who now choose not to venture to Old Trafford so often (or even at all) any lesser fans; they still spend money on buying the shirts and other merchandise; they are just as passionate as they always were. After all, only 76,000 can fit into Old Trafford in any one game; millions from around the world, not just Ireland, would love to be there. So it should come as no surprise that MUSCs in Ireland are in good health, with more than 70 of them spread across the land, a greater number than any other club can boast. They help ensure that United's popularity remains strong, even if there are now fewer Irish players at the club than at many times in the past, a trend that is likely to continue as top-level football attracts players from all over the world.

Con Murphy from Bagenalstown, County Carlow, the founder member of Bagenalstown Red Devils, told me how he formed that branch of the MUSC, one of the more recent ones to be founded: 'In May 2007, I tried to get a club up and running. We created a website, and once that was going, a letter of invitation to the inaugural branch meeting was posted out to over sixty known United fans in the locality. All were urged to tell every United supporter they knew to come along. The first meeting proved to be an outstanding success when ninety-eight members signed up on the night. Since then our numbers have swelled to over two hundred and seventy members – and it is still growing.

'On Sunday 16 December 2007, United legend Pat Crerand was unveiled as our new Honorary Club President. The club is both honoured and delighted to have such a legend as Pat associated with our club. In 2009, we were accepted as an Official Manchester United Supporters' Club, and recognised by Old Trafford, which further increased membership. The club can now apply directly to Old Trafford for tickets and also receive many extra benefits as part of their new official status.'

Since the start of the new millennium, in this HD, 3D era, the Irish player who has appeared most for United is John Francis O'Shea. He was born on 30 April 1981 in Waterford and grew up a Liverpool fan and jokingly comments: 'Well, I was a bit of a glory hunter back then and, to be fair, they were a pretty good side in the late eighties and early nineties.'

He began his career with home-town side Waterford Bohemians and soon collected Under-16 and Youth international caps for the Republic of Ireland. After he was spotted by a United scout, he signed professional forms with United on 3 August 1999. 'I could not believe my luck in signing for United, who had just won the Treble; and being able to train with Denis Irwin and my own boyhood favourite, Roy Keane, every day was extra special,' he recalls.

Two months after arriving at Old Trafford, he was given his United debut in a 3–0 League Cup third round defeat away to Aston Villa on 13 October 1999. With United already well stocked with centre-halves (Henning Berg, Jaap Stam, Ronny Johnsen, David May), he was sent out on loan to AFC Bournemouth in January 2000. O'Shea made ten appearances for the Cherries in Division Two and scored once.

That League Cup tie against Aston Villa saw another Irishman make his debut for United, coming on as a substitute. David Jonathan Healy was born in Killyleagh, County Down, on 5 August 1979 and played for Crossgar, Lisburn Youth and Down Academy High School in Downpatrick before United brought him across the Irish Sea in August 1999, just four days after his 20th birthday. Healy was bought as a back-up to established strikers Andy Cole, Teddy Sheringham, Ole Gunnar Solskjaer and Dwight Yorke, and in early 2000 he went out on loan to Port Vale.

He gained valuable experience with the Valiants and scored three times in 16 league games. At the end of the 1999–2000 season, he returned to Old Trafford and made his second appearance for United in a fourth round League Cup 2–1 defeat against Sunderland on 28 November 2000. Once again he was used by United as a substitute (coming on in the 90th minute), though there was extra time at the Stadium of Light. His third and last appearance for United was a Premier League home game against Ipswich Town on 23 December, which United won 2–0. Six days later he joined Preston North End on loan, and very soon after the move to Deepdale was made permanent when the club agreed to pay United £1.5 million for him.

Healy spent three years with Preston scoring 44 league goals in 139 games, although he was sent out on loan to Norwich City in 2003. In October 2004, he signed for Leeds United for £650,000, and despite joining the Yorkshire club three months into the season he ended the 2004–05 campaign as their top goalscorer (seven goals). Following Leeds United's relegation to League One at the end of the 2006–07 season, he joined Fulham in July 2007 in a transfer deal worth £1.5 million.

A year after moving to Fulham (four goals in 30 league games), he was on his travels again, this time to Sunderland on a three-year contract for an undisclosed fee, estimated at £1.2 million. In January 2010, Sunderland allowed him to join Ipswich Town on loan, and in November 2010 he went on loan to Doncaster Rovers before he signed for Glasgow Rangers in January 2011.

Healy made his international debut for Northern Ireland on 23 February 2000 against Luxembourg away and began his international career in style, scoring twice for his country in a 3–1 win. Although eight goals in his first 29 internationals was a decent return, Healy soon began to develop the sort of goalscoring record for his country that would stand comparison with the best. On 6 June 2004, he won his 35th cap and celebrated by scoring twice in a friendly international away to Trinidad & Tobago, his 13th and 14th goals for his country, thereby overtaking Colin Clarke's record for Northern Ireland.

He scored one of the most memorable goals of his career on 7 September 2005 when he netted the only goal of the game in a 1–0 victory over England at Windsor Park in a qualifying game for the 2006 World Cup finals. It was the first time Northern Ireland had beaten England since 1972. He won his 50th cap versus Finland in August 2006 and scored his 20th international goal in the game. The following month, he became the first player since Colin Clarke to score a hat-trick, when Northern Ireland famously defeated Spain 3–2 at Windsor Park in a Euro 2008 qualifier. Six months later, he recorded his second hat-trick in a 4–1 win over Liechtenstein to become the first player to score two hat-tricks for Northern Ireland. When Healy found the net against Denmark on 17 November 2007, it was his 13th goal in 11 games for Northern Ireland in the qualifiers for Euro 2008. This feat made him the highest-ever goalscorer in a European Championship qualifying campaign. His record of 35 goals for his country in 89 internationals may never be surpassed.

He was awarded an MBE in the Queen's 2008 Birthday Honours List for services to football. Speaking of his award Healy said: 'It's an unbelievable honour. Goalscoring records are there to be broken, but when you are given something like the MBE you are always going to have it. It's a great honour not only for myself, but for my mum and dad at home in Killyleagh in Northern Ireland and also my wife and children.'

In 2000–01, though he played a couple more League Cup ties, O'Shea also went out on loan, in his case to Belgium to gain experience with Royal Antwerp, but unlike Healy he had the chance to return. With Berg and Stam no longer at United the following campaign, he made his Premier League debut on 4 November 2001 against the team he supported as a boy. Liverpool were leading the game 3–1 with just six minutes remaining when he came on as a substitute. He recalls: 'By this time I was now a Manchester United fan and I could not wait to get on to play against Liverpool. The Kop gave me loads of abuse and stick, but all in good banter. Of course I got the normal welcome for a player making his debut as they all started to sing "Who the hell are you?"'

With Healy gone, O'Shea soon had another Irishman for company trying to make his way into the regular line-up to join Irwin and Keane. Roy Eric Carroll was born on 30 September 1977 in Enniskillen, County Fermanagh. He grew up in the Tamlaght area of Enniskillen and began his career with a local side, Fivemiletown United, before moving on to play for Ballinamallard United. In early September 1995, he joined Hull City as a trainee under the

Youth Training Scheme (YTS) and less than two months later he made his debut for the Tigers. He went on to make 46 appearances for Hull, but was sold to Wigan Athletic on 16 April 1997. The transfer fee of £350,000, at the time a club record for the Latics, was much-needed by the Humberside club to ease their financial problems.

However, Carroll had to wait seven months before he made his debut for Wigan, when he replaced their first-choice goalkeeper, Lee Butler, in a 2–1 away loss at Watford in Division Two on 29 November 1997. He helped the club to Football League Trophy success in 1998–99, and stayed there for four years, playing 169 games for the club. In 1999–2000 he was voted the best goalkeeper in Division Two, and helped the club to the play-offs that season and the next, though on both occasions they missed out on promotion. His performances drew the attention of United, among other clubs, and in July 2001 the Reds paid an undisclosed fee, believed to be in the region of £2.5 million (a record for Wigan at the time), to sign him up.

Carroll joined United as the back-up goalkeeper to Fabien Barthez, with Raimond van der Gouw also standing in his way of making the United first team. Despite this competition, he made his United debut on 26 August 2001 against Aston Villa at Villa Park in the Premier League. Within four minutes of the start he had conceded his first goal, although the game finished 1–1. He did not appear again for United until 13 October and by the end of 2002–03 he had made just 26 appearances for the club. However, with Barthez under pressure, his hopes of being first-choice goalkeeper in 2003–04 were high.

While Carroll was struggling to secure a regular place, O'Shea featured regularly in the United team that won the Premier League in season 2002–03, making 52 appearances in all competitions. His great advantage was that he was capable of playing in a number of positions, and it was his versatility at left-back, right-back, centre-back and central midfield that saw him become a regular in the side. When Rio Ferdinand missed part of the

2003–04 season for failing to attend a drugs test in January 2004, O'Shea slipped into his centre-half spot and helped United reach the 2004 FA Cup final where they recorded a 3–0 win over Millwall at the Millennium Stadium. That season, he played more games for United (49) than anyone else.

For Carroll, however, there was disappointment. In the summer of 2003, United paid $4 million for the American goalkeeper Tim Howard from the MetroStars, which ultimately resulted in Barthez leaving Old Trafford in October 2003 to join Olympique de Marseille. Howard was Sir Alex's first-choice goalkeeper, though Carroll did pick up an FA Cup winners' medal with United in 2004 when he came on as a substitute for Howard in the 84th minute.

With more competition for places, coupled with a slight dip in form, season 2004–05 saw O'Shea linked with a move away from Old Trafford, with Liverpool and Newcastle United said to be interested in acquiring his services. However, just as he had done before, he knuckled down and set about impressing Sir Alex to include him in the side. He certainly impressed Patrick Devanay from County Mayo during that famous Keane–Vieira Arsenal game that season when he scored United's fourth goal: 'John O'Shea (of all people!) finally helped me understand why people call it "the beautiful game". Taking down a wonderfully weighted through-ball from Scholes, he caressed the ball with conviction over the advancing Almunia and the expression on his face was a mixture of disbelief and delight.'

But for Carroll, the 2004–05 season would be his last at the club. He played 34 times for United, almost as many first team appearances as in the three previous seasons put together (38). But, unfortunately for him, he made a number of errors that season, including one notorious howler against Tottenham Hotspur at Old Trafford on 4 January that he somehow got away with. The score was 0–0 when Pedro Mendes lobbed Carroll from just inside the halfway line in the dying seconds of the game. Carroll scrambled back and dropped the ball, which clearly fell across the goal line. He scooped it out of the net, and unbelievably none of the match officials realised that a goal had been scored.

His last game for United was the 2005 FA Cup final against Arsenal at the Millennium Stadium in Cardiff (Keane and O'Shea also played). Although Carroll kept a clean sheet, he ended up on the losing side as Arsenal won the penalty shoot-out. He was allowed to leave Old Trafford on 27 May, when his contract expired and he opted to sign for West Ham United. He stayed with the Hammers for two seasons (35 games, 2005–07) before moving on to Glasgow Rangers (1 game, 2007–08), Derby County (27 games, 2008–09), Odense in Denmark (2009–11) where he initially displaced future United keeper Anders Lindegaard, and finally OFI Crete at the start of the 2011–12 campaign.

Carroll made his international debut for Northern Ireland on 21 May 1997 against Thailand in a 0–0 away draw and went on to make 19 appearances for his country, 11 of them as a substitute. His last match for his country was that famous 3–2 victory over Spain in 2006.

While the 2004–05 season was a last campaign for Carroll, for another Irishman it was his first. William Peter 'Liam' Miller was born in Cork on 13 February 1981 to a Scottish father and Irish mother. He went to Coachford College, in the Lee Valley, 18 miles west of Cork. He began his football career with a local junior side, Ballincollig. A prodigious young talent, he worked his way through various junior Republic of Ireland national teams, culminating in the Under-17 European Championship finals victory in 1998 in Scotland, coached by Brian Kerr.

By that stage, he had already signed for Glasgow Celtic, but it wasn't until the end of the 1999–2000 season that he made his debut for the Scottish giants, then managed by Martin O'Neill, coming on against Dundee United on 21 May 2000. In 2001, O'Neill allowed Miller to go out on loan to the Danish side, Aarhus, and he played 18 games for them. Such was the impression he made at Aarhus that they tried to sign him, but Celtic wanted to keep the young midfielder. Following his return from Denmark, he was soon a regular in the Celtic side during 2003–04, helping them to the SPL title. Several English clubs began to take notice of the young Irishman, as his performances in the 2003–04 Champions League campaign stood out. That summer Sir Alex signed him up on a 'Bosman' free transfer after Miller refused to sign a new contract with the Glasgow club.

He was given an early chance to impress, coming on as a substitute midway through the second half against Dinamo Bucharest in a Champions League qualifying round tie in the Romanian capital on 11 August 2004, helping the Reds to a 3–2 victory. In his first season at Old Trafford, he made 19 appearances for United, many as a substitute. On 26 October, he scored his first goal for United in a 3–0 win in the third round League Cup tie at Crewe Alexandra. After scoring against Barnet in a home League Cup third round 4–1 win on 26 October 2005 (his 22nd and last game for United), he was sent out on loan to Leeds United in November 2005.

He ended up staying with the Elland Road club for the remainder of the 2005–06 season. With a regular place in Sir Alex's team looking unlikely, he was bought by Roy Keane for Sunderland on 31 August 2006, a deal that surprised many. He stayed with Sunderland for two and a half seasons, making 57 league appearances (three goals), before joining Queens Park Rangers in a free transfer in January 2009. He was released by the London outfit at the end of the 2008–09 season, and so signed for Hibernian, again on a free transfer, and started superbly for the club. However, during the 2010–11 season, he found himself edged out of the side and in June signed a two-year contract with Australian side Perth Glory.

Miller made his debut as a substitute for the Republic of Ireland on 31 March 2004 in a friendly 2–1 victory over the Czech Republic at Lansdowne Road. He made a total of 22 appearances for Ireland, nine of them from the bench. He scored only one goal for Ireland, a great strike in the 3–0 win over Sweden in a friendly at Lansdowne Road on 1 March 2006.

With Keane, Carroll and Miller gone, O'Shea suddenly found himself as the only Irish regular in the side during 2005–06. He was part of the team that won the League Cup 4–0 at the Millennium Stadium against Wigan, and there was a real sense when the team finished runners-up to Chelsea that the side was only going to get better.

Even though the Irish contingent at the club was diminishing, United were still attracting new fans. Teenager Brendan Ryan Donovan from Cork, who comes from a United-mad family, hadn't really been bitten by the bug, despite receiving his middle name in honour of a certain famous Red. But he remembers the moment it all changed: 'It wasn't until 2006 when I truly became the madly obsessed United fan that I am today. And it all came about as a result of a United versus Liverpool game at Old Trafford. I distinctly remember the pre-match banter being a bit more aggressive than usual. I remember Rio Ferdinand clearing a shot off the line and then in the last minute of the game he scored the winner. True ecstasy! The next days in school were fuelled with arguments about how United were lucky and so there it was: the hook that finally landed me.'

There was a surprise during the summer when Ruud van Nistelrooy was sold to Real Madrid, but this served merely to allow the Reds' young deadly duo up front, Cristiano Ronaldo and Wayne Rooney, the chance to blossom. O'Shea was used much more from the bench in 2006–07, but his adaptability was put to its greatest test on 4 February. When Edwin van der Sar was taken off with a broken nose late on during United's Premier League game away to Tottenham Hotspur, the Reds had already used all three of their substitutes and were leading 4–0 at the time.

O'Shea went in goal (the latest in a long line of emergency Irish keepers for United) and managed to keep a clean sheet, having made a superb save from his Irish international team-mate, Robbie Keane, near the end of the match. After the save, the travelling Red Army started chanting 'Ireland's number one', much to his amusement. 'I tell you what, I got some stick from the boys in the dressing-room after the game, and it was brilliant to hear our fans help me get through what was a pretty nerve-racking experience. But there was no danger of me wanting to play in goal regularly, not even in training.'

The following month O'Shea endeared himself to United fans forever after he scored the only goal of the game in a 1–0 win over Liverpool at Anfield in the fourth minute of injury time. United were down to ten men, following the dismissal of Paul Scholes, and O'Shea, who came on as a substitute for Rooney, clinched three vital Premiership points for United with his goal in front of a stunned Kop.

'After the game I recall Gazza [Gary Neville] telling me how lucky I was to score the winning goal in a United v Liverpool game, let alone doing it away from home in front of the Kop. Gazza was really jealous, as he said he had always dreamed of doing what I had just done, but he was ecstatic with our victory. He was well pleased for me, as were all of the lads, particularly wee Scholesy. I must admit that I did have a big head in training the following week and constantly asked my team-mates what they thought of my magnificent goal!'

Just over two months later, United were confirmed as Premier League champions for the ninth time – it was O'Shea's second title medal. But the chance of a fourth Double was lost when Chelsea beat them 1–0 in the first FA Cup final in the new Wembley (O'Shea came on as a substitute). Brendan Donovan was there to join in the title celebrations on his first visit to Old Trafford, when United took on West Ham in the final game of the season: 'I arrived at Old Trafford at eleven o'clock and soaked in the atmosphere. I even got my United shirt signed by Edwin van der Sar and I had my photo taken with Chris Eagles! United already had the title wrapped up and the atmosphere was spectacular. Even though West Ham won the game 1–0 (thanks to Carlos Tévez), nothing could spoil the day for me. Just seeing the lads lift the trophy was sufficient to make me very happy. I will always remember that after the game the rain lashed down and my father and mother were concerned for my safety among such a huge crowd (even though there was really no reason to be). We had no idea how we would get back to our hotel, which was some six or eight miles away. So, instead of jumping in a taxi, we walked the whole way, only to find out there was a bus which could have taken us to the front door of the hotel!'

But before the new season got under way, United (and O'Shea) were back in Ireland, visiting Belfast on 8 August 2007 to play a pre-season friendly against Glentoran, who they beat 3–0 at The Oval in front of a crowd of 14,500.

O'Shea's adaptability continued to be vital, and when the Reds had an injury crisis among their forwards, Sir Alex had no hesitation in pushing John up front as an emergency striker, giving him the unique distinction of having played in every position for the club. On 26 September, he captained United for the first time, but it was an occasion to forget as Coventry City beat United 2–0 at Old Trafford in a third round League Cup tie.

Despite that upset, the season turned into one of the best campaigns for United, and by April they were looking at a possible Premier League and Champions League double. Paul O'Neill from Antrim remembers the night when United won through to the Champions League final in Moscow: 'The Spanish side's stars were all there: Messi, Deco, Iniesta and captain Puyol, while United were without Vidić and Rooney. It was going to be a long night. The Stretford End was bouncing, the loudest I have ever heard it roar, and all of the United fans held up cards in the East Stand to reveal the word "Believe" in large red letters. I believed!

'The singing spread around the ground and the game began. It didn't take long for the deadlock to be broken; it was in the fourteenth minute when an error in the visitors' defence let in Scholes to unleash a trademark strike into the top-left corner of the net past Víctor Valdés. It just had to be Scholes, the loyal servant who harshly missed the previous final. The crowd were ecstatic while the volume increased louder and louder, almost causing the roof of each stand to come away from its fixings.

'However, we all knew we had a long way to go in the game before we could even think about the final in Moscow. When the fourth official held aloft the injury time board and it showed a further six minutes to be added, I turned round to gauge how my friend Brendan was feeling. But he just looked at me, a nervous wreck, and he left his seat saying "I can't handle this" as he made his way to the concourse to watch the rest of the game on the TV screens where many other very anxious Reds had congregated. The volume got louder and the United fans started to wave their scarves in the air. With seconds to go, the noise was deafening while the scarves rotated much quicker in the air. Then the final whistle went and we had made the final. And so the crowd began to sing "Follow, Follow, Follow, For United are going to Moscow." What a night to remember! It was just one of those "I was there" nights and I *was* there.'

After that, United secured the title on the last day of the season, beating Wigan away 2–0. O'Shea hadn't played in either leg of the semi-final against Barcelona, but he had made 38 appearances in all competitions ahead of the final in the Luzhniki Stadium in Moscow on 21 May 2008. Sadly, he was an unused substitute in that game, and watched on as van der Sar made the crucial save that secured a third Champions League title for the club, after a penalty shootout with Chelsea.

Marc Dallas of Jordanstown was watching the game in Northern Ireland: 'My most cherished memory as a United fan simply has to be the 2008 Champions League final in Moscow in which United defeated Chelsea 6–5 on penalties. I remember watching the entire game at the Belfast Boat Club, which had been hired out for the evening and I will never ever forget that moment that Edwin van der Sar saved Nicolas Anelka's penalty to make sure that this night belonged to United. The Belfast Boat Club erupted into scenes of joy as we all went berserk with sheer delight. Every time I go to the Belfast Boat Club now, it always brings back proud and happy memories of that special night that I will never forget.'

After two seasons when O'Shea had been the only Irishman to play for United in the Premier League, that changed in 2008–09 when two more joined the first-team ranks. Jonathan Grant 'Jonny' Evans was the first to get his Premiership career under way. Born in Belfast on 2 January 1988, he began his football career with Greenisland. He was just nine years old when he was invited to attend Manchester United's Centre of Excellence. He went to Belfast High School, close to his family home in the Newtownabbey area of North Belfast. In order to improve their son's chances of fulfilling his boyhood dream of playing for the club he had always supported, the Evans family moved to Manchester in 2004, thereby allowing him to join United's highly successful youth academy. A bright lad, he attained nine GCSEs, with all of them at A* or A grade, but his real focus was on getting into the United team.

After gradually working his way through the United youth set-up, he played in two of United's three pre-season friendlies during their 2006 summer tour of South Africa. But at the start of the 2006–07 season he was sent out on loan to United's nursery club, Royal Antwerp. He had Derry-born Darron Gibson, along with Fraizer Campbell and Danny Simpson for company. When he returned from Belgium, in December, new Sunderland manager Roy Keane took the tall Irish defender on loan. He went on to help the Black Cats clinch the Championship title and with it promotion to the Premier League, and was voted the club's Young Player of the Year. He returned to Old Trafford in the summer of 2007.

On 26 September 2007, Sir Alex gave Evans his United debut in that 2–0 home defeat to Coventry City in the League Cup, and he made two appearances in the Champions League group stages, before returning on loan to Sunderland in January for the second half of the 2007–08 season, taking him up to 33 league appearances for the club.

Evans returned to United at the end of the season, but it was not until 21 September 2008 that he finally made his Premier

League debut for United, replacing the injured Nemanja Vidić in their 1–1 draw with Chelsea at Stamford Bridge. As ever, Sir Alex was willing to throw in young players into the toughest of games. In December, Evans played in both United's Club World Cup ties, picking up a winners' medal following a 1–0 victory over LDU Quito from Ecuador in Yokohama, Japan. He collected a second winners' medal with United in their League Cup final win over Tottenham Hotspur, and added a third when United won the 2008–09 Premier League title. A fantastic year was capped off for him when he was voted the Northern Ireland International Personality of the Year for 2009.

For Darron Thomas Daniel Gibson that first season in the United side was not quite so spectacular. Born on 25 October 1987 in Derry, Gibson attended St Columb's College and played junior football in the local Derry and District League. As his ability developed, he joined Irish Premier League side Institute, and in 2004 he signed for United.

On 26 October 2005, he got a belated 18th birthday present from Sir Alex when he made his debut for United in the same League Cup tie which witnessed Liam Miller's last game for the club. He came on as a substitute for Lee Martin in the 4–1 victory at Old Trafford, his only senior appearance for United in season 2005–06, though that season he helped United Reserves win the Treble. His performances for the Reserves earned the young Irishman the prestigious Jimmy Murphy Award, presented to United's best youth player of the year.

In the summer of 2006, he joined Evans on loan for Royal Antwerp and played 33 times for them, scoring one goal. In October 2007, United sent him out on loan again, this time to Wolverhampton Wanderers, who were managed by the former Republic of Ireland manager, Mick McCarthy. He played 24 games for Wolves in all competitions, and scored one goal.

Back at United for 2008–09, Gibson made his Premier League debut for the Reds on 15 November, coming on as a second-half substitute in a 5–0 thumping of Stoke City at Old Trafford. He was included in the United squad that travelled to Japan for the Club World Cup and, although he did not play in any of the games, he collected a winners' medal.

He scored his first goal for United on 4 January 2009 in United's 3–0 FA Cup third round win over Southampton at St Mary's Stadium, and then picked up his second winners' medal with United playing in their League Cup final victory over Tottenham. He played the full 90 minutes of the game, which ended 0–0, and was replaced at the start of the first period of extra-time by Ryan Giggs. The match finished 0–0, but United won the resulting penalty shootout 4–1. On 24 May, in his first Premiership start, he scored his first league goal for United in the final game of the 2008–09 season, a 1–0 win away to Hull City as Sir Alex rested several players ahead of the Champions League final against Barcelona. O'Shea, who had battled with Wes Brown and Gary Neville for the position for much of the season, played at right-back that day, but couldn't prevent Barça from winning 2–0.

On the opening day of the 2009–10 Premier League season United welcomed Birmingham City to Old Trafford, and O'Shea was handed the captain's armband for the second time in his United career, and United won 1–0. The following month, O'Shea marked his 350th game for United with a goal in a 2–0 Premier League win over Stoke City at Old Trafford on 26 September. Sadly, his season was interrupted by injury, so he made only 15 league appearances for the Reds, and had to watch on for much of the campaign as United were pipped to the title by Chelsea, who thus denied the Reds what would have been a record-breaking fourth consecutive league title.

Gibson agreed a new three-year contract to stay at Old Trafford during the summer of 2009, and on 28 February 2010 he earned his second League Cup winners' medal, when he came on as an 85th-minute substitute in United's 2–1 win over Aston Villa at Wembley Stadium. Evans started that game in the heart of United's defence alongside Vidić, and indeed, of the three

Irishmen, it was Evans who played the most times for the Reds that season (27).

The arrival of Chris Smalling at the start of the 2010–11 season meant that there was additional competition for Evans in central defence, while a fit-again O'Shea had the da Silva twins lining up to play at right-back. For Gibson, too, there was no easy way into the side in the centre of midfield. Despite being a well-built and industrious midfielder with a powerful long-range shot, there is always a fight for places. However, the Irish midfielder had become something of a cult figure with the Old Trafford crowd after scoring a series of stunning goals from around the edge of the box, and was constantly urged by the fans to shoot from seemingly any distance.

On 4 August 2010, United played a friendly at the Aviva Stadium (formerly known as Lansdowne Road) and beat an Airtricity League XI 7–1, with Evans among the goals. A bumper crowd of 49,861 watched the game, and afterwards O'Shea (who played for United in the game) commented: 'I love playing for Manchester United, and I really do enjoy going back home to Waterford to spend some time with my family and friends. I particularly love playing in friendlies in Ireland and it never ceases to amaze me just how much support we have back home. Our fans are always so enthusiastic wherever we go in the world, but for me personally I think the Irish will always have a slight edge in terms of their passion for United which is probably down to the fact that so many of my fellow countrymen have pulled on the same shirt as I have.'

In what turned out to be his final season with United, O'Shea made 32 appearances for United, helping them to a 12th Premier League title and, famously, a 19th league title, as United finally overhauled Liverpool's long-held record of championship triumphs. It was his fifth league winners' medal in a long and successful career for the club. He had made 393 appearances for United (only five Irishmen have totalled more – Tony Dunne, Denis Irwin, Roy Keane, George Best and Sammy McIlroy). He signed for Steve Bruce's Sunderland during the summer of 2011 (along with long-time defensive partner Wes Brown).

Certainly United's most versatile player of recent times, O'Shea is a shining example of selflessness and professionalism. He was always happy to race up and down the wing to the cries of 'When Johnny goes marching down the wing' from the United fans. And who will ever forget his cheeky nutmeg of Luís Figo in a Champions League game? ('I used to do the Cruyff turn all the time when I was growing up. It looks perfect if it comes off, but if it doesn't you want the ground to open up. You have to pick and choose when to do it,' he comments.)

O'Shea has always been a footballing defender, blessed with beautiful balance, crisp passing and formidable upper-body strength, which enables him to slip effortlessly into midfield and anywhere across the back four. As Sir Alex commented: 'I could play John anywhere. He has great passing awareness, two good feet, he is quick, and he is balanced. He's athletic, big and gets around well.' A former United player who knows a thing or two about defending, Paul McGrath, had this to say about him: 'His coolness can be very annoying for forwards trying to get the better of him. It's not an arrogance he has, he's just so unflustered. Nothing seems to bother him. He oozes class.' From one of the classiest defenders Ireland ever produced, that was quite a compliment.

O'Shea won his first senior cap for his country on 15 August 2001, coming on as an 84th-minute substitute at home to Croatia. 'We were winning 2–1 when I came on, but then I gave away a penalty in injury time which the visitors scored to level at 2–2,' he recalls. On 19 August 2003, he scored his only international goal to date in a 2–1 win over Australia at Lansdowne Road. He has gone on to make 70 appearances for his country.

Gibson's international career got off to a complicated start when, despite having been born in Northern Ireland, and representing them at Under-16 level, he chose to play for the Republic of Ireland. The IFA tried to prevent this, but the island of Ireland holds a unique position in world football whereby anyone born in Ireland, north or south of the border, is entitled to class themselves as a citizen of the Republic of Ireland. Which was how he ended up playing for the Republic.

On 22 August 2007, Gibson made his debut as a substitute for the Republic of Ireland in a friendly against Denmark in Aarhus in a 4–0 victory, and the following month made his first competitive appearance in 2–2 draw with Slovakia in Bratislava in a Euro 2008 qualifier. On 8 February 2011, he scored his first goal for his country in a 3–0 win against Wales and in August 2011 made his 17th appearance for his country.

But the summer of 2011 was a time when there were many newspaper reports that he was due to be transferred away from United. However, when he picked up an injury, any chance of a move was put on hold, and Gibson faced a spell battling to win back his place when he returned to full fitness.

Evans, on the other hand, made his debut for Northern Ireland on 6 September 2006, despite not having yet played a competitive game for United. As we have seen, it was a special game, with Spain being beaten 3–2 and former United stars Healy and Carroll both being a part of that great performance. Evans has been ever-present in the Northern Ireland squad since his debut, winning 27 caps by September 2011, and scored his first goal for his country in a 3–2 home win over Poland on 28 March 2009 in a World Cup qualifier.

A tall, agile and intelligent centre-back, he combines an uncompromising physical approach with an easy ability to pass the ball out from the back. He has blossomed into one of the most promising young defenders around. Whenever called upon, his ice-cool calm is immediately apparent and he handles pressure very well. By his own admission, however, the 2010–11 season was not his best for United. In an interview with the *Daily Mail*, he commented: 'I didn't hit the form I wanted. I went away and thought maybe I have another year, if I had another season like that I am sure the manager wouldn't want me around. I wasn't playing consistently to a good enough standard for Manchester United, so I have gone back to basics and worked hard.'

With the departure of Brown and O'Shea there was clearly a belief that the young Irishman still had plenty to give, even though the arrival of Phil Jones from Blackburn Rovers meant there was more competition for places in the heart of the defence. However, when both Vidić and Ferdinand were injured early in 2011–12, Evans took his opportunity well, playing alongside Jones, as United got off to a thrilling start to the new campaign, including a historic 8–2 home victory over Arsenal, as the manager showed his faith by picking one of the youngest Premier League line-ups of his career. As ever with United and this manager, the focus was on winning today while also building for the future. And as so often throughout United's history, there was an Irishman on the pitch and many more in the crowd.

Afterword

'Since the club's inception in 1878 as Newton Heath Lancashire and Yorkshire Railway Club, many players have crossed the Irish Sea to play for Manchester United and a great many of them have served the club with distinction. A truly special bond exists between the Irish and Manchester United, a strong bond built on family ties over generations of support for Manchester United, and in many ways it is a quite unique bond. The Irish are, and always will be, part of the lifeblood of Manchester United and I thank them for their eternal and unwavering loyalty to me and my team.'

Sir Alex Ferguson's words reflect a special relationship that exists between United and the Irish, and the manager thinks he knows why this may be the case: 'Manchester United understands the family connections between the Irish people and Manchester United. From time to time, I get an Irish boy over on trial and invariably the young boy will get quite homesick at the beginning. But my staff and I fully understand what Irish people are like, and we know that the family is a key part of life in Ireland. The Irish enjoy a great family unity, and many children grow up with their mother as the matriarch and we at Manchester United know this. Just as Sir Matt Busby did with George Best, then we too take the boy's feelings into consideration and let the boy have his own time to decide what he wants to do with his life. Manchester United will always fully support the boy's decision.'

It is one of the remarkable things that a club as big as United can still be a family club, but that remains one of the keys to its success and also goes towards explaining why the link with Ireland continues to be so strong. Those links have been spun like a spider's web; they started somewhat haphazardly in the club's early days, but after much hard work, they have been crafted into a mesmerising creation that is not only beautiful but also surprisingly strong and resilient. Stretching the length and breadth of the country, the web of United covers the villages, towns and cities, uniting the ordinary man, woman and child who follow the legendary names that have been woven into football history.

And who can deny the passion of the Irish in supporting their club. Certainly not Sir Alex: 'The Irish are an emotional race anyway, and they are like the Scots in that both races follow their national teams with passion and pride. The Irish's support for United is in their DNA, you can't change it, because it is in their lifeblood. These things are in every Celtic person, and the Welsh are exactly the same. When we Celts support a team, we do so with commitment. But of course, Manchester United has many wonderful and passionate fans all over the world.

'Manchester United is the biggest club in the world and most fans of Manchester United have supported the club from a very early age, with many following their father's support of the team or indeed their grandfather's support of United. You know, there are two things you cannot change about a man: you cannot change the way he walks and you cannot change the team he supports. So that's what you get with the Irish nation and the Celtic nations: a passion and a love of football, as they are all brought up watching the game. No other sport really dominates a person's thoughts and shapes their everyday lives as much as football does.'

Sir Alex sees this support in action every time United play at home – and not just at the obvious times: 'I am always the last to leave Old Trafford after a game and you can bet your life that when I walk out of the directors' entrance into the Munich Tunnel, the last sound I will hear before I get into my car is "Go on, Sir Alex, just one more autograph. I am from Ireland." The thing about the Irish is not just their support for Manchester

United, but many of them actually commit and sacrifice their lives to the club. Every time I go to Ireland, whether it is north or south of the country, the fanaticism the Irish fans show for Manchester United is extraordinary. It just seems that no matter what part of the country we play in, it is all Manchester United crazy. For me personally that is fantastic and a testimony to just how much Manchester United means to its Irish fans.'

This link is recognised not just by the manager, but also by chief executive David Gill, who sent a message of support to the George Best Carryduff MUSC on its 20th anniversary: 'As you celebrate this landmark, you should reflect on what you have achieved in the last two decades following this great club of ours. In that time Carryduff has become one of the most well-known branches in the United family, and your dedication, loyalty and hard work, all done on a voluntary basis, has been fantastic. The network of supporters' branches throughout the country, in Ireland and right around the world, is a remarkable illustration of the club's popularity and nowhere is that better demonstrated than in Northern Ireland. The historic links between the island and United are strong. Thanks for your fantastic support.'

Fans understand what the club means to them. Let Brendan Donovan from Cork explain: 'I go to many United games and I have to say the support from the Irish is fantastic. How anyone could say we are "glory hunters" is beyond me. I thought I was one of only a few to be a season ticket-holder from overseas, but quickly discovered how foolish I was to think this. I have heard of some fellow Irish United fans who have gone to nearly every game, travelled overseas and have been doing it for years.

'Sometimes I ask myself why is there such a connection between the Irish and Manchester United. Well, having read up on United's history, I would say: an Irishman named Johnny Carey would have got things started. Then, as Irish people love to support the underdog and will always help people in need, I think a lot would have started supporting United after the Munich Air Disaster in 1958 and then gone on to become lifelong fans. Put simply, Manchester United are the greatest club in the world, with the greatest fans in the world, and we Irish are a part of that and we always will be.'

Many young Irishmen have been fortunate to cross the Irish Sea in search of glory, hoping to impress those who rule the Old Trafford roost and to start their careers in the very best surroundings. Others were determined in their attempt to become a part of the continuing saga that is Manchester United's story. The rank and file, the Red Army foot-soldiers followed, knowing full well that they would never pull on that famous red shirt, but, brought up on tales of Carey, Whelan, Gregg and the rest, were keen to enrol into the United family. Fans and players may now travel from around the world to be at Old Trafford, but among them, there are still the Irish, carrying the banner first raised a lifetime ago.

But for all the historical background, and for all the recent success, there is one other factor that cannot be forgotten. Ireland and Manchester United can hardly be mentioned in the same sentence without also including two other words: George Best.

Best's performances mesmerised millions, either on the terraces or on television. Countless women, previously uninterested in football, were also dragged into the ever-growing United family, transfixed by the Belfast Boy. Even in the years after he tormented defenders, frustrated managers and team-mates alike, Best could still capture the headlines.

On the field, he showed no sense of restraint; he went for the jugular of his opponent every time and he seldom came out of that encounter as the loser. His confidence and joy entranced us all. Wherever in the world Best went, doors opened for him, people hung on his every word, things happened in his presence – and all because of his genius with a ball at his feet. How could anyone cope with all of that?

At the start of his United career, Best's father Dickie told him: 'Just remember that you were born with a gift, son, and keep your feet on the ground.' But then he became the outstanding British footballer of his generation, indeed of any generation. When he took the decision to step off the carousel of glamour and glory on New Year's Day 1974, he would have been justified in using the words that Richard Nixon used after an election defeat back in 1962: 'As I leave, you just think how much you are going to miss me. You are not going to have Nixon to kick around any more.' But alas, he was still in the press's line of fire and they continued to write their stories about him.

Best may have travelled all over the world to ply his trade after he left United, but the imprint of his place of birth, Belfast, was forever emblazoned on his soul. Following his death, Dickie asked the fans to remember George as a down-to-earth bloke, who didn't make a big deal of who or what he was. Dickie said he was very proud of his son, who had nothing against people because of their class, colour or creed; he had no interest in politics, people's religion or their beliefs. So not only did Best fulfil all our dreams on the football pitch, especially at Old Trafford, he also kept to his father's wishes as well. Like so much of the story of United and Ireland, Best was true to his family.

Hopefully the pages of this book have helped unite the players and the supporters who have made the journey from their homes across the Irish Sea, or indeed simply followed the fortunes of Manchester United from afar. As we have seen, United and the Irish are a family. And I believe that, despite what you may have read in newspapers and seen on the TV down the years, Ireland is Red. Manchester United Red.

Appendix

A – Z of All United's Irish Players

A full statistical breakdown of all Irish players to appear for Newton Heath or Manchester United, listed alphabetically. (The page reference refers to the start of their personal profile.)

Trevor Anderson   1973–74 (see page 151)
Position: Forward
Debut: 31 March 1973 v Southampton (a)
                            Division 1
Totals: Appearances: 13 (6)   Goals: 2
International caps: 22 (Northern Ireland)   Goals: 4

Henry Baird   1937–38 (see page 48)
Position: Forward
Debut: 23 January 1937 v Sheffield Wednesday (a)
                            Division 1
Totals: Appearances: 53   Goals: 18
International caps: 1 (Northern Ireland)   Goals: 0

William 'Billy' Behan   1934 (see page 45)
Position: Goalkeeper
Debut: 3 March 1934 v Bury (h) Division 2
Totals: Appearances: 1   Goals: 0
International caps: None

George Best   1963–74 (see page 113)
Position: Forward
Debut: 14 September 1963 v West
                                   Bromwich Albion (h) Division 1

Totals: Appearances: 470   Goals: 179
International caps: 37 (Northern Ireland)   Goals: 9

John 'Jackie'
Blanchflower   1951–57 (see page 66)
Position: Half-Back
Debut: 24 November 1951 v Liverpool
                                   (a) Division 1

Totals: Appearances: 117   Goals: 27
International caps: 12 (Northern Ireland)   Goals: 1

Derek Brazil   1989–90 (see page 224)
Position: Defender
Debut: 10 May 1989 v Everton (h) Division 1
Totals: Appearances: 0 (2)   Goals: 0
International caps: None

Thomas 'Tommy' Breen   1936–39 (see page 47)
Position: Goalkeeper
Debut: 28 November 1936 v Leeds United (a)
                                   Division 1

Totals: Appearances: 71   Goals: 0
International caps: 9 (Northern Ireland)   Goals: 0
                                   5 (Ireland)   Goals: 0

Seamus 'Shay' Brennan   1958–70 (see page 93)
Position: Full-Back
Debut: 19 February 1958 v Sheffield Wednesday (h)
                                   FA Cup Rd 5

Totals: Appearances: 358 (1)   Goals: 6
International caps: 19 (Republic of Ireland)   Goals: 0

Ronald 'Ronnnie' Briggs 1961–62 (see page 103)
Position: Goalkeeper
Debut: 21 January 1961 v Leicester City (a)
                           Division 1
Totals: Appearances: 11   Goals: 0
International caps: 2 (Northern Ireland)   Goals: 0

David Byrne   1933–34 (see page 44)
Position: Forward
Debut: 21 October 1933 v Bury (a) Division 2
Totals: Appearances: 4   Goals: 3
International caps: 3 (Free State)   Goals: 1

Noel Cantwell   1960–67 (see page 123)
Position: Full-Back
Debut: 26 November 1960 v Cardiff City (a)
                           Division 1
Totals: Appearances: 146   Goals: 8
International caps: 36 (Republic of Ireland)   Goals: 14

Johnny Carcy   1937–53 (see page 50)
Position: Full-Back
Debut: 25 September 1937 v Southampton (a)
                           Division 2
Totals: Appearances: 344   Goals: 17
International caps: 7 (Northern Ireland)   Goals: 0
                           29 (Ireland)   Goals: 3

Joseph 'Joe' Carolan 1958–61 (see page 97)
Position: Full-Back
Debut: 21 November 1958 v Luton Town (h)
                           Division 1
Totals: Appearances: 71   Goals: 0
International caps: 2 (Republic of Ireland)   Goals: 0

Roy Carroll   2001–05 (see page 271)
Position: Goalkeeper
Debut: 26 August 2001 v Aston Villa (a)
                                 Premier League

Totals: Appearances: 68 (4)   Goals: 0
International caps: 19 (Northern Ireland)   Goals: 0

Thomas Connell   1978 (see page 181)
Position: Full-Back
Debut: 22 December 1978 v Bolton Wanderers (a)
                                 Division 1

Totals: Appearances: 2   Goals: 0
International caps: 1 (Northern Ireland)   Goals: 0

Gerard 'Gerry' Daly   1973–77 (see page 167)
Position: Midfielder
Debut: 25 August 1973 v Arsenal (a) Division 1
Totals: Appearances: 137 (5)   Goals: 32
International caps: 48 (Republic of Ireland)   Goals: 13

Bernard Donaghy   1905–06 (see page 27)
Position: Forward
Debut: 4 November 1905 v Lincoln City (h)
                                 Division 2

Totals: Appearances: 3   Goals: 0
International caps: 1 (Ireland)   Goals: 0

Mal Donaghy   1988–92 (see page 225)
Position: Defender
Debut: 30 October 1988 v Everton (a) Division 1
Totals: Appearances: 98 (21)   Goals: 0
International caps: 91 (Northern Ireland)   Goals: 0

Anthony 'Tony' Dunne   1960–73 (see page 121)
Position: Full-Back
Debut: 15 October 1960 v Burnley (a) Division 1
Totals: Appearances: 534 (1)   Goals: 2
International caps: 33 (Republic of Ireland)   Goals: 0

Patrick Dunne   **1964–65** (see page 126)
Position: Goalkeeper
Debut: 8 September 1964 v Everton (a) Division 1
Totals: Appearances: 67   Goals: 0
International caps: 5 (Republic of Ireland)   Goals: 0

Jonny Evans   **2007–** (see page 280)
Position: Defender
Debut: 26 September 2007 v Coventry City (h)
                            League Cup Rd 3
Totals*:   Appearances: 77 (10)   Goals: 0
International caps**:   27 (Northern Ireland)   Goals: 1
* Up to the end of the 2010–11 season.
** Includes Northern Ireland's 4–1 loss away to Estonia on 6 September
2011.

John Feehan   **1949–50** (see page 62)
Position: Goalkeeper
Debut: 5 November 1949 v Birmingham City (h)
                            Division 1
Totals: Appearances: 14   Goals: 0
International caps: None   Goals: 0

Darron Gibson   **2005–** (see page 281)
Position: Midfielder
Debut: 26 October 2005 v Barnet (h)
                            League Cup Rd 3
Totals*:   Appearances: 35 (23)   Goals: 10
International caps**:   17 (Republic of Ireland)   Goals: 1
* Up to the end of the 2010–11 season.
** Includes the Republic of Ireland's 0–0 draw away to Russia on
6 September 2011

John 'Johnny' Giles   **1959–63** (see page 98)
Position: Forward
Debut: 12 September 1959 v Tottenham Hotspur (h)
                            Division 1
Totals: Appearances: 115   Goals: 13
International caps: 59 (Republic of Ireland)   Goals: 5

Keith Gillespie   1993–95 (see page 239)
Position: Winger
Debut: 5 January 1993 v Bury (h) FA Cup Rd 3
Totals: Appearances: 7 (7)   Goals: 2
International caps: 86 (Northern Ireland)   Goals: 2

Daniel 'Don' Givens   1969–70 (see page 140)
Position: Forward
Debut: 9 August 1969 v Crystal Palace (a) Division 1
Totals: Appearances: 5 (4)   Goals: 1
International caps: 56 (Republic of Ireland)   Goals: 19

Henry 'Harry' Gregg   1957–66 (see page 90)
Position: Goalkeeper
Debut: 21 December 1957 v Leicester City (h)
                             Division 1
Totals: Appearances: 247   Goals: 0
International caps: 25 (Northern Ireland)   Goals: 0

Ashley Grimes   1977–83 (see page 183)
Position: Midfielder
Debut: 20 August 1977 v Birmingham City (a)
                             Division 1
Totals: Appearances: 77 (30)   Goals: 11
International caps: 18 (Republic of Ireland)   Goals: 1

Mickey Hamill   1911–14 (see page 30)
Position: Forward
Debut: 16 November 1911 v West Bromwich
                             Albion (a) Division 1
Totals: Appearances: 60   Goals: 2
International caps: 7 (Ireland)   Goals: 1

David Healy   1999–2000 (see page 269)
Position: Forward
Debut: 13 October 1999 v Aston Villa (a)
                         League Cup Rd 3
Totals: Appearances: 0 (3)   Goals: 0
International caps*:   89 (Northern Ireland)   Goals: 35
Includes Northern Ireland's 4-1 loss away to Estonia on 6 September 2011.

Denis Irwin   1990–2002 (see page 230)
Position: Full-Back
Debut: 18 August 1990 v Liverpool (n)
                         Charity Shield
Totals: Appearances: 511 (18)   Goals: 33
International caps: 56 (Republic of Ireland)   Goals: 4

Tommy Jackson   1975–77 (see page 162)
Position: Midfielder
Debut: 16 August 1975 v Wolverhampton
                         Wanderers (a) Division 1
Totals: Appearances: 22 (1)   Goals: 0
International caps: 35 (Northern Ireland)   Goals: 0

Roy Keane   1993–2005 (see page 236)
Position: Midfielder
Debut: 7 August 1993 v Arsenal (n) Charity Shield
Totals: Appearances: 458 (22)   Goals: 51
International caps: 67 (Republic of Ireland)   Goals: 9

Patrick Kennedy   1954 (see page 68)
Position: Full-Back
Debut: 2 October 1954 v Wolverhampton
                         Wanderers (a) Division 1
Totals: Appearances: 1   Goals: 0
International caps: None

David Lyner   1922 (see page 39)
Position: Outside-Left/Outside-Right
Debut: 23 September 1922 v Coventry City (a)
                             Division 2

Totals: Appearances: 3   Goals: 0
International caps: 6 (Ireland)   Goals: 0

David McCreery   1974–79 (see page 173)
Position: Midfielder
Debut: 15 October 1974 v Portsmouth (a)
                             Division 2

Totals: Appearances: 57 (53)   Goals: 8
International caps: 67 (Northern Ireland)   Goals: 0

Noel McFarlane   1954 (see page 69)
Position: Forward
Debut: 13 February 1954 v Tottenham Hotspur (h)
                             Division 1

Totals: Appearances: 1   Goals: 0
International caps: None

Pat McGibbon   1995 (see page 235)
Position: Centre-Half
Debut: 20 September 1995 v York City (h)
                             League Cup Rd 2

Totals: Appearances: 1   Goals: 0
International caps: 7 (Northern Ireland)   Goals: 0

Christopher McGrath   1976–80 (see page 177)
Position: Midfielder
Debut: 23 October 1976 v Norwich City (h)
                             Division 1

Totals: Appearances: 15 (19)   Goals: 1
International caps: 21 (Northern Ireland)   Goals: 4

Paul McGrath 1982–89 (see page 202)
Position: Defender/Midfielder
Debut: 10 November 1982 v Bradford City (a)
  League Cup Rd 3
Totals: Appearances: 192 (7) Goals: 16
International caps: 83 (Republic of Ireland) Goals: 8

Samuel 'Sammy'
McIlroy 1971–82 (see page 155)
Position: Midfielder
Debut: 6 November 1971 v Manchester City (a)
  Division 1
Totals: Appearances: 391 (28) Goals: 71
International caps: 88 (Northern Ireland) Goals: 5

Samuel McMillan 1961–62 (see page 104)
Position: Forward
Debut: 4 November 1961 v Sheffield Wednesday (a)
  Division 1
Totals: Appearances: 15 Goals: 6
International caps: 2 (Northern Ireland) Goals: 0

Walter McMillen 1933–36 (see page 42)
Position: Half-Back
Debut: 16 September 1933 v Brentford (a) Division 2
Totals: Appearances: 29 Goals: 2
International caps: 7 (Ireland) Goals: 0

Michael 'Mick' Martin 1973–75 (see page 160)
Position: Midfielder
Debut: 24 January 1973 v Everton (h) Division 1
Totals: Appearances: 36 (7) Goals: 2
International caps: 52 (Republic of Ireland) Goals: 4

Liam Miller   2004–05 (see page 274)
Position: Midfielder
Debut: 11 August 2004 v Dinamo Bucharest (a)
                             Champions Lg Q

Totals: Appearances: 11 (11)   Goals: 2
International caps: 21 (Republic of Ireland)   Goals: 1

Kevin Moran   1979–88 (see page 193)
Position: Centre-Half
Debut: 30 April 1979 v Southampton (a) Division 1
Totals: Appearances: 284 (5)   Goals: 24
International caps: 71 (Republic of Ireland)   Goals: 6

Thomas Morrison   1902–04 (see page 24)
Position: Forward
Debut: 25 December 1902 v Manchester City (h)
                             Division 2
Totals: Appearances: 36   Goals: 8
International caps: 7 (Ireland)   Goals: 0

Philip Mulryne   1997–99 (see page 246)
Position: Forward
Debut: 14 October 1997 v Ipswich Town (a)
                             League Cup Rd 3
Totals: Appearances: 4 (1)   Goals: 0
International caps: 27 (Northern Ireland)   Goals: 3

James 'Jimmy' Nicholl   1975–82 (see page 172)
Position: Full-Back
Debut: 5 April 1975 v Southampton (a) Division 2
Totals: Appearances: 235 (13)   Goals: 6
International caps: 73 (Northern Ireland)   Goals: 1

James Nicholson   1960–62 (see page 101)
Position: Half-Back
Debut: 24 August 1960 v Everton (a) Division 1
Totals: Appearances: 68   Goals: 6
International caps: 41 (Northern Ireland)   Goals: 6

Liam O'Brien   **1986–88** (see page 222)
Position: Midfielder
Debut: 20 December 1986 v Leicester City (h)
                          Division 1

Totals: Appearances: 17 (19)   Goals: 2
International caps: 16 (Republic of Ireland)   Goals: 0

Patrick O'Connell   **1914–15** (see page 35)
Position: Half-Back
Debut: 2 September 1914 v Oldham Athletic (h)
                          Division 1

Totals: Appearances: 35   Goals: 2
International caps: 6 (Ireland)   Goals: 0

Thomas O'Shaughnessy **1890** (see page 19)
Position: Forward
Debut: 25 October 1890 v Bootle Reserves (a)
                          FA Cup 2Q Rd

Totals: Appearances: 1   Goals: 0
International caps: None

John O'Shea   **1993–2011** (see page 268)
Position: Defender/Midfielder
Debut: 13 October 1999 v Aston Villa (a)
                          League Cup Rd 3

Totals: Appearances: 301 (92)   Goals: 15
International caps*:   70 (Republic of Ireland)   Goals: 1

*Includes the Republic of Ireland's 0–0 draw away to Russia on
6 September 2011*

John Peden   **1893–94** (see page 20)
Position: Forward
Debut: 2 September 1893 v Burnley (h) Division 1
Totals: Appearances: 32   Goals: 8
International caps: 24 (Ireland)   Goals: 7

James Robinson   1919–22 (see page 38)
Position: Outside-Left
Debut: 3 January 1920 v Chelsea (h) Division 1
Totals: Appearances: 21   Goals: 3
International caps: None

Patrick 'Paddy' Roche 1975–81 (see page 176)
Position: Goalkeeper
Debut: 8 February 1975 v Oxford United (a)
                          Division 2
Totals: Appearances: 53   Goals: 0
International caps: 8 (Republic of Ireland)   Goals: 0

John 'Jackie' Scott   1952–56 (see page 67)
Position: Forward
Debut: 4 October 1952 v Wolverhampton
                          Wanderers (a) Division 1
Totals: Appearances: 3   Goals: 0
International caps: 2 (Northern Ireland)   Goals: 0

Thomas Sloan   1978–81 (see page 180)
Position: Midfielder
Debut: 18 November 1978 v Ipswich Town (h)
                          Division 1
Totals: Appearances: 4 (8)   Goals: 0
International caps: 3 (Northern Ireland)   Goals: 0

Frank Stapleton   1981–87 (see page 197)
Position: Forward
Debut: 29 August 1981 v Coventry City (a)
                          Division 1
Totals: Appearances: 267 (21)   Goals: 78
International caps: 71 (Republic of Ireland)   Goals: 20

William 'Billy' Toms
Position:
Debut:

1919–20 (see page 37)
Forward
4 October 1919 v Middlesbrough (h)
Division 1

Totals:
International caps:

Appearances: 14   Goals: 4
None

Anthony Whelan
Position:
Debut:

1980 (see page 186)
Centre-Half
29 November 1980 v Southampton (a)
Division 1

Totals:
International caps:

Appearances: 0 (1)   Goals: 0
None

Liam 'Billy' Whelan
Position:
Debut:

1955–57 (see page 70)
Inside-Right
26 March 1955 v Preston North End (a)
Division 1

Totals:
International caps:

Appearances: 98   Goals: 52
4 (Republic of Ireland)   Goals: 0

Norman Whiteside
Position:
Debut:

1982–89 (see page 200)
Midfielder/Forward
24 April 1982 v Brighton &
Hove Albion (a) Division 1

Totals:
International caps:

Appearances: 256 (18)   Goals: 67
38 (Northern Ireland)   Goals: 9

Bibliography

Articles:

'John Peden: An Early Irish Soccer Hero', *Soccer History* magazine, Issue No.11

Peter Lane, Club Historian of Peterborough United, interview with Kate Sheffield (daughter of Noel Cantwell) at London Road, Peterborough – 24 April 2010

Books:

Charlton, Bobby, with James Lawton: *My Manchester United Years – The Autobiography* (Headline, 2007)

Doolan, Paul, and Robert Goggins: *The Hoops: History of Shamrock Rovers* (Gill & Macmillan, 1993)

Dykes, Garth: *The United Alphabet – A Complete Who's Who of Manchester United* (ACL & Polar Publishing, 1994)

Engels, Friedrich: *The Condition of the Working Class in England in 1844* (Oxford World's Classics, New Edition, 1999)

Gregg, Harry: *Harry's Game – The Autobiography* (Mainstream Publishing, 2002)

Keane, Colm: *Ireland's Soccer Top 20* (Mainstream Publishing, 2004)

Keane, Roy, with Eamon Dunphy: *Keane: The Autobiography* (Michael Joseph, 2002)

McCartney, Iain: *Irish Reds* (Britespot Publishing, 2002)

Morrison, Ian & Alan Shury: *Manchester United: A Complete Record 1878–1992* (Breedon Books, 1992)

White, John D.T.: *The Official Manchester United Miscellany* (Carlton, 2005)

White, John D.T.: *The Official Manchester United Almanac* (Orion, 2008)

Williams, Mike, with D.A. Farnie: *Cotton Mills in Greater Manchester* (Carnegie Publishing Limited, 1992)

Charles Zahra, Joseph Muscat, Iain McCartney and Keith Mellor: *Manchester United Pictorial History & Club Record* (Temple Nostalgia, 1986)

TV Programmes:
Nixon in the Den – BBC Four, narrated by David Reynolds, Professor of International History at Cambridge University

Websites:
The following websites were among those consulted during my research for this book:
www.bbc.co.uk
www.belfasttelegraph.co.uk
www.dailymail.co.uk
www.englandfootballonline.com
www.givemefootball.com
www.guardian.co.uk
www.independent.co.uk
www.irishmemories.co.uk
www.irishpost.co.uk
www.irishtimes.com
www.lisburntoday.co.uk
www.manchester-united-fans-site.com
www.manchesterirish.com
www.manutd.com
www.manutdtalk.com
www.menmedia.co.uk
www.mufc.info.com
www.prideofmanchester.com
www.red11.org
www.redcafe.net

www.rednews.co.uk
www.soccer-history.co.uk
www.soccer-ireland.com
www.soccerbase.com
www.soccerscene.ie
www.stretfordend.co.uk
www.talkfootball.co.uk
www.trulyreds.com
www.waterford-news.ie
www.wikipedia.com
www.yourirish.com

Acknowledgements

I wish to pay special thanks to the following people who were of a tremendous help with my book:

My wife, Janice, and our two sons, Marc and Paul, who have been a rock and a pillar of strength to me throughout the writing of my book.

My mum, Rosaleen Doherty White, and my mother-in-law, Ruth McWilliams, for their constant encouragement.

Eamonn Holmes for his magnificent Foreword.

Sir Alex Ferguson for his very kind words about my book and for taking the time to speak to me in his office at Carrington.

Jonny Evans and John O'Shea for their wonderful interviews at Carrington.

Harry Gregg, Sammy McIlroy and Kevin Moran for taking the time to speak to me about their time at United.

Steve Bruce, Paddy Crerand, Jonny Evans, David Gill, Harry Gregg, Sammy McIlroy, Kevin Moran, Jimmy Nicholl, John O'Shea and Norman Whiteside for their supportive quotes about the book.

Bill Clarkson from Hyde for his memories of Johnny Carey and every Irish United player who followed Gentleman John; Mike Hartley for his memories of United during the 1970s; Father David McGarry from Saint Catherine of Siena Roman Catholic Church, Didsbury, for his memories of Johnny Carey and Liam Whelan.

Adrian 'Addy' Dearnaley from Stalybridge for sharing his memories of watching United over the past 45 years with me.

Barry Moorhouse, Player Liaison Manager at Manchester United, and James White, for their help in setting up interviews with United players past and present.

Ian Marshall for offering me the chance to write this book.

Damien Friel, my elder son Marc, JD, Heather Torrens, Malachy & Teresa McMahon, Kevin Banks, Adrian Abbott, Stuart Anderson and Robbie Robinson for their unwavering support and commitment as committee members of the George Best Carryduff MUSC.

My good mate John Dempsey for his companionship over the past 20 years on our numerous jaunts across the Irish Sea to see our beloved United play.

All of the staff at the Village Hotel, Hyde (especially the two Annes, Carol, Chris, Claire, Dan, Debbie, Elaine, Eva, James, Joanne, Julie, the two Katies, Kayleigh, the two Lindsays, Rebecca, Ryan and all the rest of the staff) for always being so friendly to me, my family and the members of the George Best Carryduff MUSC when we are in Manchester to see United play.

For their help with the research:

John Kiberd from www.soccer-ireland.com who helped me with many of the player biographies; Ian Nannestad from *Soccer History* magazine, www.soccer-history.co.uk, for permitting me to use parts of his article: 'John Peden: An Early Irish Soccer Hero', *Soccer History* magazine, Issue No.11; Mark Gibson, from the George Best Carryduff Manchester United Supporters Club, for his help with Manchester United's Northern Ireland international players and Manchester United games played at Windsor Park; Chris Goodwin at www.englandfootballonline.com for his assistance in unravelling the history of international football in Ireland and other topics; Steph Doehler at www.football-united-blogs.com for issuing a notice on the website inviting stories from Irish Reds about how they fell in love with Manchester United; Peter Lane, Peterborough United club historian for his help with my Noel Cantwell entry; Chris Ryder, Carryduff, County Down – a former journalist with the *Sunday*

Times; Andrew Conn, webmaster at Linfield FC; Martin Hamer, digital editor, the *Lancashire Evening Post*; Iain McCartney – author of *Irish Reds*, plus many other books on Manchester United and my mentor when I was writing this book; Roy McGivern, Linfield FC media committee member; Michael Drohan at Waterford United; Pat McNally, webmaster at www.soccerscene.ie.; Becky Grice, editor of the *East Cork Journal*; Ashley Wragg, club secretary, Lisburn Distillery FC; David Scrannage at Sporting Heroes (http://www.sporting-heroes.net/) for permitting me to use the website's lists of international games for Irish Manchester United players; Geoff Snape at the West Bromwich Albion Former Players' Association – http://www.old-baggies.com/cms/; Dawson Simpson, club historian, Lisburn Distillery FC; Sue Walsh at the Professional Footballers' Association and the PFA Magazine – www.givemefootball.com; Barry and Bill at http://red11.org/index.html; Ted MacAuley, sports journalist – *Daily Star Sunday*; Johnny Hero, U105 Radio, Belfast.

Matt Keane from the *Munster Express*; Stephen Beacom, sports editor at the *Belfast Telegraph*; and Alan Keegan, Manchester United's matchday announcer.

Karl Evans, Sam Kelleher and Michael Leneghan at Manchester United's Membership & Ticket Office, for looking after the members of the George Best Carryduff MUSC over the past 20 years, Michael Grey and Mark Sullivan at MUTV, and Gemma Thompson at *Inside United* and the *United Review* for all their help. Lynne Laffin and Rachael Cross in Sir Alex's office, and Kathleen Phipps at Manchester United's Carrington Training Centre.

I couldn't have made this the book it is without the help of so many Irish Reds, especially those from the George Best Carryduff MUSC:

Adrian and Andrew Abbott, Loughgall; Marshall and Billy Angus, Bangor; Kevin Banks, Belfast; Stephen Black, Belfast; Eugene Bryson, Derry; Gerald Burns, West Belfast MUSC; Mark

Connolly, Belfast; John Conran, Clonmel MUSC; Jimmy Copeland, South Belfast MUSC; Marc and Robert Dallas, Jordanstown, County Antrim; Patrick Devaney, County Mayo; Colm Devine, Aghyaran, County Tyrone (now living in Rochdale); Michael Devine, Aghyaran, County Tyrone; Billy Dickson, Newtownards, County Down; Frankie Dodds, Falls Road, Belfast; Walter Donaldson, Cregagh Estate, Belfast; Ryan Donovan, Cork; David Edwards, Dublin; Philip Ferguson, Newtownards, County Down; Vicky Fisher, Castlereagh, Belfast; Noel Flannery, Mount Eagles, Belfast; Jim Forbes, Ballysillan, Belfast; Damien Friel, Lifford, County Donegal; Liam Friel, Donegal MUSC; Patrick Hanrahan, Tipperary (now living in Bethpage, Long Island, New York, USA); Ted Healy, Waterford; Jim Hetherington, Andersonstown, Belfast; John Hinds, Newtownbreda, Belfast; Jim Hunter, Sion Mills MUSC; Noel Johnston, Ballynahinch; Jim Kyle, Belfast; Bert Lewis, Muckamore MUSC; Billy Irvine, Belfast; Matthew Leydon, Belfast; Paddy Lowe, Waterford; Danny McDonald, Belfast; Dylan McDonnell, Short Strand, Belfast; Stevie McMenemy, Belfast; Jim Morgan, Belfast; Mickey & Pat Morrison, Newry, County Down; Cathal Mullan, Belfast; Lynsey Mowbray, Lisburn (now living in Derry); Con Murphy, Begenalstown MUSC; Paul O'Neill, Antrim; Philip O'Neill, Belfast; Ed O'Riordan, Skeheenarinky, County Tipperary; Robbie Robinson, Belfast; Kevin Smith, Dunboyne, County Meath; Jim Wallace, City of Derry MUSC; Robin Wallace, Temple, County Down (now living in Jedburgh, Roxburghshire, Scotland); Dessie and Marty Roche, Derry; Matthew Scharfenberg, Belfast; Danny Young, Short Strand, Belfast.